CRITICAL INSIGHTS

The Immigrant Experience

CRITICAL INSIGHTS

The Immigrant Experience

Editor
Maryse Jayasuriya
University of Texas, El Paso

SALEM PRESS
A Division of EBSCO Information Services, Inc.
Ipswich, Massachusetts

GREY HOUSE PUBLISHING

Publisher's Cataloging-In-Publication Data
(Prepared by The Donohue Group, Inc.)

Names: Jayasuriya, Maryse, editor.
Title: The immigrant experience / editor, Maryse Jayasuriya, University of
        Texas, El Paso.
Other Titles: Critical insights.
Description: [First edition]. | Ipswich, Massachusetts : Salem Press, a division
        of EBSCO Information Services, Inc. ; Amenia, NY : Grey
        House Publishing, [2018] | Includes bibliographical references
        and index.
Identifiers: ISBN 9781682176924 (hardcover)
Subjects: LCSH: Immigrants' writings, American--History and criticism. |
        Emigration and immigration in literature. | American
        literature--Minority authors.
Classification: LCC PS508.I45 I46 2018 | DDC 810.809220691--dc23

First Printing

PRINTED IN THE UNITED STATES OF AMERICA

Contents

About This Volume

Maryse Jayasuriya

The essays in this volume draw upon a vast range of immigrant experiences, precisely because immigrant writing in the United States and beyond brings together people of various nationalities, cultures, languages, immigration statuses, and social and economic classes. These essays also consider a wide array of genres: poetry, fiction, nonfiction, drama, and even hybrid forms, like graphic novels. The book begins with a broad overview of the field of immigrant writing by Maryse Jayasuriya, including a substantial survey of immigrant writing that extends the works discussed in the individual essays.

Critical Contexts

The critical contexts section begins with Ezra Cappell's sweeping survey of Jewish American immigrant writing, from the nineteenth century to the present day. Jewish immigration from Eastern Europe to the United States is one of the defining models for the immigrant experience in the United States. Cappell argues that immigration has been a major theme in early twentieth-century Jewish American literature and has continued to influence late twentieth-century and contemporary Jewish American literature as well.

Umme Al-wazedi considers South Asian immigrant writing through the lenses of postcolonial and feminist criticism and theory, showing that South Asian women writers, as well as their characters, have to negotiate their hybrid and multiple identities in the new world in which they find themselves. Al-wazedi analyzes how these writers focus on issues of belonging and forming or transforming identity through fiction, collages of memory, and critical essays.

Asha Jeffers highlights the range of critical responses to one central work of immigrant fiction, Junot Diaz's *The Brief Wondrous Life of Oscar Wao* even as she advances her own understanding of this very important novel. Jeffers considers the nature and role of myth in the novel, arguing that the different kinds of myths featured, including comic books and science fiction—which she calls "myths of the future"—frame the lives of the second-generation immigrant characters.

Cynthia Leenerts compares two important immigrant graphic memoirs: GB Tran's *Vietnamerica: A Family's Journey* and Thi Bui's *The Best We Could Do*, both of which delineate family and national narratives. Based on how these two memoirs depict the immigrant experience in the United States as well as the reasons for emigration from Vietnam and the hold the homeland continues to have on the narrator/artists and their respective families, Leenerts argues that the process of anamnesis—of recovering and reconstituting memory, which is crucial both to finding one's identity and to discovering and speaking one's unique and compelling voice—is central to both narratives.

Critical Readings

The immigrant experience can provide inspiration for non-immigrant writers as well as immigrant writers, and some of the most eloquent texts on the immigrant experience in the United States were written by a fourth-generation Jewish American poet, Emma Lazarus, who came to identify powerfully with both her Sephardic and German Jewish immigrant ancestors and her Russian Jewish immigrant contemporaries. Brian Yothers considers how Lazarus's poetry came to speak so powerfully for impoverished immigrants despite her own relatively elite status in "Emma Lazarus's Poetic Representations of the Immigrant Experience."

Writings about the immigrant experience can be very inventive, idiosyncratic, and even hybrid in form. Robert C. Evans explores an early example of such writing by the Asian American author Edith Eaton (also known as Sui Sin Far)—a series of articles published in the *Los Angeles Express* newspaper over a five-month period in 1904, which purportedly recounted a cross-continental trip narrated in the voice of "Wing Sing," an imaginary Chinese American businessman from Los Angeles. Evans argues that by inventing a male persona to voice what Sui Sin Far herself experienced in the course of her travels, this female writer is able to provide important insights that are not available elsewhere regarding the Asian immigrant experience in North America.

Nalini Iyer, in her essay, provides an overview of literary works by immigrants in the United States from South Asian countries, including India, Pakistan, Sri Lanka, Bangladesh, Nepal, Afghanistan, and the Maldives. She discusses the evolution of South Asian American writing over a period of almost a century, identifying three distinct phases—South Asian "pioneers" from the 1890s to the end of World War II, the immigration boom from 1965 to 2000, and the post 9/11 era—that influenced the major themes in writing by South Asians in the United States. She argues that South Asian American writing reflects and resists the politics of American imperialism.

From an overview of South Asian American literature we move to an overview of Arab American literature. In her essay, Mejdulene B. Shomali discusses the difficulty of defining the category "Arab American" and delineates the three waves of Arab immigration to the United States (1800s–1925, 1945–1967 and 1965–present) as well as the corresponding three movements of Arab American literature. Through an analysis specifically of poet Marwa Helal's chapbook, Shomali discusses how Helal, as a representative of contemporary Arab American writers, considers issues of movement, space and time, and ancestry.

Marion Christina Rohrleitner, in the analysis of the fiction and creative nonfiction of Haitian American writer Edwidge Danticat, discusses how immigration can be an act of, in the words of philosopher Jonathan Lear, "radical hope." By exploring the role of a variety of art—including narrative literature, music, sculpture, and visual art—in the lives of the protagonists of Danticat's literary works, Rohrleitner demonstrates how creative imagination and daily artistic practice enable immigrants to go beyond the limitations of the present and express faith in a better future.

The link between immigration and creativity is also the focus of the first-generation Chinese American immigrant writer Ha Jin in his first novel about the Chinese diasporic community, *A Free Life*, in which the protagonist, a Chinese immigrant to the United States, has to negotiate between the material success usually associated with the American Dream and his own determination to become a poet in English. Te-hsing Shan examines how the novel deals with issues concerning the homeland and loyalty, the poetic ideals and practices of the protagonist along with their significance, and the way in which the protagonist is able to pursue his creative aspirations.

The complexities of undocumented life provide the focus of Marta Caminero-Santangelo's essay. She delineates a move away from depictions of such immigrants as "deserving" and "meritorious" who only see the United States as "home," which was common during the first decade of the 2000s. Since the implementation of DACA in 2012, she argues, DREAMer narratives have been more fully fleshed-out, veering away from the "good immigrant" stories and emphasizing belonging in the US as well as a multiplicity of places through memory, through the body, and through relationships. In the post-DACA era, she forecasts a continuation of DREAMer narratives that will contest and complicate prevailing negative stereotypes of undocumented immigrants as well as the life narratives prevalent earlier in the millennium.

R. Joseph Rodríguez considers how issues relating to migration and immigration, specifically among Latina/o youth, are depicted in the flourishing genre of young adult literature. His essay examines nonfiction, fiction, and poetry, with a particular focus on the depiction of undocumented immigration, and argues that such literary works both make visible and humanize the experiences of young immigrants who see themselves as new Americans and want their voices to be heard.

Like Caminero-Santangelo and Rodríguez, Maryse Jayasuriya examines the representations of undocumented immigrants—from Central Africa in this case—and their aspirations in Cameroonian novelist Imbolo Mbue's novel *Behold the Dreamers*. The essay notes the relative paucity of writing on undocumented immigrants from Africa and Asia, and it shows how Mbue presents an undocumented immigrant family as strivers who first are drawn by the hegemonic American Dream and gradually become disenchanted with it, turning ultimately to a dream of success in their home country supported by their earnings from abroad.

African immigration is also the focus of Brian Yothers's "Contemporary African Immigration and the Legacy of Slavery in Yaa Gyasi's *Homegoing*," which considers Yaa Gyasi's 2016 novel *Homegoing* as a response to the experience of twentieth-century African immigrants to the United States and the complex relationship between recent African immigrants and the historic African American community. The essay shows that Gyasi's novel, although only explicitly about immigration towards the end, is engaged with questions of migration and immigrant identity throughout. The essay is particularly concerned to show how Gyasi uses the legacy of slavery in both Africa and the Americas to frame the twentieth and twenty-first-century African immigrant experience in the United States and thus demonstrates that this immigrant-authored novel speaks powerfully, if not exclusively, to the immigrant experience.

The essays in this volume, then, deal with works and authors across many national and generic boundaries, illustrating the richness of the literature of the immigrant experience in the United States today. That they also span three centuries, from Emma Lazarus, Abraham Cahan, and Sui Sin Far to the stunning array of narratives and poems being published today, suggests how urgent narrating the immigrant experience has been and continues to be in the literature of the United States.

On the Immigrant Experience_____

Maryse Jayasuriya

The United States has often been called a "nation of immigrants."
It is no wonder, then, that there are so many narratives about the
immigration experience in the United States in so many different
genres—fiction, creative nonfiction, poetry, and drama. Although
the essays in this volume cover a broad range of immigrant writing,
there is a large body of material that goes beyond the scope of
any individual volume. I mention these additional texts in this
introduction to give readers an idea of the vast scope of the field of
immigrant writing.

Broadly speaking, migration is the result of people moving from
one location to another. Mass migrations have occurred as a result of
war, persecution, famine, and other natural disasters as well as those
caused by colonialism, imperialism, and slavery, which force people
to move from their land of origin, their homeland, to a new location,
a hostland. In other cases, people have chosen to migrate in order to
seek a better life, more resources and opportunities, perhaps a higher
standard of living.

Numerous terms have been used for immigrants, including
exiles, expatriates, refugees, asylum seekers, and diasporics. The
term "diaspora" has often been conflated with immigration. The
original use of the term was in relation to the Jewish diaspora, and
the term has also long been applied to the Armenian and Greek
diasporic communities. According to Khachig Tölölyan, the term
was initially used for very specific contexts—where groups of people
were forced to move from one location to another but maintained
their affiliation with each other and to their homeland, preserved
their culture, traditions and a collective memory, and patrolled
communal boundaries (7). Now the term "diasporic" is also used
as a catchall for people who live away from their homeland in a
hostland, in groups or as individuals.

The United States has been a particular locus of desire for immigrants. As Anupama Jain points out, "The American Dream is one of the most familiar and persistent narratives of Americanization. This is the rags-to-riches, pull-yourself-up-by-the-bootstraps story of a strong (Protestant) work ethic. Few people would argue that this 'dream' is not one of the most recognizable signifiers for allegedly unique immigrant possibilities in the United States" (65) despite the fact that "the meaning of the dream remains as troublingly elusive as its attainment is for many Americans" (65).

In his essay "Imaginary Homelands," Salman Rushdie asserts that "America, a nation of immigrants, has created great literature out of the phenomenon of cultural transplantation, out of examining the ways in which people cope with a new world" (20). Literary works about immigration have tended to focus on certain issues that immigrants have typically had to encounter. People who are forced or decide to move from one land to another face the difficulty of getting accustomed to a new, strange, unfamiliar location. They experience culture shock and are very often homesick, yearning for a homeland whether it continues to exist or not, and for the family and friends they have left behind or from whom they have been separated. They deal with feelings of loss and alienation. Frequently they struggle to survive in the new location, meaning that they have to find work, deal with poverty, and loss of status. They might have difficulties as a result of not being familiar or fluent with the dominant language or protocols of the hostland. They might also face racism, discrimination, and prejudice from the new society in which they find themselves, which might make them feel by turns invisible in the new environment or all too visible and exposed to racial or ethnic slurs, threats, and intimidation. Their narratives speak of courage and determination—of the will to survive, to persist, and to endure suffering and numerous obstacles for the sake of a better life and more opportunities—if not for themselves, then at least for their children. Such narratives include collections of short stories such as *Who's Irish?* by Gish Jen, *The Thing Around Your Neck* by Chimamanda Ngozi Adichie, and *The Refugees* by Viet Thanh Nguyen; novels such as *Lucy* by Jamaica Kincaid, *The*

Beautiful Things That Heaven Bears by Dinaw Mengestu, *Native Speaker* by Chang-Rae Lee, and *We Need New Names* by NoViolet Bulawayo; memoirs such as *The Woman Warrior* by Maxine Hong Kingston and *The Weight of Shadows: A Memoir of Immigration and Displacement* by José Orduña.

Yet, as Edward Said has argued, immigrants have a unique way of seeing their experiences:

> Most people are principally aware of one culture, one setting, one home; exiles are aware of at least two, and this plurality of vision gives rise to an awareness of simultaneous dimensions, an awareness that—to borrow a phrase from music—is contrapuntal. . . . For an exile, habits of life, expression or activity in the new environment inevitably occur against the memory of these things in another environment. Thus both the new and the old environments are vivid, actual, occurring together contrapuntally. (186)

A related benefit, as R. Radhakrishnan observes, is that immigrants "experience distance as a form of critical enlightenment or a healthy 'estrangement' from their birthland, and to experience another culture or location as a reprieve from the orthodoxies of their own 'given' cultures" (126). Like travel narratives, immigration narratives show how self-fashioning is thereby possible in the new milieu, as illustrated, for instance, in Bharati Mukherjee's novel *Jasmine*. Immigrants who have succeeded in their fields in the United States have written memoirs—such as Meena Alexander's *Fault Lines* or *'Tis* by Frank McCourt—relating their literal and metaphorical journeys from homeland to hostland. Some narratives are somewhat lighthearted, such as *Funny in Farsi* by Firoozeh Dumas and *Stealing Buddha's Dinner* by Bich Minh Nguyen. Some immigrant memoirs concentrate more on delineating the often traumatic reasons for departure from the land of origin, including *Long Way Gone: Memoirs of a Boy Soldier* by Ishmael Beah.

As they attempt to settle in, first-generation immigrants are faced with the challenge of deciding to what extent they should maintain ties to, and preserve the traditions of, the homeland and to what extent they should adapt to and assimilate into the culture of the hostland. While it is necessary to make adjustments, accommodations and compromises in order to survive and even thrive in the new context, immigrants are faced with the dilemma of doing so without completely losing the culture and traditions of their land of origin. They fear loss of identity and dissolution and might observe the new mores of the hostland with confusion or suspicion. Some might cling to the traditions that existed in the homeland at the time of their departure or exile and be surprised when they return there after years or decades away to find that the culture of the homeland has changed in the intervening period.

This dilemma tends to be exacerbated by the arrival of the second generation. These offspring of immigrants are born and raised in the hostland. They have the advantages of being familiar from the beginning with the mores of the hostland but are faced with the dominance of one culture in the family home and another outside. Very often they find themselves straddling two cultures and perhaps two or more languages. They might act as interpreters—of both the culture and the language—for their parents. Unlike first-generation immigrants, in whom the culture of their land of origin might be ingrained, the second generation might be torn between two cultures or wish to embrace one and resent the imposition on them of the other, resulting in a divided identity. These difficulties can often lead to tensions between the first-generation parents and the second-generation offspring and are depicted in novels such as Amy Tan's *The Joy Luck Club*, Jhumpa Lahiri's *The Namesake*, Julia Alvarez's *How the Garcia Girls Lost Their Accents*, Taiye Selasi's *Ghana Must Go*, and in poems such as "Assimilation" by Eugene Gloria and "Translation for Mamá" by Richard Blanco.

Conversely, there might be immigrants who have chosen to leave the land of origin due to conflicts with the sociopolitical or cultural context there and decide to assimilate completely to the hostland, fully embracing new cultural and societal norms. It might be the case that the children of such immigrants might be eager to discover the culture and traditions of their parents' homeland, which also creates intergenerational problems. Second-generation immigrants might become emotionally invested and politically involved in their parents' homeland and try to influence what happens there, as detailed in novels such as V. V. Ganeshananthan's *Love Marriage*.

Immigrant parents and diasporic communities might have difficulties reconciling themselves to Stuart Hall's assertion that

> cultural identity [. . .] is a matter of 'becoming' as well as 'being.' It might belong to the future as much as to the past. It is not something which already exists, transcending place, time, history, and culture. Cultural identities come from somewhere, have histories. But, like everything which is historical, they undergo constant transformation. Far from being eternally fixed in some essentialized past, they are subject to the continuous 'play' of history, culture and power. (236)

First- and second-generation immigrants thus have to deal with the difficult reality of ongoing and unceasing negotiation entailed by cultural hybridity, which, according to Homi K. Bhabha is "[the] interstitial passage between fixed identifications" (4).

It is not only first- and second-generation immigrants that face difficulties. Third- and fourth-generation immigrants might also face issues based on race and ethnic or religious affiliations. These difficulties are heightened during times of conflict and war in the hostland if those conflicts and wars are with the land of origin of the immigrants or descendants of such immigrants. During World Wars I and II, immigrants to the United States from Germany, for example, had to show their loyalty to the hostland by anglicizing their names and switching from German to English at home for fear of repercussions. Japanese Americans were infamously interned during World War II and were also pressured to prove their loyalty to the hostland. Conflicting loyalties are depicted in John Okada's novel *No-No Boy*, in which a young man answers "no" twice to a questionnaire asking whether he, a second-generation Japanese American, would be willing to serve in the US military and pledge loyalty to the United States; his refusal stems from his resentment at the fact that he and his family were interned. He is sent to prison for two years as a result and has to face hostility from his family and community afterwards. Following the events of 9/11, Arab Americans, Muslim Americans, Sikh Americans and other peoples of color have had to face increased scrutiny and racial profiling as well as persecution and hate crimes, as illustrated in novels such as Mohsin Hamid's *The Reluctant Fundamentalist*.

Over the years, changing immigration policies have also meant that certain immigrants have had to deal with restrictions such as not being able to bring their families to the United States, leading to enforced and prolonged separations along with isolation and alienation, while some groups faced quota systems for decades. Undocumented immigrants have also had to live secret lives, in perpetual fear of deportation.

While the United States has been the desired location for many immigrants and is the focus for this collection, there are many literary works about other locations that have drawn immigrants. Novels such as Sam Selvon's *The Lonely Londoners*; Hanif Kureishi's *The Buddha of Suburbia*; Zadie Smith's *White Teeth*, Buchi Emecheta's *Second Class Citizen*; Andrea Levy's *Small Island*; Monica Ali's *Brick Lane*; Leila Aboulela's *Minaret*; and Kamila Shamsie's *Home Fire* are set in the United Kingdom, which has its own multicultural society as a result of the arrival of immigrants from its former colonies. Marjane Satrapi's graphic novel *Persepolis 2* details the hardships of the protagonist when she leaves her homeland of Iran and tries to find a sense of belonging in Vienna. Michael Ondaatje in his poetry collection *Handwriting* and M. G. Vassanji in his novel *The In-Between World of Vikram Lall* both write about multiple displacements and affiliations: Sri Lanka, England, and Canada in the case of the former and India, Kenya, and Canada in the case of the latter. Yasmine Gooneratne's novel *A Change of Skies* focuses on Sri Lankans reinventing themselves in Australia, while Channa Wickremesekera's novel *Distant Warriors* depicts a diasporic community in Australia that is divided on ethnic lines and, ironically, replicates the tensions of the homeland that many of them sought to escape through emigration.

As the range of novels, poems, and memoirs discussed in this essay and in the volume as a whole makes clear, the immigrant experience is vast in both scope and variety. Immigration has been a defining feature in the literature of the United States throughout its history, and immigrant literature continues to expand as an increasingly substantial part of literary production and criticism in the United States. Beyond the boundaries of the United States, there are many literary works that deal with the immigrant experience around the globe, and some of the works listed in this essay can serve as an opportunity for further reading that explores the literature of the immigrant experience as both American literature and, indeed, world literature.

Works Cited

Aboulela, Leila. *Minaret*. Bloomsbury, 2005.

Adichie, Chimamanda Ngozi. *The Thing Around Your Neck*. Anchor, 2010.

Alexander, Meena. *Fault Lines: A Memoir*. The Feminist Press at CUNY, 2003.

Ali, Mona. *Brick Lane*. Scribner, 2004.

Alvarez, Julia. *How the Garcia Girls Lost Their Accents*. Algonquin Books, 2010.

Bhabha, Homi K. *The Location of Culture*. Routledge, 1994.

Beah, Ishmael. *Long Way Gone: Memoirs of a Boy Soldier*. Sarah Crichton Books, 2008.

Blanco, Richard. "Translation for Mamá." *Directions to the Beach of the Dead*. U of Arizona P, 2005, pp. 24-26.

Braziel, Jana Evans, and Anita Mannur, editors. *Theorizing Diaspora*. Blackwell, 2003.

Bulawayo, NoViolet. *We Need New Names*. Back Bay Books, 2014.

Dumas, Firoozeh. *Funny in Farsi: A Memoir of Growing Up Iranian in America*. Random House, 2006.

Emecheta, Buchi. *Second Class Citizen*. George Braziller, 1974.

Ganeshananthan, V. V. *Love Marriage*. Random House, 2008.

Gloria, Eugene. "Assimilation." *Returning a Borrowed Tongue: Poems by Filipino and Filipino American Writers*, edited by Nick Carbó, Coffee House Press, 1995, pp. 102-3.

Gooneratne, Yasmine. *A Change of Skies*. Picador, 1991.

Hall, Stuart. "Cultural Identity and Diaspora." *Theorizing Diaspora*, edited by Jana Evans Braziel and Anita Mannur, Blackwell, 2003, pp. 233-246.

Jain, Anupama. *How to be South Asian in America*. Temple UP, 2011.

Jen, Gish. *Who's Irish?: Stories*. Vintage, 2000.

Kincaid, Jamaica. *Lucy*. Farrar, Straus and Giroux, 2002.

Kingston, Maxine Hong. *The Woman Warrior: Memoirs of a Girlhood Among Ghosts*. Vintage, 1989.

Kureishi, Hanif. *The Buddha of Suburbia*. Penguin, 1991.

Lahiri, Jhumpa. *The Namesake*. Mariner, 2003.

Lee, Chang-Rae. *Native Speaker*. Riverhead, 1995.

Levy, Andrea. *Small Island*. Picador, 2010.

McCourt, Frank. *'Tis: A Memoir*. Simon and Schuster, 2000.

Mengestu, Dinaw. *The Beautiful Things That Heaven Bears*. Riverhead, 2007.

Mukherjee, Bharati. *Jasmine*. Grove Press, 1999.

Nguyen, Bich Minh. *Stealing Buddha's Dinner: A Memoir*. Penguin, 2008.

Nguyen, Viet Thanh. *The Refugees*. Grove Press, 2017.

Okada, John. *No-No Boy*. U of Washington P, 1976.

Ondaatje, Michael. *Handwriting: Poems*. Vintage, 2000.

Orduña, Jose. *The Weight of Shadows: A Memoir of Immigration and Displacement*. Beacon P, 2016.

Radhakrishnan, R. "Ethnicity in the Age of Diaspora." *Theorizing Diaspora*, edited by Jana Evans Braziel and Anita Mannur, Blackwell, 2003, pp. 119-31.

Rushdie, Salman. "Imaginary Homelands." *Imaginary Homelands: Essays and Criticism 1981–1991*. Granta, 1991, pp. 9-21.

Said, Edward. *Reflections on Exile and Other Essays*. Harvard UP, 2002.

Satrapi, Marjane. *Persepolis 2: The Story of a Return*. Pantheon, 2005.

Selasi, Taiye. *Ghana Must Go*. Penguin, 2014.

Selvon, Sam. *The Lonely Londoners*. Longman, 1989.

Shamsie, Kamila. *Home Fire*. Riverhead, 2017.

Smith, Zadie. *White Teeth*. Vintage, 2000.

Tan, Amy. *The Joy Luck Club*. Penguin, 1989.

Tölölyan, Khachig. "Rethinking *Diaspora*(s): Stateless Power in the Transnational Moment." *Diaspora* vol. 5, no. 1, 1996, pp. 3-36.

Vassanji, M. G. *The In-Between World of Vikram Lall*. Vintage, 2005.

Wickremesekera, Channa. *Distant Warriors*. Perera-Hussein, 2005.

CRITICAL
CONTEXTS

"The Hope for the Better": Immigrants in Jewish American Literature

Ezra Cappell

The Steerage, 1907 Alfred Stieglitz (American, 1864–1946)
Photogravure on vellum; 12 11/16 x 10 3/16 in. (32.2 x 25.8 cm)
Alfred Stieglitz Collection, 1933 (33.43.419)

It is only through an act of forced immigration that the Jewish people can become a nation. God tells Abram: "'Get thee out of thy country, and from thy kindred, and from thy father's house, unto the land that I will show thee. And I will make of thee a great nation, and I will bless thee, and make thy name great; and be thou a blessing'" (Genesis 12: 1-2). While this might be the first immigration story in Jewish literature, it certainly isn't the last. Some of the most iconic Jewish poems and prayers are immersed in migration stories, either by divine edict or by the evil decree of ancient rulers. In the twelfth century, for example, living in Spain, Yehudah Halevi pens his most iconic poem, a lyric suffused with the split reality of the life of an immigrant. As Jonathan Rosen says in his foreword to a collection of Halevi's poems that was recently published, "Halevi was born in Spain at the height of its Golden Age, but though he was celebrated as a master of the poetic forms of this most poetic era, enjoying wealth and fame as a poet, physician, and sage, in 1140, then in his late sixties, he turned his back on Spain and sailed for Crusader-ruled Palestine" (1). Here is Halevi's poem, "My heart is in the East":

> My heart is in the East, and I am at the ends of the West;
> How can I taste what I eat and how could it be pleasing to me?
> How shall I render my vows and my bonds, while yet
> Zion lies beneath the fetter of Edom, and I am in the chains of Arabia?
> It would be easy for me to leave all the bounty of Spain—
> As it is precious for me to behold the dust of the desolate sanctuary. (21)

This idea of being split in two—of being physically in one place while dreaming of another—is deeply connected to the Jewish experience.

When discussing Jewish exile and immigration there are a number of possible topics to consider: what constitutes a homeland (and leaving a homeland) for people who have spent millennia being uprooted from one country after another? Is home a physical place or is it a shared culture? Is it adherence to a shared set of beliefs? For those without land, can a language constitute a home for the displaced and uprooted? For generations of Jewish people, the

Torah, the Hebrew Bible, and its thousands of commentaries and holy texts, constituted a portable homeland for a people dispersed throughout the nations of the world.

Towards the beginning of his Holocaust memoir, Italian Jewish writer and chemist Primo Levi watches the mourning rituals of a group of Jews from Tripoli who had moved to Italy and were now about to be transported by cattle car to Auschwitz. They all gather together to light yahrzeit[1] candles for themselves: "We collected in a group outside their door and we experienced within ourselves a grief that was new for us, the ancient grief of the people that has no land, the grief without hope of the exodus which is renewed every century" (16).

This duality and split has continued to be a hallmark of the literature that immigrants and the children of immigrants created in America. It is, therefore, fitting that when we speak of American immigration literature we think immediately of the Jewish experience on these "alien shores." Between the years of 1881 and 1924, when the United States passed anti-immigrant legislation, over two million Jews emigrated from the pale of settlement in Europe to the "goldena medina,"[2] to the promised land of America. Writers like Mary Antin and Anzia Yezierska, Abraham Cahan, and Henry Roth all made immigration their theme and the source of their art. Jewish American immigrant writers dramatized the tremendous promise of the new world; their novels and memoirs highlight the relief of newly-arrived people who have left behind the seemingly endless discrimination and anti-Semitism of life in Europe, a life often defined by violence and pogroms. Yet these narratives, even while giving voice to the great promise of America, also concurrently dramatize the crushingly difficult lives the immigrants faced upon re-settling in America. Most of the Jewish immigrants, who made the journey in the steerage compartment of steamships, settled on the Lower East Side of Manhattan—a neighborhood composed of the poorest tenement buildings in NYC that by the 1890s was swarming with waves of Italian American, Irish American, and Jewish American immigrants all competing for air and light in a neighborhood that was the most densely populated place on Earth.

Jacob Riis, a Danish immigrant himself, attempted to educate the upper- and middle-classes about the horrors of the Lower East Side and the plight of immigrants in America. In 1890, he published his most well-known book of essays and photographs, *How the Other Half Lives*, and in his chapter titled "Jewtown," he describes the Jewish section of the Lower East Side:

> The tenements grow taller, and the gaps in their ranks close up rapidly as we cross the Bowery and, leaving Chinatown and the Italians behind, invade the Hebrew quarter. . . . So thoroughly has the chosen people crowded out the Gentiles in the Tenth Ward that, when the great Jewish holidays come around every year, the public schools in the district have practically to close up. Of their thousands of pupils scarce a handful come to school. Nor is there any suspicion that the rest are playing hookey. They stay honestly home to celebrate. There is no mistaking it: we are in Jewtown. It is said that nowhere in the world are so many people crowded together on a square mile as here. The average five-story tenement adds a story or two to its stature in Ludlow Street and an extra building on the rear lot, and yet the sign "To Let" is the rarest of all there. Here is one seven stories high. The sanitary policeman whose beat this is will tell you that it contains thirty-six families, but the term has a widely different meaning here and on the avenues. In this house, where a case of small-pox was reported, there were fifty-eight babies and thirty-eight children that were over five years of age. In Essex Street two small rooms in a six-story tenement were made to hold a "family" of father and mother, twelve children and six boarders. The boarder plays as important a part in the domestic economy of Jewtown as the lodger in the Mulberry Street Bend. These are samples of the packing of the population that has run up the record here to the rate of three hundred and thirty thousand per square mile. The densest crowding of Old London, I pointed out before, never got beyond a hundred and seventy-five thousand. Even the alley is crowded out. Through dark hallways and filthy cellars, crowded, as is every foot of the street, with dirty children, the settlements in the rear are reached... Life here means the hardest kind of work almost from the cradle. The world as a debtor has no credit in Jewtown. Its promise to pay wouldn't buy one of the old hats that are hawked about Hester Street, unless

backed by security representing labor done at lowest market rates. (Riis 128-129)

The very best of the immigrant writers make an attempt to balance the great promise of America, a land built upon founding documents guaranteeing equality and liberty for all, with the harsh reality of a poverty-laden existence filled with back-breaking manual labor and the anguish of dislocation, which defined the immigrant experience for so many.

Yet for the immigrant writer, these challenges are balanced by unique aesthetic possibilities. As Eva Hoffman, a Jewish writer who as a young girl emigrated from Poland in 1959 to Vancouver, British Columbia, suggests:

> For the immigrant writer the process of coming to know a new world involves the attempt to imagine and to enter into other subjectivities, and the subjectivity of another language. At the same time, literature more than perhaps any other form of human activity can give us insight into other subjectivities, fates, and lives. (246)

So, given the many nationalities that came to America in great numbers, why is it that we turn to the Jewish American experience as somehow being representative of the larger multi-ethnic group that collectively make up "the immigrant class"? The Statue of Liberty might provide us with an answer.

When the Statue of Liberty rose in New York harbor, it was meant as a symbol of nationalism. Yet a few years later, once the immortal words of Emma Lazarus, a Jewish American poet and descendent of immigrants to America, wrote her poem "The New Colossus," and once those words were inscribed on the base of "Lady Liberty," the public began to connect the Statue of Liberty with immigration and, more specifically, with Jewish American immigration.

A small boy shows his parents the Statue of Liberty from Ellis
Island U.S. immigration station in New York Harbor.
[ca. 1930], photographic print. Reproduction Number: LC-DIG-ds-03375
(digital file from original item) LC-USZ62-50904 (b&w film copy neg.)

Photo by Ezra Cappell

Given its iconic status in the field of Jewish immigration we will quote Lazarus's sonnet in its entirety:

Not like the brazen giant of Greek fame,
With conquering limbs astride from land to land;
Here at our sea-washed, sunset gates shall stand
A mighty woman with a torch, whose flame
Is the imprisoned lightning, and her name
Mother of Exiles. From her beacon-hand
Glows world-wide welcome; her mild eyes command
The air-bridged harbor that twin cities frame.
"Keep, ancient lands, your storied pomp!" cries she
With silent lips. "Give me your tired, your poor,
Your huddled masses yearning to breathe free,
The wretched refuse of your teeming shore.
Send these, the homeless, tempest-tost to me,
I lift my lamp beside the golden door!"

Following Emma Lazarus's lead, many Jewish immigrant writers wrote of their joy at finding America and being able to finally breathe free in a country that didn't persecute them simply for being born Jewish. Here is Mary Antin writing in her bestselling autobiography, *The Promised Land*:

In after years, when I passed as an American among Americans, if I was suddenly made aware of the past that lay forgotten,—if a letter from Russia, or a paragraph in the newspaper, or a conversation overheard in the street-car, suddenly reminded me of what I might have been,—I thought it miracle enough that I, Mashke, the granddaughter of Raphael the Russian, born to a humble destiny, should be at home in an American metropolis, be free to fashion my own life, and should dream my dreams in English phrases. But in the beginning my admiration was spent on more concrete embodiments of the splendors of America; such as fine houses, gay shops, electric engines and apparatus, public buildings, illuminations, and parades. My early letters to my Russian friends were filled with boastful descriptions of these glories of my new country. No native citizen of Chelsea took such pride and delight in its institutions as I did. It required no fife and drum corps, no Fourth of July procession, to set me tingling with patriotism. Even the common agents and instruments of municipal life, such as the letter carrier and the fire engine, I regarded with a measure of respect. I know what I thought of people who said that Chelsea was a very small, dull, unaspiring town, with no discernible excuse for a separate name or existence. (156)

Despite this beautiful image of a beacon in New York harbor welcoming immigrants, the actual immigrant story varied considerably from the version often portrayed in prose and poetry. Therefore, by the 1930s, many Jewish immigrant writers described the immigrant experience in decidedly darker tones. In his 1934 modernist masterpiece, *Call it Sleep*, Henry Roth writes of the moment the immigrant family gains their first glimpse of the Statue of Liberty:

> The spinning disk of the late-afternoon sun slanted behind her, and to those on board who gazed, her features were charred with shadow, her depths exhausted, her masses ironed to one single plane. Against the luminous sky the rays of her halo were spikes of darkness roweling the air; shadow flattened the torch she bore to a black cross against flawless light—the blackened hilt of a broken sword. Liberty. The child and his mother stared again at the massive figure in wonder. (14)

The early generation of immigrant writers attempted to capture the striving of the Jews who managed to make it over to America. An exchange between two recent Jewish immigrants in Anzia Yezierska's short story "Hunger" exemplifies this yearning and the desire to better oneself, a major theme of Yezierska's stories, as well as the work of many other Jewish American immigrant writers. In this scene, Shenah Pessah is out on a date with her sweatshop co-worker Sam Arkin:

> Through streets growing black with swarming crowds of toil-released workers they made their way. Sam Arkin's thick hand rested with a lightness new to him upon the little arm tucked under his. The haggling pushcart peddlers, the newsboys screaming, "Tageblatt, Abenblatt,

Herold," the roaring noises of the elevated trains resounding the paean of joy swelling his heart.

"America was good to me, but I never guessed how good till now." The words were out before he knew it. "Tell me only, what pulled you to this country?"

"What pulls anybody here? The hope for the better. People who got it good in the old world don't hunger for the new." (Yezierska 25)

This scene gives readers not just a vivid description of the yearning for a better life that, beneath the glow of the Statue of Liberty's torch, brought many millions of Jewish immigrants to the shores of the new world. Yezierska also gives her readers a visceral feel for the noise, confusion, and crowded streets of the turn-of-the-century Lower East Side.

This sweatshop world of garment workers is powerfully brought to life in an Abraham Cahan short story, "A Sweatshop Romance." In this story, Cahan describes the backbreaking work that most of the new immigrants experience. They may "hunger for the new," but if there is anything that Jewish American immigrant literature underscores for its readers, it is that the rewards of the new world were hard-won and often not experienced until the next generation, the second generation of immigrants in America who were able to rise out of the ghetto and make a better life for themselves. In the following passage, Abraham Cahan describes the typical day of a Jewish American immigrant sweatshop worker:

Lippman's was a task shop, and according to the signification which the term has in the political economy of the sweating world, his operator, baster, and finisher, while nominally engaged at so much a week, were in reality paid by the piece, the economical week being determined by a stipulated quantity of made-up coats rather than by a fixed number of the earth's revolutions around its axis; for the sweatshop day will not coincide with the solar day unless a given amount of work be accomplished in its course. (191)

What this meant was that most of the Jewish American immigrant workers in the sweatshops (as well as the thousands of Irish American and Italian American immigrant workers who toiled alongside them) routinely worked sixteen-hour days to make their daily quota of garment pieces. This hardly constituted "the good life" or "the hope for better" that inspired millions of immigrants to, following the biblical patriarch Abram's lead, "lech l'cha," to go forth and find a new life. Yet despite the many obstacles they encountered, these immigrants persevered, and their sweat and labor created many unimaginable opportunities for the next generation of Jewish Americans. This second generation was written about by postwar Jewish American writers: Saul Bellow, Bernard Malamud, and Philip Roth, who represented a great flowering of Jewish American letters.

Writing about that second generation of Jewish writers, historian and literary critic Irving Howe famously opined that once the generation of immigrant writers and their children passed, Jewish American literature as a genre would wither and die. In 1977, Irving Howe edited an anthology called *Jewish-American Stories*. In his introductory remarks, Howe worried about the future of Jewish writing in America, a future without the benefit of its great sustaining theme: immigration. Howe wrote: "My own view is that American Jewish fiction has probably moved past its high point. Insofar as this body of writing draws heavily from the immigrant experience, it must suffer a depletion of resources, a thinning-out of materials and memories" (16). For Howe, Jewish literature took place on the streets and in the tenements of the Lower East Side.

Yet here we are forty years after Howe's pronouncement and, rather unpredictably, a new group of Jewish immigrants have re-invigorated the field of Jewish American literature. Over the past few decades these many Jewish immigrants have come over to the US from Russia and the former Soviet Republics. Writers like Gary Shteyngart, Lara Vapnyar, Boris Fishman, and David Bezmozgis (Jewish Canadian), to name just a few, have been creating new stories of Jewish immigration and writing a new chapter to the immigrant experience in Jewish American fiction.

At the outset of his 2006 novel *Absurdistan*, Gary Shteyngart reverses the paradigmatic Jewish American immigration tale.

Shteyngart's hero Misha Vainberg has been living in America for many years; however, during a trip back to Russia to attend his father's funeral, he ends up stuck in bureaucratic limbo after the terrorist attacks of 9/11. Throughout the novel, Vainberg remains exiled in his ancestral homeland of Russia. Shteyngart's hero does not attempt to make it "to" America like so many of Shalom Aleichem's characters, nor is he concerned with making it "in" America as so many of Abraham Cahan's characters are; rather, Shteyngart ironically tropes on this theme, focusing on Vainberg's attempt to re-integrate himself, to make it "back" into a post-9/11 America.

As a hip-hopping millionaire in a post-Soviet-era St. Petersburg, all Misha Vainberg wants is for the American embassy officials to allow him to return to the pre-9/11 idyll of New York City's cultural melting pot that he left behind when he went back to St. Petersburg to attend his murdered father's funeral. Therefore, unlike the immigrants dreaming of the *goldena medina* in early twentieth-century Jewish American fiction, Shteyngart's Vainberg—having been schooled in a top US liberal arts university, "Accidental College," modeled on Shteyngart's own undergraduate institution of Oberlin—is fully cognizant of what he has been deprived of in the 9/11 attacks: the great promise of American freedom and the opportunity to pursue his happiness and his hip-hop dreams and desires, all unimaginable pursuits in twenty-first-century Russia, where an ascendant anti-Semitism still persecutes Vainberg at every opportunity. Not only is Vainberg's mother's grave vandalized by marauding neo-Nazis, in several memorable scenes Shteyngart's hero suffers through vicious anti-Semitic assaults. Vainberg never reaches his adopted New York City homeland within the novel; instead there is an endless deferral of this mythical Eden. As a result, the actual New York City becomes replaced by an imaginative act, a reimagining of a fictional city and invented homeland. To this new mode of ironic Jewish American immigration novels, we could add Michael Chabon's 2007 novel *The Yiddish Policeman's Union*, which tells the story of Jews who have emigrated from Europe to Alaska once America has helped save them from the horrors of the

Holocaust—help, which in cold, hard, and brutal reality, was never forthcoming to the European Jews.

There is yet another group of recent Jewish American writers who are re-inventing and expanding our conception of an immigration story. Writers like Shulem Deen, Leah Vincent, Deborah Feldman, Shalom Auslander, and Leah Lax have been called *Off the Derech* (OTD), which literally means "off the path." The term refers to people who no longer follow the "derech," the life path, which according to rabbinic authority is the only legal and moral way to live one's life. Many individuals born into ultra-Orthodox communities who lose their faith and no longer adhere to the many strict communal rules and customs either end up leaving on their own or are forced to leave their birth communities. Usually this is a painful and bewildering rupture, as "OTD" people are cut off from their families and forced to remake their lives on the "outside" in the secular world.

Over the past few decades, many of these "OTD" individuals have written memoirs and novels dealing with their experiences of leaving the ultra-Orthodox communities of their birth for a far more bewilderingly modern existence in the outside world[3]. Whereas previous Jewish immigrants traveled for weeks in steerage over thousands of treacherous nautical miles in their journey from the Old World of Europe to the shores of America, many of these OTD individuals are physically just a short subway ride away on the 4 train from their ultra-Orthodox birth communities in Crown Heights, Brooklyn, for example, to the East Village in Manhattan. Although the physical space is not nearly as distant to travel for this new group of writers, the cultural and linguistic displacement can be even vaster than the oceans crossed by their immigrant ancestors generations ago. These OTD narratives, I believe, can be viewed as a new iteration of the Jewish immigrant experience in America.

We see this immigration motif quite clearly in Leah Lax's OTD memoir, *Uncovered: How I Left my Hasidic Life and Finally Came Home*: such is the seemingly unbridgeable space between her Hasidic community and the secular world of America that she feels completely like an immigrant. She uses many of the same tropes of

---

bewilderment we find in the first-generation immigrant writing of Abraham Cahan or Henry Roth. Lax, despite being raised her entire life in America, with her limited English proficiency, finds herself unable to make sense of the conversations she overhears at school. In a candid moment in her memoir, Lax discovers that she is just like the millions of Jewish immigrants who, a century earlier, came over in steerage from the old country.

> I'm changing in other ways. Maybe it's reading all those books, each with a different standpoint and philosophy, each with a different heart, forming in my mind a new collection of voices that aren't a Group in lockstep. Maybe it's all the time I'm spending outside of Hasidic land in heady academic freedom. I don't know. But now I can see that religious life has filled me with grandiose convictions, made me believe I knew God's words and thoughts and that I truly changed the world with the strike of a match or the proper tying of shoes. Now I just feel small and ineffective. Is that what the world out there is? No clear path—just an enormous jumble of conflicting beliefs, events, personalities, desires—and nothing I do will change it? I'll die, a blip, and leave no mark at all. And it doesn't matter how I tie my shoes.
>
> Yet, after all these years in black and white, I still don't know what color is.
>
> Although I can see paradox and irony everywhere I turn, I'm ill prepared to deal with it. In the secular world, I'm a child, or a new immigrant, without insight or reference points.
>
> In class and in the student lounge, I sidle up to conversations, but they talk about movies and television shows and politics and I don't know most of what they're talking about. Students meet and hang out in bars and coffee shops and restaurants, where I wouldn't know how to order or how to figure a tax and a tip. (Lax 283)

In this powerful new group of Off the Derech memoirs and narratives, we see that the great theme of the immigrant experience has once again moved to the forefront of Jewish American writing. Although back in the 1970s Irving Howe tolled the death knell for Jewish American literature, we see how this topic of immigration still suffuses and enlivens a new generation of Jewish writers, to

---

the delight of a new generation of readers discovering the joys and perils of being transplanted from one world and culture into the vast, swirling American present. Far from being closed, the topic of immigration continues to enliven Jewish American literature well into the twenty-first century and beyond. United States Poet Laureate Philip Levine, in his poem "The Mercy" (1999), shows the numerous ways that late twentieth century and contemporary Jewish American writers are reinventing and reimagining the immigration motif for a new audience.

The poem begins with Levine telling the story of his mother's harrowing journey from the old country to America and his efforts, many decades later, at researching and discovering as many details as he can about his mother's trip and the ship that brought her over to the new world. Here are the opening lines of the poem:

> The ship that took my mother to Ellis Island
> Eighty-three years ago was named "The Mercy."
> She remembers trying to eat a banana
> without first peeling it and seeing her first orange
> in the hands of a young Scot, a seaman
> who gave her a bite and wiped her mouth for her
> with a red bandana and taught her the word,
> "orange," saying it patiently over and over. (1-8)

The poem begins by dramatizing the deprivation and poverty faced by Jews in the shtetls of Europe. Levine's mother had apparently, at the age of nine, never seen a banana or an orange before. Although she is undertaking this great journey all by herself, at least Levine's mother has the help and generosity of another person, "a young Scot" (5) who gives her a taste of the promise of the new world.

Yet much like the immigrant experience in America, the voyage quickly turns dark, and smallpox rages among the passengers in steerage. Levine reports that while researching his mother's story at the New York Public Library, he discovers that disease was so rampant the ship was forced to sit in quarantine for a full month offshore before the passengers were allowed to disembark.

Through his powerful conclusion to the poem, Levine takes the Jewish immigrant experience in new directions, reinventing the form. Levine writes that while his mother's ship sat in quarantine, other ships continued to arrive, each filled with immigrants from around the world seeking a new, better life. According to Levine, the list of ships arriving in America "goes on for pages" (28) as "November gives/ way to winter, the sea pounds this alien shore" (28-29).

After alluding to Psalm 137 with the line "this alien shore," Levine connects his mother's story of traveling alone across America, to the story of other, different ethnic immigrant groups and their difficult experiences in the new world. Levine tells his readers about Italian miners from Piemonte, who: "dig / under towns in western Pennsylvania / only to rediscover the same nightmare / they left at home" (30-33).

Once Levine shows his readers the life of backbreaking and soul-crushing manual labor that awaits so many of the new immigrants to these "alien shores," he concludes with that moment of mercy with which he began his poem:

A nine-year-old girl travels
all night by train with one suitcase and an orange.
She learns that mercy is something you can eat
again and again while the juice spills over
your chin, you can wipe it away with the back
of your hands and you can never get enough. (33-38)

We see Philip Levine meditating in his poem not just on his Jewish mother's difficult passage to America, but, unlike the earlier generation of Jewish American immigrant writers, he takes her story a step further and connects her experience of dislocation and fear, but also of kindness and mercy, to the experience of other ethnic groups who also toiled on these "alien shores," a reference to Psalm 137. This Psalm tells an earlier story of Jewish forced migration into their long and difficult exile:

Psalm 137 King James Version (KJV)

1 By the rivers of Babylon, there we sat down, yea, we wept, when we remembered Zion.

2 We hanged our harps upon the willows in the midst thereof.

3 For there they that carried us away captive required of us a song; and they that wasted us required of us mirth, saying, Sing us one of the songs of Zion.

4 How shall we sing the Lord's song in a strange land?

5 If I forget thee, O Jerusalem, let my right hand forget her cunning.

6 If I do not remember thee, let my tongue cleave to the roof of my mouth; if I prefer not Jerusalem above my chief joy.

7 Remember, O Lord, the children of Edom in the day of Jerusalem; who said, Rase it, rase it, even to the foundation thereof.

8 O daughter of Babylon, who art to be destroyed; happy shall he be, that rewardeth thee as thou hast served us.

9 Happy shall he be, that taketh and dasheth thy little ones against the stones.

Psalm 137 tells the story of the Jews being taken into exile in Babylon after the sacking of Jerusalem and the destruction of the holy temple. As the Jews were being taken into captivity, their captors, wanting to make sport of their slaves, demanded that they sing them a song. This cruelty elicited one of the most famous retorts in all of Hebrew literature: "How shall we sing the Lord's song in a strange land?" (l. 4). The Jewish survivors refused a song for their captors and, hanging their harps on the willow trees, they vowed to always raise the memory of the destruction of Jerusalem even above their highest joy.

In his poem, "The Mercy," Levine glosses this psalm with his reference to "alien shores," yet rather than perpetuate this endless cycle of retributive violence, Levine ironically reverses this message. In his poem, Levine suggests that with a little bit of mercy (sometimes all it takes is an orange), immigrants might just make it in America after all.

In Psalm 137, the speaker wishes to visit upon the captors what they had done during the destruction of Jerusalem. The poet cries: "Happy shall he be, that taketh and dasheth thy little ones against the stones" (9). In Levine's poem, instead of horrific violence, dashing a young girl's head against the rocks, there is the merciful offer of a gift, a hope-inducing orange. In Levine's immigration narrative, people from vastly different ethnicities and religious backgrounds help one another, supporting one another through compassion and mercy. Just like violence will always beget more counter-violence, mercy, too, will beget ever more goodness—and Levine suggests that immigrants, just like the rest of us, can never truly have enough mercy and generosity.

Levine imagines the Jewish American immigrant experience as a template upon which to view the suffering and difficulties of other ethnic groups as well: his mother's story is interwoven with the tale of Italian American miners from Piemonte who, instead of finding "hope for the better" as Anzia Yezierska's characters do, "rediscover the same nightmare they left at home" (30-33). It is this cycle of unending violence that Levine suggests is the flipside of American mercy and freedom. For Emma Lazarus, the Statue of Liberty represents the dream and promise of a new, better life for the millions of immigrants streaming beneath her raised torch, but Philip Levine's poem "The Mercy" suggests that all too often these immigrants will awake to the difficult reality of poverty and unending physical labor in the new land of America.

Levine's paradox, the great promise of America versus the reality as experienced by the vast majority of new immigrants to this land, is at the heart of the Jewish American literary experience in the twentieth century, and, as we have seen, it still animates much of Jewish literary production today. Despite this reality, the title of Levine's poem leaves readers with the salient image of one vulnerable person, a young Scotsman, showing mercy to another even more vulnerable Jewish immigrant—a nine-year old girl, all alone on her way to a new world where she did not speak the language and knew almost no one. Levine's poem stridently informs us that if immigrants are going to succeed in the new world, they must rely upon one another and not wait for governmental or institutional compassion or support.

Levine, in his fin de siècle poem of immigration, complicates the Jewish American experience by connecting it powerfully to another equally compelling story of immigration and hardship, the story of coal miners from Piemonte. Unlike Irving Howe, who felt that with the death of the immigrant generation, Jewish American literature had passed its "high water mark," Levine's poem, recent Russian Jewish tales of immigration, and the Off the Derech narratives considered earlier, remind us that "the past is never dead. It's not even past" (Faulkner 73). Immigration narratives continue to inspire new ways of thinking and writing about the continuing saga of the Jewish experience in America.

Notes

1. A yahrzeit candle is a memorial candle that is lit in memory of the dead.

2. The phrase *goldena medina* literally means "the golden land" or "the golden state." Brochures advertising steamship passage to the new world often exaggerated the wealth of America, claiming the US was so rich that its streets were paved with gold.

3. Keeping with our theme of "the hope for the better," one tool being used to help OTD individuals is a series of videos titled "It Gets Besser." *Besser* is the Yiddish word for "better," and the group is dedicated to instilling hope and belief in recent "immigrants" from ultra-Orthodox communities that, over time once they acclimate to their new world, life will indeed get better. The "It Gets Besser" videos feature "before" and "after" pictures of OTD individuals, showing them first as ultra-Orthodox people and then wearing secular garb.

Works Cited

Antin, Mary. *The Promised Land*. Houghton Mifflin Company, 1912.

Cahan, Abraham. *Yekl and the Imported Bridegroom*. Dover, 1970.

Chabon, Michael. *The Yiddish Policeman's Union*. Harper Perennial, 2007.

Faulkner, William. *Requiem for a Nun*. Vintage, 2012.

Ghert-Zand, Renee. "A Video Message to the Ultra-Orthodox: 'It Gets Besser.'" *The Forward*, 12 Jul. 2011, forward.com/schmooze/139753/a-video-message-to-the-ultra-orthodox-it-gets/. Accessed 21 Dec. 2017.

Halevi, Yehudah. *The Selected Poems of Yehuda Halevi*. Edited by Hillel Halkin, Nextbook, 2011.

Hoffman, Eva. Afterword. *The Writer Uprooted: Contemporary Jewish Exile Literature*, edited by Alvin H. Rosenfeld. Indiana UP, 2008, pp. 234-246.

Howe, Irving. *Jewish-American Stories*. Edited and introduction by Irving Howe. New American Library, 1977.

Lax, Leah. *Uncovered: How I left Hasidic Life and Finally Came Home*. She Writes P, 2015.

Levi, Primo., S. J Woolf, and Philip Roth. *Survival in Auschwitz: The Nazi Assault On Humanity*. 1st Touchstone ed. New York: Simon & Schuster, 1996.

Levine, Philip. "The Mercy." *The Mercy: Poems*. Knopf Doubleday, 2011, p. 73.

Riis, Jacob. *How the Other Half Lives*. Bedford, 1996.

Roth, Henry. *Call it Sleep*. Farrar, Straus and Giroux, 1994.

Shteyngart, Gary. *Absurdistan*. Random House, 2007.

Yezierska, Anzia. *How I Found America: Collected Stories of Anzia Yezierska*. Persea Books, 1991.

Who We Are: South Asian Women Writing Life and Identity_____

Umme Al-wazedi

> She says to herself if she were able to write she could continue to
> live.
>
> (Theresa Hak Kyung Cha, *Dictee*)

Immigrant women writers have struggled to address the most crucial
aspect of their identity—that of belonging. These writers have
grappled with many questions: How does one belong? Where does
one belong? What is wrong in being considered an American instead
of a hyphenated American? Their writing is about their identity as
much as it is about their characters, and they refuse to be "otherized"
and "objectified" (Mukherjee 33). The idea of identity is complex
because it is not simply "a transgression or just a matter of identity
formation," as Sara Ahmed argues; often these writers need to
negotiate their identities (96). The burden of negotiating identities,
which can be hybrid and multiple, is also complex because the world
that these women writers live in introduces to them the complicated
notions of race and ethnicity, faith and interracial marriages, sexism
and homophobia. South Asian immigrant women writers have their
own way of reacting to these issues; some explore them through
stories—often romantic stories—while some create collages of
memory and others analyze these issues through critical essays.

Tahiri Naqvi is a Pakistani American writer who has written
about Pakistani women in Pakistan as well as in the United States.
In Naqvi's short story "Brave We Are," the narrator, a Pakistani
American woman, tries to define the word *hybrid* to her son, Kasim.
While defining the word, she continues cooking her own hybrid
food arrangement of Pakistani spaghetti. She thinks nothing of her
son associating different items together to arrive at the meaning of
hybridity until he connects the concept to a human being:

"Mom, Ammi," he asks, [. . .] "What does hybrid mean?"
"Hybrid?" [. . .]
"Yea, hybrid. Do you know what it means?" [. . .]
"It's a sort of mixture, a combination of different sorts of things," I
say wisely, with the absolute knowledge that "things" is susceptible
to misinterpretation. I rack my brain for a good example. If I don't
hurry up with one he's going to move away with the notion that his
mother doesn't know what hybrid means.
"You mean if you mix orange juice with lemonade it's going to
become hybrid juice?" [. . .]
"Well, that too." [. . .] "The word is used when you breed two different
kinds of plants or animals, it's called cross-breeding." (Naqvi 57)

After explaining this definition, she gives an example of a hybrid
apple to her son, concluding that the new apple will probably have a
name like Macintosh-Yellow. Kasim retorts, "Does that mean Mary
is also hybrid?" Kasim's voice crashes into the narrator's thoughts
because she has not anticipated that he would apply the meaning of
hybridity to his friend, Mary. Kasim doesn't repudiate the definition
of hybridity but comes to a conclusion that Mary, the daughter of
a Pakistani father and an English mother, is a hybrid. The narrator
is definitely shocked at her son's attempt at linking the concept of
hybridity to his friend's racial identity. While the narrator seems
to resist the application of the word hybridity to Mary, her food
preparation tells a greater "truth" about hybridity than her perception
of Mary's hybrid genealogy.

If a hybrid identity is explained through a biological,
essentialized definition, then that hybridity becomes negative,
such as the case of the mulatto. Yet if it is seen as positive, it still
does not mean that two wholes combine into a simple third whole.
Rather, hybridity creates a dynamic being who is a part of a more
heterogeneous group. Naqvi points out through the above scene in
her story, the challenge faced by a mother who tries to define a hybrid
identity without creating a stereotype "that can neither be waved
nor be dismissed with flippant ambiguity" (59). The narrator tries to
evade her son's question about Mary's hybrid identity tactfully, yet
through her utterances, Naqvi seems to emphasize that the issue of

hybridity cannot be ignored. The narrator is aware of the fact that the biological definition of hybridity may cause a problem. As readers, we are able to connect the narrator's reluctance to let Kasim apply the term hybrid to Mary to the history of mixed-race children being called "halfies" and "half-breeds" in the United States. Genealogy becomes problematic in this scene, and the narrator definitely sees such an identity as negative. We can see this through her recounting of a conversation she had with Mary's English mother, Helen, about Mary's father's ideas concerning his children's lives. Mary's father, as Helen communicates to the narrator, is reluctant to let his children choose the mainstream lifestyle, such as having a girlfriend or a boyfriend, which is against Islamic culture. Yet the narrator remembers that Mary's father named his daughter Marium because "it's a name everyone knows" (Naqvi 58). The narrator thinks he chose it because it is familiar, convenient, and tri-religious (58), but perhaps it is also because people will not ask any questions about Mary's looks. Mary's father's attitude indicates there are difficulties in raising mixed-race children.

What complicates the narrator's position on the idea of hybridity is her own hybrid creation of food. While she makes the spaghetti during her conversation with Kasim, she is using South Asian ingredients as well as ingredients that are particular to the dish in the United States. In the end, she makes sure that "the spaghetti isn't squelched. The strands must remain smooth, elusive, separate" (Naqvi 60). The main ingredient must be pure. This image reflects back to the idea that "hybridity continues to be haunted by an idea of fusion or mixture that implicitly assumes 'the prior existence of pure, fixed, and separate antecedents'" (Kawash 5). So, through Naqvi's story, readers are aware of the fact that there is newness in the identity but that newness can't be named because it is something in-between, belonging to both the homeland and the host-land and neither.

Belonging to the new world that these writers have made their home and carrying the stories and experiences of the home country are also the subjects of Meena Alexander's writings. Alexander, who has lived in India, Sudan, England, and the United States, uses poems, explanations of poems, stories of her grandmother and her ancestral place, and history to construct her identity. In "House of a Thousand Doors" in the collection *The Shock of Arrival*, Alexander portrays the condition of a woman who can't enter the house:

She kneels at each
of the thousand doors in turn
paying her dues.
Her debt is endless.
I hear the flute played in darkness,
A bride forked thing,
I watch her kneel in all my lifetime
Imploring the household gods
Who will not let her in. (30)

In a vignette before the poem she talks about a "grandmother figure" who is not allowed in her father's house. Alexander says the reason for this exclusion is because she is "a female and a married woman" who "has to leave her mother's house" but can't come back again (28). If she tries, she is denied entry to the house she grew up in. Alexander feels that her situation is similar to that of this grandmother: when she married and came to America, she couldn't go back and enter her father's house. This poem has two meanings about belonging: one South Asian, that is, a woman's ultimate place is in her in-laws' house, while the other is that of an immigrant—an immigrant is an exile or, as she feels in her own heart, what W.E.B. Du Bois has said: "two souls, two thoughts . . . in one dark body" (Alexander 2). When she began living in America, she felt she was living in a place "where she has no history" (63). Her history is here constructed through the stereotypical, exotic image of the western gaze—she is often seen as a Latina, a Guyanese, a Trinidadian, or a Fijian. Thus, she writes, "What does it mean to find one's place in America? What does finding a place mean for an Asian-American artist who bears within him- or herself the mark of radical migrancy?" (161).

Her questions lead her to focus on the famous woman freedom fighter in undivided India during the British colonial period, Sarojini

Naidu. Alexander talks about Naidu's struggle with having to speak English. Alexander writes of Naidu, "Born of Bengali parents in the city of Hyderabad, she spoke not Bengali but Urdu, the Islamic language of culture in her city. Living at the edge of Bengali and espousing Urdu, Naidu added English to her store, the language of British India" (172). Naidu used the English language in her political life as she gave speeches in English. So, she used the master's language to fight against the master. Alexander seems to say that she harbors the spirit of Naidu in the sense that she, as well, has made English her own language instead of writing in her mother tongue, Malayalam.

Similar to Meena Alexander, Chitra Banerjee Divakaruni also creates a dual self in her collection of short stories *Arranged Marriage*. She talks about women who come to America after their marriage and try to live in both worlds. Sometimes for the purpose of living a meaningful life, her characters assimilate completely to the new life in America. The characters often anticipate their American Dream. Alexander's short story "Clothes" chronicles the life of a young woman, Sumita, who is married to Somesh Sen. Somesh runs a 7-Eleven store in the United States. While still in India, Sumita dreams of this store—"Soft American music floated in the background as I moved between shelves stocked high with brightly colored cans and elegant-necked bottles, turning their labels carefully to the front, polishing them until they shone" (Divakaruni, *Arranged* 23). Her American Dream is to work in the store; however, when she reaches America, her life is no different from those of her friends who were married and continue to live in India. She has to live with her parents-in-law and remain at home and prepare food for the people who come to visit the parents and try on American clothes at night. She wears "American" clothes like shirts, skirts, and jeans and "marvel[s] at the curves" of her hips and thighs while Somesh promises to take her to the park where they can ride the roller coaster. Sumita's desire, though, is to go to the store and work there. She, sometimes together with Somesh, dreams of moving into her own home. But one night her dream is shattered as her husband is killed by a gunman who robs the 7-Eleven shop, thus robbing her dream with it.

The story continues when Sumita is thinking about the kindness of her in-laws, who give her a white sari to wear, as is the tradition for a widow, and break her bangles but don't ask her to cut her hair, blame her for their son's death, or send her away. While the parents-in-law decide to go back to India, Sumita decides to stay in "this new, dangerous land" (Divakaruni, *Arranged* 33). Divakaruni ends the story with Sumita's confidence that she will be able to survive in this country: "In the mirror a woman holds my gaze, her eyes apprehensive yet steady. She wears a blouse and skirt the color of almonds" (33). Thus, "Clothes" raises the question of stereotypes about arranged marriages and breaks that stereotype as well. It equally raises questions about the Indian woman and her agency: Couldn't Sumita wear saris and still be independent? Is the writer's message that one has to wear western clothes to be able to have empowerment? "Is the metaphor of clothes troubling in what it celebrates: America as liberation, India as stifling tradition?" questions Pallavi Rastogi (37).

From Sumita in the short story to Tilottama in the novel *The Mistress of Spices*, the story of making this new place home continues in the work of Divakaruni. Tilottama's story is told through magic and spices. The novel opens with a single line: "I am a mistress of spices" (Divakaruni, *Mistress* 3). Tilo runs a spice store in Oakland, California, which is magical as she can use the power of the spices to help people. She can sense the illness, the loneliness and alienation, the homesickness and the heartbreaks of the people around her and accordingly gives them remedies, but no one knows this:

> "The store. Even for those who know nothing of the inner room with its sacred secret shelves, the store is an excursion into the land of might-have-been. A self-indulgence dangerous for a brown people who come from elsewhere, to whom real Americans might say *Why?*" (6).

Tilo loves to help people, but she yearns for love in her life, so when she meets Raven, a Native American, she is divided within herself. If she falls in love, then she will lose the power of the spices; the spices will be angry, and she will be unable to help people. Tilo observes the lives of immigrants, who pass by her with all their troubles. She also feels their pain. Divakaruni talks about the violence that immigrants sustain to exist in this country through the story of Mohan and Veena. Mohan sells kababs and samosas in a cart, and he and his wife are planning to buy another cart and expand their business. He is attacked late at night by two white males and severely beaten up; "broken in body broken in mind by America," Mohan is traumatized and has psychological problems (Divakaruni, *Mistress* 182). In the end, his friends gather some funds and send Mohan and Veena back to India, thus bringing the couple's American Dream to an end. Tilo also feels very close to the women in her society; she feels the pain of Lalita, Ahuja's wife, and Geetha. These women talk about the abuse in their houses, their longing for a better life in a new world—America. Tilo hears, "Silence and tears, silence and tears, all the way to America. Bloated sack of pain swelling inside her throat until at last today turmeric untied the knot and let it out" (107).

Susana Vega-González argues that Divakaruni draws on the magical power of women that exist in her culture (3). From literature to the real world, Divakaruni believes in materializing that power. Thus, in an interview she says, "At Berkeley, I volunteered at the women's center. [. . .] As I got more involved, I became interested in helping battered women—violence against women crosses cultural borders and educational levels. Then, slowly, I focused on women in my community." In 1991, with a group of friends, she founded a help-line to provide services to Indian American women. The most important things the help-line volunteers do is listen and be an empathetic presence. Inspired by the life stories of these women, Divakaruni published a short story collection, *Arranged Marriages*, which told of their abuse—and their courage (Softky).

The pursuit of the American Dream continues in the stories of Bharati Mukherjee, who emphasizes that the journey is not always easy. In a *Massachusetts Review* interview, she affirms

. . . we immigrants have fascinating tales to relate. Many of us have lived in newly independent or emerging countries which are plagued by civil and religious conflicts. We have experienced rapid changes in the history of the nations in which we lived. When we uproot ourselves from those countries and come here, either by choice or out of necessity, we suddenly must absorb 200 years of American history and learn to adapt to American society. Our lives are remarkable, often heroic. (Mukherjee, "An Interview" 654)

Mukherjee, born a Brahmin in Kolkata and living in an extended family, was surrounded by her girl cousins in India. However, she always felt that she was different from her cousins as she didn't adhere to her father's wish, which was to "marry the perfect Bengali bridegroom selected by him" (Mukherjee, "Beyond" 29). Like her, her fictional character Jasmine in her novel *Jasmine* didn't want to get married to a groom chosen by her grandmother, at all—she wanted to be a doctor and have her own clinic. Jasmine, whose given name was Jyoti, grew up in a village in India before she came to America. Mukherjee shows the struggle of an undocumented immigrant who definitely achieves agency; yet, as Kristin Carter-Sanborn argues, Jasmine is someone who first transforms according to the fantasies of the men whom she meets (579). For instance, her husband Prakash changes her name to Jasmine: "He wanted to break down the Jyoti I'd been in Hasnapur and make me a new kind of city woman, to break off the past, he gave me a new name: Jasmine" (Mukherjee, *Jasmine* 77). Prakash dies in a terrorist attack, and then Jasmine leaves for America. The man who helps her to enter the US, Half-Face, fantasizes about her as a poor Third World woman who has nobody to protect her—"I have been to Asia and it's the armpit of the Universe" (112)—and he believes that this idea gives him the right to rape her. Then Jasmine meets Lillian Gordon, who calls her "Jazzy." Then she becomes Jase, the caregiver. The next man she meets, Bud, calls her Jane. Each naming is an attempt by others to give her a new identity, and sometimes these identities are racialized. For example, Jasmine tells the readers that Bud himself "courts me because I am alien. I am darkness, mystery, inscrutability" (200). She becomes racially a strange and exotic body.

Jasmine's life in America is filled with violence and hardship, but the novel ends with optimism and the re-emphasis of the complex nature of the identity of a woman in exile; as Jasmine notes, "Time will tell if I am a tornado, rubble-maker, arising from nowhere and disappearing into a cloud" (Mukherjee, *Jasmine* 241). From the very beginning Jasmine refused to accept her future: ". . . an astrologer . . . foretold of my widowhood and exile" (3). Now she is ready to face other obstacles and journey toward the next transformation, thus presenting to us a remarkable and heroic life.

What is striking about Mukherjee's writing and what separates her from her compatriots is her dialogue about multiculturalism and hyphenated identity in North America and her controversial positon on these issues. In her article "Beyond Multiculturalism," she talks about nationalism—Indian as well as Canadian and American. She feels that the traditional concept of the nation state is "violently destabilizing" (Mukherjee, "Beyond" 32). She tells us that to her father, identity was linked to the soil and family origins: "I was first a Mukherjee, then a Bengali Brahmin, and only then an Indian" (30). She critiques "the artificial retentions of 'pure race' and 'pure culture'" while talking about the other Indian expatriates' reaction to her self-declared identity as an American (33): "My rejection of hyphenization has been deliberately misrepresented as 'race treachery'" (33). She is skeptical of some first-generation Indian immigrants who, "embittered by overt anti-Asian racism and by unofficial 'glass-ceilings,' construct a phantom more-Indian-than-Indians-in-India" as a mechanism to fight against marginalization. However, she is equally critical of the American nationalism that is driven by the fear of what she calls, in the words of Daniel Stein, Executive Director of the Federation for American Reform, "cultural transmogrification" (32). She fiercely condemns the Eurocentrist and ethnocentrist view of only "like-looking, like-speaking, like-worshipping" people as members of a nation state. She is unable to see how the Canadian model, "the multicultural mosaic," could be successful when the country still holds onto its "fixed, exclusivist national identity" (31).

Unhappy with the racial profiling in Canada, she moved to the United States—a country she saw as a "stage for the drama of self-transformation" (Mukherjee, "Beyond" 29). What moves the readers most is her optimistic thought about Americans who "believe that one's station in life—poverty, education, family background—do not determine one's fate" (29). She was not oblivious to race-related hatred in America, as she noted the rise of physical and fatal attacks on Asian Americans in the 1990s. She reminds the mainstream Americans that "America's complexion is browning daily" (31). Critics were skeptical of Mukherjee when she "drape[d] herself in the stars and stripes in an Iowa corn field for the lead photo for her essay 'American Dreamer' in *Mother Jones* in 1997." Yet her response to criticism is curt and straightforward: "I choose to describe myself on my own terms, that is, as an American without hyphens" (33). Her reason is that by using hyphenization we give others the opportunity to marginalize us again; she asks, "Why is it that hyphenization is imposed only on non-white Americans?" She contends that hyphenization accentuates the categorization of the American landscape into a "center" and "periphery," and she championed the obliteration of this categorization (33). Why is it important to seriously ponder what Mukherjee is saying here even though she might appear as paradoxical as she also talks about her nostalgia for her Bengali culture? She discourages the retention of cultural memory if the aim of that retention is "cultural balkanization" (33). She wants to sensitize her readers "to think of culture and nationhood not as an uneasy aggregate of antagonistic *them's* and *us's*, but as a constantly re-forming, transmogrifying *we*" and invent "a new vocabulary that demands, and obtains, an equitable power-sharing for all the members of the American community" (33). This piece that she wrote in 1996 holds true to our time. As immigrant writers fight to retain their identity as Asian Americans and as Americans on their terms, as they are repeatedly criticized for owning the American Dream, and perpetually considered as outsiders through the closed border rhetoric, Mukherjee's very idealistic and optimistic conclusion seems to convey a positive note for the future: "I prefer that we forge a national identity that is born of our acknowledgement of the steady de-Europeanization of the American population, that constantly synthesizes—fuses— the disparate cultures of our country's residents, and that provides a new, sustaining, and unifying national creed" (34).

Naqvi, Alexander, Divakaruni, and Mukherjee speak multiple languages and carry with them multiple cultures. As they weave the powers of women in their writing, not only do they create new stories but also talk about the influence of the past, which can be seen as complex, with tradition and modernity at war every step of the way. Echoing what Theresa Hak Kyung Cha says in the epigraph that these writers lived by writing about these experiences, I conclude that at the same time they were successful in showing the triumphs in living through the struggles.

Works Cited

Ahmed, Sara. "'She'll Wake Up One of These Days and Find She's Turned into a Nigger': Passing through Hybridity." *Performativity and Belonging*, Edited by Vicki Bell, Sage, 1999, pp. 87-106.

Alexander, Meena. *The Shock of Arrival: Reflections on Postcolonial Experience*. South End P, 1996.

Carter-Sanborn, Kristin. "'We Murder Who We Were': Jasmine and the Violence of Identity." *American Literature*, vol. 66, no. 3, 1994, pp. 573-593.

Cha, Theresa Hak Kyung. *Dictee*. California UP, 2001.

Divakaruni, Chitra Banerjee. *Arranged Marriage*. Doubleday, 1995.

_____. *The Mistress of Spices*. Random House, 1998.

Kawash, Samira. *Dislocating the Color Line: Identity, Hybridity, and Singularity in African-American Narrative*. Stanford UP, 1997.

Mukherjee, Bharati. "An Interview with Bharati Mukherjee." With Alison Carb. *The Massachusetts Review*, vol. 29, 1998, pp. 645-54.

_____. "Beyond Multiculturalism: Surviving the Nineties," *Journal of Modern Literature*, vol. XX, no.1, 1996, pp. 29-34.

_____. *Jasmine*. Grove P, 1989.

Naqvi, Tahera. *Dying in a Strange Country*. TSAR, 2001.

Rastogi, Pallavi. "Pedagogical Strategies in Discussing Chitra Banerjee Divakaruni's *Arranged Marriage*." *Asian American Literature: Discourse & Pedagogies*, vol. 1, 2010, pp. 35-41.

Softky, Elizabeth. "Cross-cultural understanding spiced with the Indian diaspora." *Black Issues in Higher Education*, vol. 14, no.15, September 18, 1997, p. 26. Academic Search Complete, EBSCOhost. Accessed 22 Oct. 2017.

Vega-González, Susana. "Negotiating Boundaries in Divakaruni's *The Mistress of Spices* and Naylor's *Mama Day*." *Comparative Literature and Culture*, vol. 5, no.2, 2003. doi.org/10.7771/1481-4374.1186/. Accessed 13 Jan. 2018.

Myth and Migration in Junot Díaz's *The Brief Wondrous Life of Oscar Wao*_____

Asha Jeffers

Junot Díaz's 2007 debut novel *The Brief Wondrous Life of Oscar Wao* is a genre-straddling story that brings together a variety of different forms of writing, including "the highbrow *New Yorker* aesthetic; the immigrant novel; the family saga; the secret history; the Latin American *novela del dictador* (dictator novel); the growing body of Dominican American literature; and, as Díaz points out in an interview with *Callaloo*, also 'the African Diaspora tradition' (Céspedes and TorresSaillant 904)" (Miller 92). At the heart of this generically complex work is the narrative of one family, whose migration from the Dominican Republic to the United States allows the novel to engage with a wide variety of social and political issues and circumstances. Although the novel is narrated by Yunior, a Dominican American man with nerdy interests but a macho exterior, it follows the de Leon family. This family consists of our titular character, Oscar, an internally and externally nerdy, virginal, US-born Dominican boy, as well as his proud sister Lola and their difficult mother Beli, whose epic and troubled family and personal history in the Dominican Republic takes up a significant portion of the novel and is shown to greatly affect the lives of Oscar and Lola. This essay will focus on *Oscar Wao* as a novel of migration. In particular, it is a novel that explores the ways that the past and the ancestral homeland influences the lives of the children of immigrants through an engagement with myths. There are several different kinds of myths in the novel, including traditional folkloric concepts of curses and blessings, mythical reconstructions of the distant and recent history of the Dominican Republic, family mythologies, and what I call "myths of the future": comic books and science fiction.

Díaz's novel has attracted a great deal of critical attention in the years since its publication, approaching it from a number of standpoints. This diversity reflects the richness and multifaceted

34

nature of the text. Much criticism of the novel is, unsurprisingly, concerned with genre, particularly in relation to science fiction, fantasy, and magical realism (Bautista, Lopez-Calvo, Miller, Hanna, Nielson). Daniel Bautista proposes that the novel creates a new genre he calls "comic book realism," which "irreverently mixes realism and popular culture in an attempt to capture the bewildering variety of cultural influences that define the lives of Díaz's Dominican-American protagonists" (42). Bautista sees this new genre as a reworking of magical realism, a genre of literature that is particularly associated with Latin America. Some well-known magical realist writers are Gabriel García Márquez, Isabel Allende, and Jorge Luis Borges. Bautista usefully points out that many writers and critics see the mystical elements of magical realism as authentic representations of traditional and indigenous beliefs' influence on Latin American society (Bautista 42-43). Bautista argues that Oscar's position as the child of Dominican immigrants gives him a complicated relationship to the Dominican Republic. For Bautista, this complicated relationship sets Oscar as a character apart from those found in Latin American magical realist novels and the novel itself apart from the magical realist genre. Bautista also defends the novel's use of speculative fiction and fantasy, arguing that it is more than window dressing and denying that it is implicitly anti-nerd, as another critic, Henry Wessell, accuses it of being (Bautista 42). He does not, however, see speculative/science fiction and fantasy as mythologies in their own right. This chapter attempts to contextualize the novel's fantastical elements as mythological in a way similar to the more traditionally mythical aspects of the text, identifying science/speculative fiction particularly as myths of the future.

Some of the other criticism focuses on the political and historical implications of the text, some in order to praise the novel's contributions to conversations about Dominican history and diasporic politics (Rader) and others to critique the novel's political lens or a perceived lack of it (Neilson). José David Saldivar's "Conjectures on 'Americanity' and Junot Díaz's 'Fukú Americanus' in *The Brief Wondrous Life of Oscar Wao*" uses the novel's concept of the *fukú americanus*, a kind of curse that will be discussed in more detail below, to consider the novel's interventions into the silenced histories of oppression in the Caribbean. While Saldivar makes some excellent points about the novel, he does not address the mystical elements of the fukú. Elena Machado Sáez sees the novel as a "foundational fiction for the Dominican American diaspora" (523). She also sees the novel as failing to confront the relationship between the novel's narrative structure and the Dominican hypermasculinity that the novel critiques. Dixa Ramirez also critically engages the novel's depiction of masculinity; she connects the hypermasculinity so present in the text with the "a distinctly circum-Atlantic discourse of magic" (384). I will be engaging more fully with Ramirez's argument below.

To ground my discussion of myth in this essay, I draw on the ideas of the Caribbean writer and theorist Wilson Harris. He describes fable and myth as "variables of the imagination" (Harris 18) and builds a strong connection between myth and metaphor; myth's figurative nature creates within and outside of texts a way of seeing that is made clearer through comparison. He also draws out the inherently creative, meaning-making nature of myth, which is a significant aspect of how the term myth is traditionally used. This can be seen even in its Oxford English Dictionary definition: "a traditional story, typically involving supernatural beings or forces, which embodies and provides an explanation, aetiology, or justification for something such as the early history of a society, a religious belief or ritual, or a natural phenomenon" ("Myth"). Myth helps people to make sense of the world, particularly those aspects of it that are most difficult to understand. There are two main parts of Harris's way of thinking about myth that make it relevant to this essay: the way that myth changes when it is moved across spaces and places and the claim that myth can help the oppressed understand and build on the past, more so than even counter-histories.

Myths migrate with the people who believe them. This movement can cause change in both the myths themselves and the ways that people relate to their myths. Wilson Harris explores this change by comparing West African and Caribbean vodun (popularly known as voodoo) practices. He points out that West African vodun practices are conservative in that they are focused on maintaining unchanging ties with ancestors, while Caribbean vodun self-consciously goes against cultural norms (Harris 26). Because vodun in the Caribbean was actively suppressed during the colonial period and even afterwards, and because it was the result of not just one community's traditional beliefs but a mixing of many groups' religious traditions, it was necessary for it to be adapted to these particular circumstances. For Wilson, this "re-assembles an inter-tribal or cross-cultural community of families" (27), a myth that creates new kinds of relationships in the diaspora. The kinds of mythical concepts and figures found in *The Brief Wondrous Life of Oscar Wao* come from this kind of mixed heritage. Díaz points this out early in the novel, when the narrator is explaining the fukú, the novel's most central mythological concept. The fukú is not distinct to the Dominican Republic; versions of it can be found all over the Caribbean: "The Puetrorocks [Puerto Ricans] want to talk about fufus, and the Haitians have some shit just like it. There are a zillion of these fukú stories" (Díaz 6). The fukú is not only something that exists in several places, it is actually created by migration.

In this novel, the fukú, "generally a curse or a doom of some kind; specifically the Curse and the Doom of the New World" (Díaz 1), is born out of the suffering of enslaved Africans and brought to the Americas where it becomes "the death bane of the Tainos" (1), the indigenous people of Hispaniola, the island which contains the Dominican Republic and Haiti, as well as several other islands. Critically for this novel, the fukú is not just contained in the Caribbean; it travels. The narrator even suggests that the fukú was what killed John F. Kennedy and lost the Americans the Vietnam War (4-5). But the fukú comes in two sorts, little and large (1). The little version, which is the fukú's more general definition as "a curse or doom of some kind," follows its subjects wherever they go. Thus, when Oscar's mother Beli moves to the United States, the fukú is not left behind but continues to resonate in her life and the life of her children. This migration creates another set of changes to the relationship between the fukú (as well as other mythical concepts) with those who inherit its legacy.

For Harris, myth can be a more helpful and powerful way of understanding the past than counter-histories, by which I mean the writing of history from the perspective of the oppressed. While official history refers to historical narratives that support the views of those who have power, such as governments and ruling classes, counter-history refers to historical narratives that try to center the experience of common people and those who lacked political power. Harris argues that counter-histories use all the same techniques and premises as official history and therefore cannot really challenge it (Harris 23). Instead, Harris states,

> it is my assumption, in the light of all the foregoing, that a certain rapport exists between Haitian Vodun and West Indian limbo which suggests an epic potential or syndrome of variables. That epic potential, I believe, may supply the nerve-end of authority which is lacking at the moment in the conventional stance of history. (28)

Oppressed writers and artists are empowered by a turn to the mythical, the legendary, and the epic. Harris contends that "the true capacity of marginal and disadvantaged cultures resides in their genius to tilt the field of civilization so that one may visualize boundaries of persuasion in new and unsuspected lights to release a different apprehension of reality, the language of reality, a different *reading* of texts of reality" (50). So, for Harris, using myth and mythical language can open up new ways of looking at the world that not only helps us to understand the past better, but also to build a better future, a future that creates "the hope for a profoundly compassionate society committed to freedom within a creative scale" (28-29).

Díaz seems to share Harris's belief in the power of myth as he weaves numerous mythical concepts and ideas into his story to explore Dominican history as well as contemporary American culture and society. Importantly, Díaz's novel does not suggest that myths need to be believed in for them to be powerful, for either good or ill. As our narrator, Yunior, says, "It's perfectly fine if you don't believe in these 'superstitions.' In fact, it's better than fine—

it's perfect. Because no matter what you believe, fukú believes in you" (Díaz 5). This passage can be read as suggesting that whether or not you believe in curses, bad things still happen to you, but it also seems to suggest that it is in the best interest of the curse for you not to believe in it. Perhaps this is because the fukú, if you accept that it exists, also has an antidote: the zafa. The zafa is described as a "surefire counterspell that would keep you and your family safe" (7). A curse of mythical proportions requires a mythical defense against it. It is significant that this defense is "a simple word" (7) as this text is deeply invested in the power of language. Indeed, the book is framed in relation to this concept: "Even now as I write these words I wonder if this book ain't a zafa of sorts. My very own counterspell" (7). By framing the novel in these terms, Díaz suggests that recognizing a "curse" is necessary for coming to terms with it, and that to have any hope of overcoming it, a creative force is required.

As I have pointed out, the concept of the fukú is grounded in the specific historical context of Hispaniola. The fukú is associated with Christopher Columbus, "the Admiral" (Díaz 1). The *fukú americanus* is associated with Columbus in two ways, as it is "also called the *fukú* of the Admiral because the Admiral was both its midwife and one of its great European victims; despite 'discovering' the New World the Admiral died miserable and syphilitic, hearing (dique) divine voices" (1). The novel's beginning therefore provides an alternative way of reading the history of the Dominican Republic, an alternative that emphasizes the supernatural. This novel is not a realist or realistic counter-narrative. Instead, it takes on the language of myth to produce a different vision of the past of the island that makes clear the ways that the past and the island maintain an influence on even those who spend their lives away from it. But the novel also reveals the ways that distance, both physical and emotional, shapes different ways of understanding and dealing with the difficult legacies that the novel addresses. Saldivar rightly points out that Díaz's "remarkable framing of the *fukú americanus* as an alternative unit of analysis beyond the unit of the nation-state further allows him to think through the US and Eurocentric structures of hegemonic thought and representation that continue to dominate the globe today" (133); the fukú is not contained by Hispaniola even if it is born there.

The fukú is also associated with another important figure from the Dominican Republic's history: its long-reigning dictator, President Rafael Leónidas Trujillo Molina, most often known throughout the text as Trujillo, although also as "El Jefe, the Failed Cattle Thief, and Fuckface" (Díaz 1). He was president from 1930 to 1938 and then from 1942 to 1952. According to Yunior, "no one knows whether Trujillo was the Curse's servant or its master, its agent or its principal, but it was clear he and it had an understanding, that them two was *tight*" (2-3). A significant chunk of the novel tells the story of Oscar's ancestor Abelard Cabral's struggles under Trujillo, who brought about the once-prosperous family's destruction. Yunior gives three possible explanations for this destruction: "an accident, a conspiracy, or a fukú" (243); one banal, one realistic but more complex, and one supernatural. Yunior notes, "Most of the folks you speak to prefer the story with a supernatural twist. They believe that not only did Trujillo want Abelard's daughter, but when he couldn't snatch her, out of spite he put a fukú on the family's ass" (243). This supernatural reading of the event makes Trujillo seem powerful, but it also makes him seem evil; it supports Dixa Ramirez's claim that "*Oscar Wao* echoes the larger Dominican society's adoption of a magical 'shorthand' for discussing the machinations of unjust power" (386). In the Dominican Republic of *Oscar Wao*, supernatural explanations provide a language for power.

The novel also uses another sort of language to explore its themes: the language of speculative fiction and fantasy. At first, it seems to make a distinction between the mythical and the speculative but then turns around to question whether this distinction really holds. Yunior questions whether Oscar would have liked his classification of the story as a fukú story, suggesting that Oscar would have seen it as more sci-fi or fantasy. After all, Yunior imagines Oscar asking, "What more sci-fi than the Santo Domingo? What more fantasy than the Antilles?" (Díaz 6). Yunior's response, "But now that I know how it all turns out, I have to ask, in turn: What more fukú?"

(6), at first seems to suggest that he sees the mythical as a more appropriate lens through which to see the events of Oscar's life and the Dominican Republic as a place. Saldivar refers to "Oscar's double sciences—the Global North's science fiction and Césaire's Global South's new science or discipline of *négritude*" (131), the latter of which I argue can be seen as including the language of myth, growing from an Afro-Caribbean spiritual cosmology, that is weaved into the novel. Yet, Yunior continues to use science fiction and fantasy allusions throughout the narrative. One of the novel's epigraphs is even from a Fantastic Four comic: "Of what import are brief, nameless lives . . . to **Galactus**??" (emphasis in the original). This choice of epigraph is not just a signal of the novel's use of comic book language; it also sets up one of the major themes of the novel. Galactus, a supervillain, does not care for brief and nameless lives, but this novel raises one such life to mythical proportions. The language of speculative fiction and fantasy are in keeping with Oscar's role as a nerd; he is a child with Star Trek dolls (Díaz 13), a teen "painting his D&D miniatures or reading the latest Stephen King" (18) and eventually a young adult planning to write "a quartet of science-fiction fantasies that would be his crowning achievement. J.R.R. Tolkien meets E.E. 'Doc' Smith" (269). But Oscar is not our narrator; Yunior is. It is Yunior who names Oscar's eventual killers Solomon Grundy and Gorilla Grod after two DC Comics villains (294). Indeed, Yunior actually acknowledges his inclusion of these discourses in the novel; "I know I've thrown a lot of fantasy and sci-fi in the mix" (285) he admits. The inclusion of speculative language in the text's narrative is just as purposeful as the use of what is considered more obviously mythical language, such as the fukú.

The narrative's use of science fiction and fantasy allusions and illustrations suggests that both approaches, the traditionally mythical and the speculative, are valid. Indeed, it seems to suggest that they are even more productive when used together. Bautista acknowledges this coming together when he states that "the notion that Oscar's love for the speculative genres actually help [*sic*] him connect with older Dominican and familial beliefs represents an important reconciliation between what had first seemed like two very distinct traditions in the novel" (49). Myth is generally seen as concerned with the past and science fiction as concerned with the future, while fantasy can work in either direction, but generally on an alternate plane. *The Brief Wondrous Life of Oscar Wao* suggests that the modern world is not where myth goes to die but rather to be reborn. The novel makes clear that comic books and science fiction are myths just as much as the fukú—myths of the future rather than myths of the past, but nonetheless myths that tell us important things about ourselves, what we think, what we value, who we are, who we want to be, and who we fear being. Even as Yunior is applying the logic of the fukú to the death of Columbus and the US's defeat in Saigon, he is comparing the inescapable nature of the fukú to "Darkseid's Omega Effect" and "Morgoth's bane" (Díaz 5), the former a DC Comic's supervillain and the latter an evil character from the fantasy works of J.R.R. Tolkien. Díaz ties together the mythology of his ancestors and the mythology of comic books, fantasy, and science fiction so that they cannot be separated. Both sets of mythical language are a means of interpreting the present, one oriented towards the past and one oriented towards the future, and both shaping his characters' reading of the world. This is significant because it reminds us of the Janus figure, facing the past and the present, and its associations with migration and diaspora. The consistent relevance of more traditional mythical language does not undermine the fact that the reality of the immigrant and second-generation characters' lives lends itself particularly well to being expressed through the language of the speculative genres: "You really want to know what being an X-man feels like? Just be a smart bookish boy of color in a contemporary U.S. ghetto. Mamma mia! Like having bat wings or a pair of tentacles growing out of your chest" (22). Speculative language gives insight into racialized second-generation experiences.

For the immigrant and second-generation characters of the novel, the power of language and the language of power are important parts of how they can understand their own lives and pasts as well as the lives and pasts of others. Importantly, for these diasporic characters, this understanding does not have to concern only blood relations. While the protagonist of the novel is Oscar, the narrator is Yunior, who tells the story of Oscar and his family. When writing about the silence that surrounds the Cabral family's past, Ramirez argues that "the mystery of the Cabral family tragedy that begins with Abelard's imprisonment becomes a traumatic silence that cannot be broken, despite Oscar's attempts to write his family's history" (390). But Yunior does write the story of the Cabral family, even if his telling of it is incomplete. The family story is transmitted, just not by a blood relation. As an outsider to the family but involved in its present moment through complex social bonds—ex-boyfriend, sometimes roommate, biographer—Yunior can hold the story for the family's next generation, Lola's daughter Isis, who is the imaginary recipient of the novel. Yunior has his own family, and he hints that they too had their run-ins with Trujillo, but it is Oscar and his family's story that has its "fingers around [Yunior's] throat" (Díaz 6) and which he chooses to transmit intergenerationally. Regardless of what we might consider to be his own reasons for needing to tell Oscar's story, Yunior's storytelling resists the silencing of the past, a silencing that is a direct result of the power Trujillo had over the people and the discourse of the Dominican Republic.

By planning to transmit the stories of not only the Cabrals but also of Oscar to Isis through the language of myth, Yunior can imagine a future in which the American-born third generation daughter of his ex-girlfriend can transcend the difficult past that comes before her. Yunior's hope in Isis is not only for Oscar's family; it is also for himself. His investment in her is deeply personal; he states, "[she] could have been my daughter if I'd been smart, if I'd been ----" (Díaz 329). This silence is one of the moments in the text that reveals Yunior's simultaneous realization of the consequences of his toxic masculinity as well as his inability to express it or to avoid acting on it. Yet despite his flaw, or perhaps because of it, he sees the importance of Isis even without a blood-relationship as the lack of it "makes her no less precious" (329). The text suggests that intergenerational relationships need not be based on bonds of blood in immigrant families; they can be based on a larger, more unstable, but also more inclusive sense of connection. In Isis there is the coming together of all of the mythical discourses that make up the novel. She is the wearer of three "azabaches," jet amulets, "the one Oscar wore as a baby, the one Lola wore as a baby, and the one Beli was given by La Inca upon reaching Sanctuary," which Yunior describes as "powerful elder magic. Three shields against the Eye" (329). Thus, she is protected by a connection to her ancestors as well as by traditional magic objects. This is "backed by a six-mile plinth of prayer. (Lola's not stupid; she made both my mother and La Inca the girl's madrinas [godmothers]). Powerful wards indeed" (329-330); the spiritual legacy of La Inca, who raised Beli, shored up by that of Yunior's mother, who is occasionally mentioned throughout the novel, is also present for Isis. All of this, however, is not enough to protect her forever.

Yunior ominously predicts that "one day, though, the Circle will fail. As Circles always do. And for the first time she will hear the word *fukú*. And she will have a dream of the No Face Man. Not now, but soon" (Díaz 330). Just as Oscar, Lola, and Yunior were not free from the forces that shaped their parents' lives, neither is Isis. The fukú and its physical form, the No Face Man, who appears to Beli, Oscar, and Lola at various points in the text, persist and still need to be grappled with even at yet another remove from their origin. The difference, this section of the text seems to suggest, is that the second generation has already created some of the groundwork for coming to terms with this complicated legacy, work that can be completed by the third. When Isis comes "looking for answers" (330), Yunior plans to be ready. This penultimate section of the novel is written as a projection into the future; there is no guarantee that these events will take place, just hope. Yunior imagines that Isis will come, and he will show her everything he has kept: "I'll take her down to the basement and open the four refrigerators where I store her tio's books, his games, his manuscript, his comic books, his papers" (330). He will have set up the basement in such a way that she can stay with all of these things as she needs to, as many nights "as it takes" (330), but as it takes to what? Yunior's great hope is that "if she's as smart and as brave as I'm expecting she'll be, she'll take all we've done and all we've learned and add her own insights and she'll put an end to it. That is what, on my best days, I hope. What I dream" (330-331). It is significant that he expects that she will come to his home to see Oscar's things; he does not plan to give them to her but rather to have her visit with them. Yunior volunteers to bear the weight of Oscar and his family's struggles so that it is available to Isis, but she is not burdened by it. She will take with her the knowledge and the spiritual legacy of her forebears, blood-related or otherwise, but without having to drag their literal baggage behind her.

After Yunior has presented his imagined future meeting with Isis, he turns once again to one of the comic books that most prominently features in the novel: Frank Miller's *Watchmen*. Yunior produces a sort of false ending for the novel through quoting the actual ending of the comic. While he has expressed hope that Isis will "put an end to it" (Díaz 331), the "it" presumably referring to the fukú, he once again seems to question his belief that this is possible, through his repetition of the comic's ending. Adrian Veidt asks Dr. Manhattan for validation for his act of killing a sizable portion of New York City's population in order to save the world by bringing people together against a common enemy, saying, "I did the right thing, didn't I? It all worked out in the end" to which Dr. Manhattan replies, "In the end? Nothing ends, Adrian. Nothing ever ends" (331). This ominous suggestion leaves the novel's perspective of the future ambiguous; both the imagining about Isis and this invocation of *Watchmen* are stories, one imagined when Yunior is feeling hopeful and the other turned to when he feels "downtrodden or morose" (331). Neither is, yet, real. Oscar fell victim to the fukú, should you choose to believe in it, and Yunior is not free of it either, whether you believe in it or not. Added to this are the two stories of the final section. One is the never-delivered package of the things that Oscar wrote while in the Dominican Republic, what he claimed was "the cure to what ails us . . . The Cosmo DNA" (333). Like the book his grandfather Abelard wrote (246), his own analysis of the Dominican condition is lost. What does reach Yunior is the final story of the novel, the story of Oscar and Ybón's weekend away. This feels like a very strange way to end the novel. Machado Sáez sees this ending as Yunior "resolving" the uncomfortable queerness of Oscar (548). However, I would argue that by ending the novel in this space of intimacy—and not just sexual penetration but

> the little intimacies that he'd never in his whole life anticipated, like combing her hair or getting her underwear off a line or watching her walk naked to the bathroom or the way she would suddenly sit on his lap and put her face into his neck. The intimacies like listening to her tell him about being a little girl and him telling her that he'd been a virgin all his life (Díaz 334)

and yet having this space be so disjointed, a supplement to the part of the text that seemed complete—suggests instead an imaginative act of wish fulfilment, a gift from Yunior to Oscar of what he most longed for, not what Yunior wanted him to have. Perhaps this story is the only way that Yunior could end his zafa; knowing as the reader does that it is his relationship with Ybón that gets Oscar killed, perhaps the novel is making clear that fukú and zafa cannot be separated from one another and that within every fukú lives the seed of its own zafa and, more unsettlingly, within every zafa is the seed of the fukú.

Like many novels focused on immigrant characters, *The Brief Wondrous Life of Oscar Wao* splits its narrative between the ancestral homeland and the site of settlement. The origins of Dominican identities and worldviews are central to the novel, but so is the Dominican American experience and the second-generation American experience more broadly. This is particularly reflected in the novel's use of both deeply Dominican mythical discourses and deeply American mythical discourses. Just as any form of the Dominican American experience is necessarily affected by both of those places, so is this Dominican American novel. Just as immigrant and second-generation lives are greatly influenced by the past, particularly the past in the ancestral homeland, they are also very much invested in the future in the site of settlement. This simultaneous grappling with the past while trying to face and prepare for the future is reflected in much immigrant writing, and Junot Díaz is able to masterfully display these two priorities through his use of both myths of the past and myths of the future.

Works Cited

Bautista, Daniel. "Comic Book Realism: Form and Genre in Junot Díaz's *The Brief Wondrous Life of Oscar Wao*." *Journal of the Fantastic in the Arts*, vol. 21, no.1, 2010, pp. 41-53.

Díaz, Junot. *The Brief Wondrous Life of Oscar Wao*. Riverhead Books, 2007.

Hanna, Monica. "'Reassembling the Fragments': Battling Historiographies, Caribbean Discourse, and Nerd Genres in Junot Díaz's *The Brief Wondrous Life of Oscar Wao*." *Callaloo*, vol. 33, no. 2, 2010, pp. 498-520.

Harris, Wilson. *History, Fable and Myth in the Caribbean and Guianas*. Calaloux Publications, 1995.

Lopez-Calvo, Ignacio. "A Postmodern Platano's Trujillo: Junot Díaz's *The Brief Wondrous Life of Oscar Wao*, More Macondo than McOndo." *Antipodas: Journal of Hispanic and Galician Studies*, vol. 20, 2009, pp. 75-90.

Machado Saez, Elena. "Dictating Desire, Dictating Diaspora: Junot Díaz's *The Brief Wondrous Life of Oscar Wao* as Foundational Romance." *Contemporary Literature*, vol. 52, no.3, fall 2011, pp. 522-555.

Miller, T. S. "Preternatural Narration and the Lens of Genre Fiction in Junot Díaz's *The Brief Wondrous Life of Oscar Wao*." *Science Fiction Studies*, vol. 38, no.1, March 2011, pp. 92-114.

"Myth." *Oxford English Dictionary*, 2015, en.oxforddictionaries.com/definition/myth/. Accessed 15 Apr. 2015.

Nielson, Him. "The Geek vs. the Goat: Popcultural Politics in Junot Díaz's *The Brief Wondrous Life of Oscar Wao*." *Contracorriente: A Journal of Social History and Literature in Latin America*, vol. 11, no. 2, 2014, pp. 256-277.

Rader, Pamela J. "'Trawling in Silences': Finding Humanity in the Paginas en Blanco of History in Junot Díaz's *The Brief Wondrous Life of Oscar Wao*." *Label Me Latina/o*, vol. 2, spring 2012, pp. 1-23.

Ramirez, Dixa. "Great Men's magic: charting hyper-masculinity and supernatural discourses of power in Junot Diaz's *The Brief Wondrous*

Life of Oscar Wao." *Atlantic Studies*, vol. 10, no. 3, 2013, pp. 384-405.

Saldivar, José David. "Conjectures of 'Americanity' and Junot Díaz's 'Fuku Americanus' in *The Brief Wondrous Life of Oscar Wao.*" *The Global South*, vol. 5, no.1, spring 2011, pp. 120-136.

Graphic Anamnesis: Redrawing the Home Country in Thi Bui's *The Best We Could Do* and GB Tran's *Vietnamerica: A Family's Journey*____

Cynthia A. Leenerts

Traveling in the genre of graphic memoirs such as Art Spiegelman's *Maus*, Marjane Satrapi's *Persepolis*, and Alison Bechdel's *Fun Home*, GB Tran's *Vietnamerica: A Family's Journey* (2010) and Thi Bui's *The Best We Could Do* (2017) diversely sketch out family and national narratives, the narrator/artists laying out their own travel paths, bringing readers to understand not only immigrants' lives (as opposed to "immigrant life," which is by no means universal) in the United States, as well as conveying the complex and compelling nature of the Vietnam that they left, and which still exerts a hold on them. Central to both novels is the process of anamnesis: of recovering and reconstituting memory—in a sense, doing what Thi Bui calls a "rewind, reverse" (23) of an immigrant process of forgetting, in the wake of leaving a nation racked by colonialism and war, to a nation whose welcome would be tepid at best. Along with others in the Vietnamese diaspora, they have little chance of returning soon, let alone often, and hence, in those pre-Internet decades, almost no communication with those left behind: realistically, for years, they have no way to keep memories alive, apart from talking with one another, a dicey prospect when the past is laden with trauma.

At the time of this writing, Tran's novel has attracted attention from several literary critics (including Rocío G. Davis, Mary A. Goodwin, and Alaina Kaus), who focus on memory and reconstitution and their graphical representation, among other concerns. Bui's more recent memoir has attracted only book reviews and interviews thus far—possibly due to its recent publication, but also because some reviewers classify it as young adult (YA) fiction, one in *Booklist* characterizing it as an "approachable presentation of difficult subject matter [that] presents excellent curriculum support for older readers" (Bostrom). Moreover, Bui's publisher notes on the inner jacket, "Teacher's guide, discussion questions, and pronunciation key [are] available at abramsbooks.com/TheBestWeCouldDo,": it is marketed as YA, which makes some critics reluctant to engage with it, a deficiency that merits correction in the short and long runs.

My intent here is to analyze both novels—to add to the critical discussion of Tran's work and to initiate critical discussion of Bui's—by comparing their redrawings of memory and considering their narrators' processes of anamnesis embodied in their narrative lines and graphic representations.

The graphic-novel genre is ideal for memoirs of all varieties, particularly for immigration narratives. As Alaina Kaus observes in "A View from the Vietnamese Diaspora: Memories of Warfare and Refuge in GB Tran's *Vietnamerica*":

> [I]n many ways, GB's self-conscious reworkings of the past could not be told in any way other than through comics. *Vietnamerica* is one of a growing body of life narratives presented in the comics medium, standing alongside major works such as Art Spiegelman's *Maus*, Lynda Barry's *One Hundred Demons*, Marjane Satrapi's *Persepolis*, and Alison Bechdel's *Fun Home*. In her study of graphic life narratives by women, Hillary L. Chute explains that these works function through what she describes as the comics medium's 'cross-discursivity,' or the dual word and image arrangement on the page, to narrate read historical events that are often traumatic. [. . .] Chute states that [. . .] [t]he authors revisit their pasts, retrace events, and literally repicture them. (1)

Kaus builds on Chute's female-focused discussion to include a graphic memoir written by a man; cross-discursivity (the presence and interactions of both word and image on a page) is simply the way that a graphic novel, any graphic novel, speaks to its reader. Kaus's observations also apply to *The Best We Could Do*: the graphic-novel genre, the marriage of word and image, likewise provides the most compelling medium for Bui's story. Having read both novels—or any graphic novel, but especially a memoir that in Chute's words revisits, retraces, and repictures—it is worthwhile trying to imagine how such works would communicate as merely words on a page. This is not to say that a "traditional" memoir cannot be transformative or moving: to the extent that a writer brings in concrete images that appeal to the senses in a style that speaks to the reader, a memoir will transform and move, but in a graphic format, what may take a traditional narrative paragraphs or pages to build often appears in a single panel or a short series of panels, as happens in both *Vietnamerica* and *The Best We Could Do*.

* * *

A note about naming: throughout this essay, I separate the names of the author as author/artist and the author as character: I refer to GB Tran as "Tran" when discussing him as author/artist and as GB when discussing him as a character; similarly, Thi Bui is "Bui" as author/artist and "Thi" as a character. I refer to the other characters by the names that Tran and Thi most commonly use.

About pagination: while Bui's pagination is consistent and trackable, with clearly defined chapter breaks, Tran's novel rarely features page numbers and does not offer traditional chapter breaks: if he does number a page, it is at a pause or shift in his narrative (not as a titled chapter) by means of a monochromatic full-page panel (generally called a splash panel) in black, brown, red, cyan, or white, followed by an isolated small panel against a monochromatic background, that page also numbered. Citing is thus problematic, but in an oddly compelling way: readers and critics must focus especially sharply on the visual, as well as on any accompanying narrative, when discussing his work. With Bui's novel, however, one may use the customary parenthetical citation. Also, throughout the essay, I typically use dashes or ellipsis dots to indicate panel transitions.

* * *

Both novels begin with a major generational event marking a transition. GB accompanies his parents (Tri and Dzung, whom he calls Dad and Mom) to Vietnam for the funerals of his paternal grandfather (Huu Nghiep) and maternal grandmother (Thi Mot), his last surviving grandparents; Thi gives birth to her son, attended by her husband Travis, with her mother (whom she consistently calls Má, as she calls her father Bố) out in the hall, overcome by emotion. Each narrator has essentially moved up a generation (GB by an ending and Thi by a beginning), and in each case, each narrator's mother opens a flood of recollection, later augmented by the more reticent father, and to a lesser extent (in Tran) by other family members and friends along the way. Parental narratives, particularly maternal, predominate by far, but those of the father (who in both texts initially resists any notion of a talking cure) often catch more attention: the fathers, each of whom is estranged from his own father, have both lived through great trauma, for which they typically compensate by shortness of words (and in Tri's case by the recurring *chk chk* of a lighter, used by him or by other men, to light cigarettes or funereal incense).

The backgrounds of Tran and Bui are similar on the surface, with a few significant differences: they both come from two-parent families, and each has three siblings: GB's are Lisa, Manny, and Vy (all of whom are born in Vietnam, while GB is born in the US); Thi's are Lan, Bích ("It's pronounced BICK, okay?" [Bui 29]), and her younger brother Tâm. Thi is the third (living) child; two additional siblings (Quyên and Tha'o), interestingly represented as shadows of adolescents, as if they had kept growing (29), have died in infancy, and her younger brother is born in a Malaysian refugee camp after the family leaves Vietnam. While Bui's family tree appears relatively uncluttered, some of Tran's relatives have multiple marriages or liaisons: GB's paternal grandmother, Le Nhi, abandoned by her husband, during the first Indochina War (between the Viet Minh and the French), enters a common-law marriage with "Le Colonel," by whom she has a son before he is killed in a marketplace bombing. Huu Nghiep also marries again. Tri himself later marries a Frenchwoman. In Tran's drawing of his family tree, her flowing blonde hair partially obscures her name, which begins with "He," with the third letter possibly an "n" or an "r." She gives birth to Lisa and Manny before leaving alone to return to France, and her very existence is kept as a family quasi-secret, GB not learning of her until adulthood. In Tran's family history, children often shift between relatives' homes, avoiding local flare-ups of war with the Japanese, the French, or the Americans, and at times, various adults take in orphans to help with the considerable daily workload of survival.

Legalistic boundaries of "family" are effaced in Tran's novel, much more so than in Bui's. Even so, in Bui's novel, family status does not guarantee intimacy. While Má speaks glowingly of her own father, she confesses about her mother, of whom she rarely speaks: "I hated it when my mother hit the servants. But she hit her children, too. We were ALL terrified of her" (Bui 142). She continues, across a few panels: "She always wore immaculate white clothes, and smoked exotic tobaccos. Sometimes I'd try to climb onto her lap and breathe in her smell . . . but she always pushed me away" (142). Even after her mother and father come to the United States when Thi is about twelve years old, their relationship remains distant (34). Not surprisingly, as a girl, Má initially does not plan to marry, telling her friends (albeit to Thi's shock when she relates it to her), "I can't picture it. I just want to study all my life. Become a doctor, if I can, and help people" (150). Thi recalls, "But I know what happened next. She married my father" (151). Their union is problematic, in many ways a casualty of the immigration process. Bố, like Má, had been a teacher in Vietnam, but in the US, like Má, he is now only offered menial jobs, so he stays at home with Thi and Tâm, leaving Má to carry the family's financial burdens, and more significantly, he isolates himself with his own demons, as yet not understood by his children. Even though at the time of her writing Bui's parents have separated, the family lives in relatively close proximity to one another—although, as Bui comments and upon which she elaborates, "proximity and closeness are not the same" (31).

Tran's family, by contrast, lives scattered around the US: Tran sketches a map showing New York (where he and Lisa live), California (where Vy lives), and Florida (where Manny lives) colored in yellow, labeled as the Federation of Free States; Arizona, colored red, is the Parent's Republic of Vietnam; the rest of the continental US, colored brown, separating siblings and parents, is the Great Cultural Divide, surrounded by the white Sea of Cultural

Loss (over which the family has flown to establish themselves in the US). As Kaus notes, "Clearly evoking the Vietnamese flag, the red and yellow chart Vietnam over the United States" (1). On the facing page, Tran observes, captioning a half-page panel of a plane crossing a dark blue, watercolor-clouded sky, "Mom and Dad fled Vietnam to keep the family together," adding, captioning a drawing of the whole (young) immigrant family (with only himself and Vy smiling), "If they hadn't, Dad would have ended up in a labor camp, Mom denied work and forced to struggle in poverty, and my sisters and brother reduced to street beggars. Who knows if I would have ever been born?"

Tran's and Bui's families' respective departures from Vietnam also account for some differences in the novels' outlooks and approaches: Tran's father, mother, and siblings are able, with the help of an American friend, to fly out of the country on April 25, 1975, five days before the iconic April 30, 1975 (known in many US history books and to South Vietnamese emigrés as the "Fall of Saigon"). The plane stops in the Philippines, in Guam, in San Diego, and ultimately in South Carolina, their eventual home: the trip takes a matter of days. Bui's family, by contrast, is unable to leave until 1978, when Thi is three years old and when Má is eight months pregnant with Tâm, and so they experience the worst of post-1975, pre-normalization Vietnam: because the parents have not clearly supported unification/liberation, they live a relatively precarious existence until they can arrange to escape with others by boat. As Bui narrates, they travel, avoiding government patrols and pirates, "one hundred kilometers east to international waters," then "seven hundred kilometers southwest to Terengganu, Malaysia" (240), thereafter waiting for months in a refugee camp for some nation in which they think they can survive to let them in. Fluency in French and competence in English help, but the Buis' journey is much more fraught than that of the Trans.

Despite their only slight difference in age (Thi is a toddler and GB yet unborn), they are of separate immigration generations: Thi of the first, and Tran of the second. Thi has a few active memories of Vietnam, as well as of her family's emigration, whereas GB has to rely upon accounts relayed by his parents and siblings, before eventually traveling to Vietnam as an adult. Because Thi has consciousness, memory, and speech when she arrives in the US, her acculturation process differs from that of GB, and so does her account thereof. Significantly, she chronicles her childhood, mostly in linear fashion, connecting her story with the recollections of her mother and father, while second-generation GB concentrates on his trip to Vietnam at age thirty, with his parents' stories forming extensive flashbacks, his own childhood a mostly irrelevant era.

Further, possibly because of greater proficiency in Vietnamese, Bui writes all Vietnamese names, places, and words with diacritical marks, whereas Tran does not. The diacritical marks reflect the tonal quality of Vietnamese. A name like Má, for example, carries a rising tone, one of the five tones used in the South, or the six used in the North, to distinguish it from other *ma* words of different tone. Bui focuses closely on language elsewhere in the novel, noting subtleties of words:

> When my mother spoke to her children, she called herself 'Mẹ," the term used in the North—a weighty, serious, more elegant word for 'Mother.' . . . We preferred the Southern word "Má," a jolly, bright sound we insisted fit her better. . . . I wonder now how I would feel if my son did something like that to me. (316)

In an inset panel on the same page, as she towels off her son after his bath, she invites him, "Call me Mama," and he retorts, "No! You are Mommy." She reflects:

> I'm no longer a kid . . . am I? Having a child taught me, certainly, that I am not the center of the universe. But being a child, even a grown-up one, seems to me to be a lifetime pass for selfishness. We hang resentment onto the things our parents did to us, or the things that they DIDN'T do for us . . . and in my case—call them by the wrong name. (317)

She pays close attention to that small but powerful word, rendered in the prestigious Northern dialect or the everyday Southern, extending to an Eastern/Western linguistic divide, and this focus also fans out to her usage of diacriticals, with their underlying tones.

* * *

To return: Tran's novel opens with death, Bui's with birth. These events release floods of memories, in both novels crossing from the frame narration to that of the mother, continuing with the father, and then moving on divergent paths. Anamnesis operates in each of the storytelling parents: the act of relating the past brings it progressively more to life to the narrator, especially in the case of the fathers, who each overcome initial reticence. Each novel's frame story also relates the anamnesis of the author. Both begin with the author's character in a moment of transition, with the father, mother, and others layering in narratives (in Tran, over several weeks in Vietnam in 2005; in Bui over a few years after the birth of her son). Throughout, the memoirs bring both into deeper understandings of who they are and where they have come from, reconstituting memory, bringing a fuller presence of Vietnam into their American or Americanized lives. What evolves is memory at one remove—mostly parental, although Bui can build on some actual childhood memories—but as the parents have experienced life in Vietnam a generation earlier, their children, now the parents' "Vietnamese" age, can begin to identify with them as adults in a way that would have been impossible for them to do as children.

Tran's frame story actually begins with the words of his mother as GB sits silently next to her on a plane: because GB would write this memoir with his name on the cover and spine, the reader may initially assume it is his narration, but as the mother continues to speak, the reader quickly discovers, seeing the words "your father," whose voice it is. Against panel backgrounds of the red, black, and pale yellow of the sky and the Saigon landscape of 1975, Dzung begins:

> "You know what your father was doing at your age? . . . He . . .
> WE left Vietnam. . . . On the morning of April 25, 1975, our family
> crammed into a U.S. cargo plane bound for America. . . . It was one

of the last to take off before the Vietcong bombs destroyed the Saigon airport later that night."

A wide central panel, wordless, depicts a destroyed airport, and then below, GB's father and mother, thirty years younger, sit pensively, as the mother voices over, "That was 30 years ago." Time jumps forward to another interior aircraft scene. As Mary Goodwin notes in "Mapping Memory in Tran's *Vietnamerica*," "the earlier trip is set in black against a red sky; on GB's later trip, however, the sky is empty and white." Tran's color scheme shifts to white, pale yellow, rust, and sky blue, and Dzung continues, while Tri sleeps, isolated by Bose headphones, "Your father was the same age as you are now. . . . Funny coincidence, don't you think?" As the narration proceeds, generations collapse into each other, especially those of fathers and sons: Tri uncannily resembles his father, Huu Nghiep, at his age—most uncomfortably, GB observes on a visit with his father to Huu Nghiep's house ("the coldest house in all of Saigon") as his grandfather's widow, who is never named, points out ("It's like my husband's sitting here in front of me"). She later grasps his arm too affectionately for his comfort level and notes, "Just as tall as your father," cuing Tri to lead an exit. Later, less disconcertingly, Tri's old friend Do, who does not make the 1975 exit and who spends six years in a re-education camp, observes the family likeness: "Same posture, same hair, same nose! . . . Act the same, too: whenever I visited Huu Nghiep after you escaped to America, he barely said a word. . . . It was just like NOT talking to you!" But resemblances are not always surface level: during this time, GB has already discovered that his grandfather, who had been a doctor, had also been a writer (ironically, given his neglect of his own son, of a book on the care of children); and on a subsequent visit to the cold house, he sees one of his father's paintings (discovering not only that his father had abandoned his painting career when leaving Vietnam, but that his seemingly cold and doctrinaire grandfather, who would have regarded his son's artwork as bourgeois, had nonetheless placed the one surviving painting—the rest had been burned in 1975—in a place of honor). While the DNA has not come out strongly in GB's appearance, it appears to have influenced his occupations as writer and artist.

Tran's graphic techniques subtly separate scenes and narratives, which is important because throughout the novel, flashbacks and flashforwards abound. He employs a variety of color palettes and techniques. The book's high-gloss paper sets off the saturated reds, blacks, and blues of battle scenes. The deep greens, blues, and browns of the countryside; the bright, cartoonish colors of some of Tri Huu's flashbacks; some stark black-and-white narratives; along with the primary red, yellow, and cyan of post-Liberation socialist-realism style splash panels; as well as the solid (or nearly solid) colored numbered pages, catch the eye, as well as replicating GB's iterative process of learning about his parents' and older relatives' pasts in Vietnam. The eye seeks a resting place now and then, but Tran's artwork keeps it moving. He uses a variety of panel shapes and sizes: some bordered, some open, some deckle-edged. Most are rectangular, but in a few instances, waving lines of smoke (generated by a burning incense stick or a flicked lighter) enclose rounded, irregular panels. His approach reaches into visual multi-media: a collage of photographs of the youthful Dzung, Tri (reminiscent of the photos that Vladek, in Art Spiegelman's *Maus*, drops on the table and the floor when he tells his son who in his family has survived and who has not [274-76]) and others forms a splash panel opposite the solid black page 137. Also facing a solid black page (Tran 159) is a map of Southeast Asia, with Laos, Thailand, and Cambodia stencil-labeled, like US military supply containers, with South Vietnam a deep trench, full of desperate men, women, and children reaching for retreating aircraft carriers and other boats. North Vietnam's trench is depicted as empty, and beyond the curved earth, the black sky over China is lit up with red rays. Tran's variety of illustration provides division, and hence momentum, to this otherwise undivided book. Tran also is careful to distinguish between narratives: he voices his mother in handwriting, his father in caps, and others in printed upper and lower case. As they speak, or are spoken of, characters age and "youth," often from panel to panel when memory rolls back the years or pushes them forward. Tran also ensures that a reader can recognize the aged, mature, youthful, or childlike depictions of any given character: characteristic features of hairline or hair ornament, eyes, and mouth stay uniform over the years, while faces and hair length and color will change with time.

In contrast, Bui's color palette throughout her novel is uniform: similarly to the color scheme of Alison Bechdel's *Fun Home* (a monochromatic grey-blue with black line), Bui makes a monochromatic wash of sienna (possibly evoking the orange house, her childhood San Diego home, or perhaps suggesting earth, red clay) with clean black lining and shading. A complementary sky blue frames the front and back cover linings and also features on the cover, which has the texture of good matte drawing stock (in comparison with Tran's glossy cover, done in the primary colors of the Vietnam and US flags). Her technique, especially when compared to that of Tran, seems simple: she does not shift color groupings, and her lettering is of a uniform font throughout, with the exception of sound effects. But the novel's chapter titles—labor; rewind, reverse; home, the holding pen; blood and rice; either, or; the chessboard; heroes and losers; the shore; fire and ash; and ebb and flow—organize her and her parents' narratives, without the need for differentiated color schemes. Moreover, Bui's novel, despite its depictions of stress, danger, and trauma, overall carries what the romantic poet William Wordsworth, in the preface to his 1800 collection *Lyrical Ballads*, could call "emotion recollected in tranquillity": despite the content of the memoir, her writing, more than Tran's, seems to arise from a sort of resolution, even serenity. She has had more time to process the stories, which emerged over a longer time period: GB's over a period of months, Thi's over a period of approximately ten years. The end of Tran's novel closes a narrative circle: time has rolled forward to the moment when his parents invite him to go with them on the trip with which he begins the novel—his delayed "yes" (provoked when he glances at his father's inscribed message in a book: "To my son, Gia-Bao Tran. 'A MAN WITHOUT HISTORY IS A TREE WITHOUT ROOTS'—Confucius") inspiring openness to change and the confrontation with history that has transpired throughout the memoir. Bui's novel ends on a note of hope, with Thi's ten-year-old son swimming blissfully underwater. GB is an adult, with transitions ahead of him; Thi, possessed of her parents' stories, has launched her own child into the future. Both novels provide tension in the form of traumatic memories, but Tran compresses his while Bui lets hers roll out over time. So the overall mood of the two novels is strikingly different: both navigate through trauma, but Tran remains edgy (frequently showing GB reacting with emotional explosions of shock or disbelief), while Bui seems to take each emotional wave in stride, perhaps because of her comparatively calmer colors and lines, but possibly because of their varying life experiences and personalities.

Under the apparent differences, Tran and Bui's techniques share some similarities. Bui's panels are mostly rectangular, some with closed borders and others open. Similarly to Tran, Bui provides photos (from the refugee camp), but rather than showing an overlapping collage, she tiles four photos (of Lan, of her father, of Bích, and of her mother holding her) evenly, captioned "We were now BOAT PEOPLE." She surrounds this family still life by sketches of other photographs, captioned "—five among hundreds of thousands of refugees flooding into neighboring countries, seeking asylum" (Bui 267).

Similarly to Tran, Bui youths her parents as they re-enter their past worlds, and she frequently juxtaposes herself and a parent at comparable ages. Her chapter 6 splash panel shows her and her young father facing away from each other, seemingly standing on the same curb, but separated by decades and an ocean. She regards the Brooklyn Bridge while he takes in a Saigon street scene, as she comments (on her side of the panel), "I imagine that the awe and excitement I felt for New York when I moved there after college" (and on his) "—must be something like what my father felt when he arrived in Sài Gòn in 1955" (Bui 173). More dramatically, Bui occasionally draws several panels, with her and her father aging and youthing as the narrative requires: Thi, as a child, observes her father (approximately forty years old, wearing a white tee-shirt and white pants, sitting at a dinette table, smoking). She reflects, "To understand how my father became the way he was"—shifting to the same child Thi, now watching her child-father (now her contemporary), wearing a black pyjama outfit, sitting at the same dinette, and still smoking—"I had to learn what happened to him as a little boy." In the next panel, a reverse-shot perspective shows both children seated at the dinette: "It took a long time"—shifting to the present, with her father, now old, and she, now mature, seated at the table (her father wearing a white tee-shirt and black pants), concluding "to learn the right questions to ask" (92).

Thi's approach to memory recovery is to actively interview her parents (whereas GB's mother initiates the cascade of recollections). Gazing at her newborn son, she reflects, "FAMILY is now something I have created—and not something I was born into— the responsibility is immense—A wave of empathy for my mother washes over me" (Bui 21-22). Having learned from her mother, "You forget how painful [childbirth] was.—I had forgotten until I saw you on that bed, and it all came back to me" (20), she seemingly feels compelled to reach out. Her mother has flown to New York to be with her when she gave birth, only to miss the moment, overcome in her own recollected pain. But their conversations in the hospital eventually culminate in Thi's moving her family to California to be near the rest, to reconnect. Once she learns the "right questions," her distant father, whom she initially sees as vaguely threatening, quietly menacing as he smokes his frustrations away at the kitchen table, unlocks himself, and "the stories poured forth with no beginning or end—anecdotes without shape, wounds beneath words" (93) and he launches himself back to 1951, to the countryside near Hai Phong. As Bui later comments, "Each of Bố's stories about childhood has a different shape but the same ending" (100): loss, accompanied by violence observed, more often suffered. His father beats him and his mother, and in 1945, his father throws his wife out. Her son never sees her again and only later hears that she has gone to China with a Nationalist soldier returning home from the war—she drops out of the narrative, over the border, later bearing three more children (117). Bố's father joins the Viet Minh, while his grandfather remains a landlord and raises the boy (with the father occasionally returning home to take out his frustrations on his son). Bui continues, "Away to the relative safety of Ha'i Phòng, a city now controlled by the French, went Bố at the age of seven," and jumping forward decades, "And in the dark apartment in San Diego, I grew up with the terrified boy who became my father" (128). She concludes, in her child persona, "Afraid of my father, craving safety and comfort, I had no idea that the terror I felt was only the long shadow of his own" (129). Looking over her artwork, her father comments to his adult daughter, "Mm. You know how it was for me. And why later I wouldn't be . . . normal" (130). In a September 2017 interview with Irene Noguchi, Bui explains:

> What I realized about my father is [that] he is a very afraid person. All through my childhood and life, he's been very afraid of everything and it's very crippling. It makes him dependent on my mom and his children to be his ambassadors in the world, and it's left him feeling unfulfilled in the United States. When I was a child, it was terrifying to be taken care of by someone who was always terrified. That passing on of fear was an unintentional lesson that the world is a terrifying place.

But as her father's stories unspool, the part of him that resisted fear, or temporarily repressed it, comes out when he relates how he was able to navigate the boat on which they escaped and save the lives of all on board. "In the end," writes Noguchi, "she paints her parents as deeply human: flawed yet persistently hopeful in their own ways." As Bui explains about the title of her memoir, "Sometimes the best we can do isn't good enough, and sometimes the best we can do is very heroic and amazing. And both those things can come from the same people" (qtd. in Noguchi).

Bui expresses more difficulty in writing about her mother, "maybe because my image of her is too tied up with my opinion of myself" (131), so she begins with her own memories of her mother, whose child self she idolized, "a princess in a home far more beautiful than mine, in a country more ancient and romantic than the one I knew" (135). Despite Má's alienation from her own mother, she still lives a privileged life, attending French schools and, unlike Bố, relatively cocooned from the conflict between the French and the Viet Minh. As the parental narratives unspool, Bui follows them forward through the years, gradually relating a national narrative of Vietnam, along with the maturing narratives of Má and Bố.

Both texts carry the twentieth-century history of Vietnam, as well as of Vietnamese families, and the political and the personal inextricably build the narratives. As Kaus writes of Tran, he

> represents the First and Second Indochina Wars from a perspective located within the Vietnamese diaspora. He thus offers a viewpoint often suppressed in popular, almost exclusively American-centric reproductions of Vietnam in the United States, from films such as Francis Ford Coppola's *Apocalypse Now* and Oliver Stone's *Platoon* to written works such as Michael Herr's *Dispatches* and Tim O'Brien's *Going After Cacciato* or *The Things They Carried*. Situating the Second Indochina War (1959–75), or the American War in Vietnam, within a much larger history of colonial violence and forced relocation, Tran [decenters] the role of the United States in his family's history, even as he presents a crucial depiction of the United States both before and after the so-termed "fall of Saigon" in April 1975.

Similarly, Bui writes from the Vietnamese diaspora, also narrating history, albeit concentrating more on the Second Indochina War. The two wars, however, both involved a liberation struggle within Vietnam (the first against France, the second against the US). Bui, like Tran, situates part of her family as complicit with the colonizers (sending the children to French schools), and she, like Tran, also shows family members questioning colonization and turning away from it, as young Má does in high school: feeling "a sense of nationalism, of pride in my own people," when despite her French fluency, she consciously chooses to speak Vietnamese and to turn away from elitism (Bui 147). But much of her history lesson focuses on the American war: in 1965, her mother relates, "American planes carpet-bombed a country dependent on agriculture with napalm and the defoliant Agent Orange" (200) and that "money ruined everything else [. . .] amidst skyrocketing inflation . . . teachers' salaries stayed fixed" (201). Reflecting on her parents' stories, Bui writes,

> I think a lot of Americans forget that for the Vietnamese . . . the war continued . . . whether America was involved or not. . . . For my parents, there was a rocket that barely missed their house . . . and killed a neighbor . . . best friends and students killed in combat. (209)

Bui portrays April 30, 1975, her panels set up in a rare diagonal arrangement: "In Việt Nam today, among the victors, it is called LIBERATION DAY. Overseas, among expats like my parents, it is remembered as THE DAY WE LOST OUR COUNTRY" (211): taking up nearly half the composition below is the iconic (to Americans, at least) scene of a helicopter atop a building, with hordes of persons, warded off by a man on the roof, captioned "This is the image that most people know of the fall of Sài Gòn" (211). In the following pages, radio bulletins, accompanied with stark images chronicling the listeners' fears, resolve in the unexpected (to Bui's parents, as well as to many American readers), as Bui explains,

> The American version of this story is one of South Vietnamese cowardice, corruption, and ineptitude . . . South Vietnamese soldiers abandoning their uniforms in the street . . . Americans crying at their wasted efforts to save a country not worth saving. . . . But Communist forces entered Sài Gòn without a fight, and no blood was shed. (216)

* * *

At this historical point, the Buis would have three more years in Vietnam, while the Trans have just left. While Tran's father does not have the literal last word, his thoughts, just before Dzung relates the story of their escape thirty years on, set that final narrative into perspective: Tri explains to GB, "You can't look at our family in a vacuum and apply your myopic contemporary Western filter to them." The caption for a panel of people warming their hands over a fire of Tri's paintings reads: "Our family wasn't alone. We weren't a special case. Everyone suffered. Everyone had to do whatever they needed to survive." Over a panel of Do embracing his wife are the words: "Years passed before families reunited." Tri continues, through scenes of rebuilding, of Thi Mot and her son putting away photos, of Huu Nghiep closing a dresser drawer and turning aside in agony from his yellow-star memorial on his wall: "Before people felt like they had a future again. By then, it was too late for my generation. Our hopes and dreams lie with our children. Every decision we made … Every sacrifice we gave … Was for their future." This narrative gives way to the scenes of the family's citizenship swearing-in ceremony, with the judge stamping their certificates and proclaiming (against a solid black panel), "Your journey has ended!" The next page, facing a solid black p. 245, shows an aircraft pulling together two land masses over the Pacific, turning the ocean into an hourglass shape (Goodwin noting that the image "[suggests] the strain the force needed to make the two sides meet, thus forming 'Vietnamerica'"). The aircraft stitches the narrow passage between the northern and southern gulfs. This suturing image is followed by the chaotic unrolling of the family's escape, introduced by Dzung, who is wiping her glasses: "We fled Vietnam on April 25, 1975, five days before the North's tanks rolled into Saigon and claimed victory" (Tran 246). Her panel is superimposed on an overpowering wall of solid black, fringed by silhouetted palm trees, with a North Vietnamese tank charging forward, backlit by a sky in multiple shades of red, striated with black (247). The airport scene is a double splash panel, two facing pages, where the eye must roam restlessly, finding nothing, or everything, sifting through a chaos that resolves into black-and-white continuation of the family's barely making it onto a plane, the aircraft doors slamming them in, a leaf blowing through the crack, making its way across three pages of blackness. As Goodwin observes, "the perspective at each stopping point is that of a prisoner, looking out from behind bars at a severely restricted view, an ironic contradiction to the text in those slices ("You're safe now!" "Freedom." "Liberty"). The exit scene (coming right after the triumphant "Your journey has ended!") fades to black, resuming with the final scene in New York, with GB reading his father's "A man without history" inscription and asking "Can I still go to Vietnam with you?"

And so GB has the literal last word in his memoir, but in response to his father and his mother. Thi also has the last word, but it is a culmination of much reflection, after having interviewed her parents over the years and now being ready to write, to relate the story. She recalls:

> My parents built their bubble around us—our home in America. They taught us to be respectful . . . to take care of one another . . . and to do well in school. . . . Those were the intended lessons. . . . The unintentional ones came from their unexorcised demons . . . and from the habits they formed over so many years of trying to survive. (Bui 295)

Bố admonishes, "Lock the door!" while Má tells them, "Always be the best in your class!" (Bui 296) But the lesson that goes deepest comes when the family has to evacuate the apartment because of a fire upstairs: Thi recalls, "This is the night I learned what my parents had been preparing me for my whole life . . . the inexplicable need and extraordinary ability to RUN when the shit hits the fan. My Refugee Reflex" (304-05).

To a deeper degree than GB, Thi works to assign lasting meanings to her parents' narratives, to ponder their implications for her, as well as for her son. She wonders:

> How much of ME is my own, and how much is stamped into my blood and bone, predestined? . . . I used to imagine that history had infused my parents' lives with the dust of a cataclysmic explosion. That it had seeped through their skin and become part of their blood. That being my father's child, I, too, was a product of war . . . and being my mother's child, could never measure up to her. But maybe being their child simply means that I will always feel the weight of their past. (Bui 324-25)

"At least," she reflects, "I no longer feel the need to reclaim a HOMELAND," understanding that "the ground beneath [her] parents' feet had always been shifting" (Bui 326). She worries whether she "would pass along some gene for sorrow . . . or unintentionally inflict damage [she] could never undo" (327). But the sight of her son at the beach, splashing and swimming fearlessly in the waves, provokes her to conclude, "I don't see war and loss . . . or even Travis and me . . ." (327). In the final splash panel, of her son gliding underwater, she writes, "and I think maybe he can be free" (328). Bui's conclusion is overtly hopeful in what she imagines for her son—not only based on what she herself has gone through, but her own continued acculturation. She is attached to a husband and to a growing child, and she clearly looks at the future, not only for her child, but for her students, many of whom are themselves immigrants.

At the time of his writing, Tran presents himself as unattached (although he would later marry and have children, his narrator at that time has not yet experienced the parental epiphany that Bui explores). His chronology—like memory, not linear—makes the novel seem to end just before the point at which he begins. He can keep working with the past and the future, and one may sense that unlike Bui's narrator, his narrator has not yet reached a resting place. Still, as Rocío Davis observes, his cover art may suggest that he has continued to transform, as the inside and outside covers

> show a family tree complete with pictures of the memoir's 'cast,' including family friends Do and Leonard (the American who helped the Tran family escape from Vietnam). The second-page spread is well structured, except for the lower left-hand corner, where Tran draws himself trying to collect and order the placards that will allow him to establish his position in the family tree. He holds his portrait with his Americanized name—[GB]—under his arm as he reaches for a board that has his full name—Gia-Bao, which he had refused to use from childhood—on it. This resonates with the entire book project, and with the quotation from Confucius that frames the narrative. Only by knowing the full history, he implies, can he occupy his place in the family tree. The urgency in the figure's movements suggests the need to know and appropriate the stories, acknowledging what this means for his own sense of self. Though the images on the front and back are identical, the feeling with which the reader approaches the second one have changed, as have those of the artist. (262)

*   *   *

In the healing of memories and in the coming to terms with oneself, with one's blood, and with one's nation (or nations), anamnesis is critical to moving forward. Romantic poet William Blake's trope of innocence, experience, and higher innocence (a construct that is neither American nor Vietnamese) can provide a way into understanding both Tran's and Bui's resolutions. Blake holds that we are born innocent, trustful, positive, secure; that life inevitably throws us into the realm of experience, a world of loss, of fear, of death; and that we can be (but too often are not) touched by beauty, by art, by the transcendent joys that lead us into the world of higher innocence. In this higher innocence, we have left behind both naiveté and nihilism and, now awakened, are connected with our inner self and with the outer world. Initially naïve (or otherwise unaware) children, both GB and Thi, matured into Tran and Bui, take up the burdens of memory (their own and those of their parents and other informants) and reach a point where they can discern (in disparate ways) what to keep, what to box up and store away, and why it is important to open up the boxes and sift through again.

Works Cited

Bechdel, Alison. *Fun Home: A Family Tragicomic.* Mariner, 2007.

Bostrom, Annie. "*The Best We Could Do.*" *Booklist*, vol. 113, no. 14, 15 Mar. 2017, p. 33. *Academic Search Complete.* Accessed 3 Oct. 2017.

Bui, Thi. *The Best We Could Do: An Illustrated Memoir.* Abrams Comicarts, 2017.

Davis, Rocío G. "Layering History: Graphic Embodiment and Emotions in GB Tran's *Vietnamerica.*" *Rethinking History*, vol. 19, no. 2, 2015, pp. 252-67. *Academic Search Complete.* Accessed 3 Oct. 2017.

Goodwin, Mary. "Mapping Memory in Tran's *Vietnamerica.*" *CLCWeb: Comparative Literature and Culture*, vol. 17, no. 3, Sept. 2015, n.p. *Literature Resource Center.* Accessed 3 Oct. 2017.

Kaus, Alaina. "A View from the Vietnamese Diaspora: Memories of Warfare and Refuge in GB Tran's *Vietnamerica.*" *Mosaic*, vol. 49, no. 4, Dec. 2016, p. 1. *Literature Resource Center.* Accessed 3 Oct. 2017.

Noguchi, Irena. "A Vietnam Story Told through the Eyes of Refugee Parents." *KQED Arts*. KQED, 1 Sept. 2017, ww2.kqed.org/arts/217/09/01/a-vietnam-story-told-through-the-eyes-of-refugee-parents/. Accessed 4 Sept. 2017.

Satrapi, Marjane. *The Complete Persepolis*. Pantheon, 2007.

Spiegelman, Art. *The Complete Maus*. Pantheon, 1997.

Tran, GB. *Vietnamerica: A Family's Journey*. Villard, 2010.

Wordsworth, William. "Preface to *Lyrical Ballads*." 1800. *Bartleby.com*, 2015, www.bartleby.com/39/36.html/. Accessed 3 Dec. 2017.

CRITICAL
READINGS

Emma Lazarus's Poetic Representations of the Immigrant Experience_____

Brian Yothers

Some of the most memorable representations of the immigrant experience are not written by immigrants, but rather by non-immigrants who have come to identify with the cause of immigrants and refugees. The case of Emma Lazarus, a poet who is frequently invoked in debates over immigration in the United States, is perhaps the most striking example of this phenomenon. Lazarus, born in 1849, was the descendant of a prosperous Sephardic Jewish family who had deep roots in the United States by the nineteenth century—as her modern biographer Esther Schor points out, she was "at least a fourth-generation American" and had at least one female poet who wrote in English among her ancestors—but she came to identify powerfully with often impoverished and persecuted Eastern European Jewish immigrants fleeing persecution in their homelands and to serve as one of their most outspoken advocates (Schor xi, 4). This identification came despite Lazarus's privileged social position (Bette Roth Young described her milieu as "aristocratic") and the fact that she, unlike the mostly religious immigrants from Eastern Europe, considered herself to be largely secular in her relation to her Jewish identity and indeed was critical of organized religion in its Christian and Jewish manifestations alike (Young x).

In addition to the fact that she was not herself an immigrant to the United States, Lazarus was not the first Jewish person in the United States to have an important role in the story of American poetry or in the related field of music. The earliest Jewish poet to be recognized in the United States was, as John Hollander has pointed out, the Southern poet Penina Moise, whose work was in general more focused on her Southern than on her Jewish identity; the humorist Bret Harte, who also wrote some light verse, was of Jewish descent (Hollander xix). In another example, the musical accompaniment to George Pope Morris's "Woodman, Spare that Tree!" described by Edgar Allan

Poe as the finest song written in the United States by the early 1840s (Poe 219), was composed by Henry Russell, a Jewish expatriate from England who lived in the United States during the 1830s, and Russell also composed the accompaniment to Sargent Epes's "A Life on the Ocean Wave," a song with a rich afterlife ranging from the United States Merchant Marine Corps to the recent history of Portugal and the United Kingdom (Scott 40, 214). Thus Jewish migration has been a part of American literary culture from a very early time indeed, even before the substantial increase in Jewish immigration that led Lazarus to compose her most famous poems. What Lazarus added to the development of the Jewish American literary tradition and the literature of the immigrant experience was her close identification of Jewishness with immigration, even for those who, like her, had ancestors who had been in the United States for generations.

Immigration and Human Rights: "1492"

Despite the substantial social and religious differences between Lazarus and the Russian Jewish immigrants that she championed, Lazarus could find grounds for empathy with Russian refugees in the deep history of her own family as members of the Jewish diaspora. This becomes especially clear in her sonnet titled "1492," which reads

> Thou two-faced year, Mother of Change and Fate,
> Didst weep when Spain cast forth with flaming sword,
> The children of the prophets of the Lord,
> Prince, priest, and people, spurned by zealot hate.
> Hounded from sea to sea, from state to state,
> The West refused them, and the East abhorred.
> No anchorage the known world could afford,
> Close-locked was every port, barred every gate.
> Then smiling, thou unveil'dst, O two-faced year,
> A virgin world where doors of sunset part,
> Saying, "Ho, all who weary, enter here!
> There falls each ancient barrier that the art
> Of race or creed or rank devised, to rear
> Grim bulwarked hatred between heart and heart!" (87, l. 1-14)

In the events of 1492, identified by Lazarus in the poem as a "two-faced year," Lazarus found precedent for the pogroms that contributed to Russian Jewish immigration during her adult life, and she also found profoundly personal connections to her own family history. As a Jewish woman of Sephardic descent, Lazarus could claim ancestry from Jewish people expelled from Spain after the Christian reconquest of the Iberian Peninsula, and so the story of 1492 is an intensely personal one for her. The year 1492 was also one in which Columbus made landfall in Hispaniola, meaning that one avenue of escape for Jewish exiles was to the Americas. The year 1492 is "two-faced" for Lazarus in that it was both a disaster for Spanish Jews and the opening of a new possibility. Lazarus does not, unfortunately, acknowledge the ways in which 1492 could be seen as a year of catastrophe for both the indigenous peoples of America or for Africans who would be enslaved in the Western Hemisphere, but she does offer a sense of the complexities of the year's events from the specific perspective of the Sephardic Jewish community. She particularly emphasizes the idea that immigration to North America could offer possibilities that were unavailable in Christian-dominated Europe and Muslim-dominated North Africa.

Lazarus's depiction of American identity in "1492" is aspirational, even prophetic. When she attributes words to the year, they echo the words of the prophet Isaiah from the Hebrew Bible: "Ho, all who weary" resembles in subject matter and cadence the opening verse of Isaiah 55 in many English-language translations. She imagines the Western Hemisphere as a place where racial and religious bigotry can be deprived of their power, and she looks to an egalitarian, pluralistic future in which "race or creed or rank" can no longer provide grounds for discrimination. Even though Lazarus's own family's immigration to North America preceded the American Revolution, she still can find grounds in that past immigrant experience for supporting the aspirations of nineteenth-century Russian Jewish immigrants who in many ways bear little resemble to an elite Sephardic New York poet.

Immigration and Exile in Texas

Perhaps one of Lazarus's most curious poems of the immigrant experience is her depiction of a Russian Jewish immigrant family in Texas, a state that Lazarus never visited. Lazarus's poem "In Exile" has been praised highly for its lyricism by John Hollander, the literary critic who edited the most readily available edition of her poems, even as it has been criticized by Lazarus's biographer Esther Schor for what Schor regarded as some clumsy archaisms (Hollander xviii). The poem begins with what Lazarus calls an "Extract from a letter of a Russian refugee in Texas": *"Since that day till now our life is one unbroken paradise. We live a true brotherly life. Every evening after supper we take a seat under the mighty oak and sing our songs"* (77). The quotation is completely idyllic in its description of the immigrant experience: the new immigrants in Texas have found relief from prior sufferings, and Texas itself seems to have become a sort of promised land for these immigrants, who maintain their distinctive religious traditions by "singing [their] songs" in exile.

This extract leads into a poem that is a mixture of conventional post-romantic nature poetry and a reflection on both the sorrows of exile from one's homeland and the hope of a better future in a hostland that seems rich with promise. The opening stanza of "In Exile" could have been written by virtually any post-romantic poet, and it is rich with the sensuousness that students of British romanticism would associate with the poetry of John Keats. The stanza sets up an agricultural scene that speaks to each of the five senses:

> Twilight is here, soft breezes bow the grass,
> Day's sounds of various toil break slowly off.
> The yoke-freed oxen low, the patient ass
> Dips his dry nostril in the cool, deep trough.
> Up from the prairie the tanned herdsmen pass
> With frothy pails, guiding with voices rough
> Their udder-lightened kine. Fresh smells of earth,
> The rich, black furrows of the glebe send forth.(77, l. 1-8)

Lazarus provides a scene that is full of visual, sonic, and tactile elements, and she even invokes the smell of the earth that her Russian immigrants in Texas are tilling. Archaisms like "kine" and "glebe," in tandem with the rich natural description in the scene, make clear that this is pastoral poetry, even as the epigraph has already indicated that Lazarus is concerned with the current situation of immigrants to the United States.

The second stanza turns from the scene itself to the subjective feelings of the immigrants, who find that Texas has offered them a kind of agricultural paradise.

> After the Southern day of heavy toil,
>> How good to lie, with limbs relaxed, brows bare
> To evening's fan, and watch the smoke-wreaths coil
>> Up from one's pipe-stem through the rayless air.
> So deem these unused tillers of the soil,
>> Who stretched beneath the shadowing oak tree, stare
> Peacefully on the star-unfolding skies,
>> And name their life unbroken paradise. (77, l. 9-16)

The Jewish immigrants in Texas are here presented as farmers who have, by means of vigorous labor, made the land yield sustenance. The expression "unused tillers of the soil" points to the fact that this runs counter both to stereotypes about Jewish immigrants and to the past of ghetto life in Eastern Europe. It also serves to reassure Lazarus's non-Jewish readers, and indeed Jewish readers from Lazarus's own social class and cultural background, that the aspirations of Russian Jewish immigrants fleeing persecution in Russia are ultimately similar to those of other Americans.

The third stanza makes a significant turn from the peaceful pastoral imagery of the first two stanzas. Now the profound experiences of loss and pain that have brought these immigrants to the United States during the nineteenth century come to the fore.

> The hounded stag that has escaped the pack,
>> And pants at ease within a thick-leaved dell;

The unimprisoned bird that finds the track
    Through sun-bathed space, to where his fellows dwell;
The martyr, granted respite from the rack,
    The death-doomed victim pardoned from his cell,—
Such only know the joy these exiles gain,—
    Life's sharpest rapture is surcease of pain. (77-78, l. 17-24)

Lazarus's dictum that "surcease of pain" is "Life's sharpest rapture" is heightened by the idyllic descriptions that make up the opening stanzas. Lazarus builds to this observation through a series of examples that reveal that these exiles have been hunted in their homelands, and therefore have a tremendous experience of pain from which to recover in their new hostland. They are like the "hounded stag" that escapes, the bird that has become "unimprisoned," the martyr for an unspecified faith, who is "granted respite" from torture, and the pardoned prisoner previously condemned to die. Each of these images builds in emotional power upon those that precede it, and Lazarus's description of the suffering of the Jewish minority in Russia provides an explanation of why exhausting manual labor in the hot Texas sun could seem like paradise.

After suggesting that the Russian Jewish immigrants she describes share similar aspirations with earlier generations of migrants to North America, she then acknowledges the religious and cultural differences between these new immigrants and those who had come previously:

Strange faces theirs, wherethrough the Orient sun
    Gleams from the eyes and glows athwart the skin.
Grave lines of studious thought and purpose run
From curl-crowned forehead to dark-bearded chin.
    And over all the seal is stamped thereon
Of anguish branded by a world of sin,
    In fire and blood through ages on their name,
Their seal of glory and the Gentiles' shame. (78, l. 25-32)

This stanza is the first point at which the Jewish identity of Lazarus's exiles is made explicit. Notably, Lazarus ties the necessity of a welcome to Jewish immigrants from Russia to the brutal history of Christian anti-Semitism and asks her readers, whether elite Jewish Americans of Sephardic and German descent or non-Jewish Americans, to admire their courage in the face of persecution, a quality for which some of the earliest migrants to North America— New England Puritans and French Huguenots—had been praised by American Protestant writers.

This invocation of shared persecution turns directly into an invocation of religious liberty. Lazarus identifies what the Jewish immigrants in Texas most desire:

> Freedom to love the law that Moses brought,
>> To sing the songs of David, and to think
> The thoughts Gabirol to Spinoza taught,
>> Freedom to dig the common earth, to drink
> The universal air—for this they sought
>> Refuge o'er wave and continent, to link
> Egypt with Texas in their mystic chain,
>> And truth's perpetual lamp forbid to wane. (78, l. 33-40)

A powerful aspect of Lazarus's account of Judaism is that it includes Spinoza, a secular figure, alongside Moses, the central religious figure in the faith. Lazarus includes the Texan immigrants in a Jewish national and intellectual tradition that is related to Judaism as a system of religious belief, but also highly independent of such a system, as Spinoza was expelled from the Jewish community in the Netherlands for his heretical religious beliefs. For Lazarus, what ultimately defines the desires of these immigrants is a combination of religious and intellectual freedom: the freedom to practice Judaism according to the Law of Moses and the freedom to deviate from religious tradition by following one's own intellectual and moral compass, like the great secular Jewish philosopher Baruch Spinoza.

In her conclusion, Lazarus returns to the emotional complexity of the immigrant experience: so much has been gained for these refugee farmers, but they still bear in mind what has been lost: a homeland in which their ancestors had lived for centuries. As a result, the triumph of these immigrants, as expressed in their songs, is tinged with melancholy:

> Hark! through the quiet evening air, their song
>   Floats forth with wild sweet rhythm and glad refrain.
> They sing the conquest of the spirit strong,
>   The soul that wrests the victory from pain;
> The noble joys of manhood that belong
>   To comrades and to brothers. In their strain
> Rustle of palms and Eastern streams one hears,
>   And the broad prairie melts in mist of tears. (78, l. 40-48)

Lazarus delves deeply into the psychology of the Russian Jewish immigrant experience here: their experiences in Texas represent a profound rupture with their life in Russia, but also a continuation of the broader experience of Jewish exile in the world of the diaspora. In this sense, the Jewish American immigrant experience as discussed by Lazarus is a continuation of a longer experience of displacement that has characterized the Jewish diaspora, even as it offers the hope that here the old story of exile can be re-written.

Lazarus's Poetic Monument: "The New Colossus"
"In Exile" is not, of course, the poem about immigration for which Lazarus is most remembered. That honor goes to "The New Colossus," the poem that appears on the base of the Statue of Liberty. Like "In Exile," "The New Colossus" is a poem that rewards close reading. In her most famous poem, Lazarus writes

> Not like the brazen giant of Greek fame,
> With conquering limbs astride from land to land;
> Here at our sea-washed, sunset gates shall stand
> A mighty woman with a torch, whose flame
> Is the imprisoned lightning, and her name
> Mother of Exiles. From her beacon-hand
> Glows world-wide welcome; her mild eyes command
> The air-bridged harbor that twin cities frame.
> "Keep, ancient lands, your storied pomp!" cries she
> With silent lips. "Give me your tired, your poor,

Your huddled masses yearning to breathe free,
The wretched refuse of your teeming shore.
Send these, the homeless, tempest-tost to me,
I lift my lamp beside the golden door!" (58, l. 1-14)

When Lazarus published a collected version of her poetry near the end of her life, as Schor points out, she chose to begin that volume with "The New Colossus," and it is, in many ways, the purest expression of her emphasis on exile and migration in her poetry. John Hollander has described this poem as an exceptionally well-crafted sonnet, in addition to its powerful cultural resonance. The poem, commissioned as a verbal companion to the Statue of Liberty, begins by distinguishing that statue from the Colossus of ancient Rhodes. Her size makes the comparison inevitable, but she offers a striking contrast: as a woman, as a token of welcome rather than conquest, she signifies a rejection of the idea that national greatness is defined by military prowess, suggesting instead that a nation that binds together immigrants can be more powerful than a nation that conquers foreign lands. The crucial epithet in Lazarus's presentation of the statue is "Mother of Exiles." As a representation of the United States, the Statue of Liberty for Lazarus represents the possibility that a nation can achieve greatness by nurturing diversity and showing compassion for those who are displaced. The words attributed to the statue, asking for the "tired," "poor," "huddled masses," the "tempest-tost" and "homeless" make the American experience synonymous with the immigrant experience, and they explicitly defy any invidious comparisons between worthy and unworthy immigrants. If Lazarus's poem has become so familiar as to be a cliché, its familiarity can obscure the power of the statement that it makes about what it means to be an American and what it suggests about the meaning of national greatness. Centrally, Lazarus's sonnet represents the United States as being distinctive precisely insofar as it welcomes immigrants of all socio-economic statuses, religious backgrounds and beliefs, and places of national origin. Lazarus's patriotism is thus defined by inclusion rather than exclusion, by a sense of the value of diversity rather than by an impulse toward homogeneity, and by a devotion to the possibility that divergent cultures and religions can strengthen American identity.

Immigration and the Living Jewish Experience in the United States

Perhaps the poem that most defines Lazarus's status as a poet of immigration is neither her celebration of Texas from the standpoint of Russian refugees nor her iconic celebration of the United States as a welcoming hostland. Rather it is a poem that she wrote directly in response to a poem by one of her most revered older contemporaries, Henry Wadsworth Longfellow.

In his poem, "The Jewish Cemetery at Newport," Longfellow had written about one of the oldest Jewish communities in the United States, one that pre-dated the American Revolution and that had famously received an affirming letter from George Washington, the first President of the United States. Washington had written to address precisely the concerns about religious discrimination that Longfellow and Lazarus would discuss in their poetry. Addressing the community at Newport as a whole, Washington wrote:

> It is now no more that toleration is spoken of as if it were the indulgence of one class of people that another enjoyed the exercise of their inherent natural rights, for, happily, the Government of the United States, which gives to bigotry no sanction, to persecution no assistance, requires only that they who live under its protection should demean themselves as good citizens in giving it on all occasions their effectual support.
>
> It would be inconsistent with the frankness of my character not to avow that I am pleased with your favorable opinion of my administration and fervent wishes for my felicity.
>
> May the children of the stock of Abraham who dwell in this land continue to merit and enjoy the good will of the other inhabitants— while every one shall sit in safety under his own vine and fig tree and there shall be none to make him afraid. (766)

This letter is frequently remembered as a landmark in the history of religious tolerance and even pluralism in the United States, but it also constitutes a gesture of welcome to a community that, while it was already present in the United States at its founding, was nonetheless frequently treated as falling outside an American mainstream that, especially in its early years, was defined religiously by Protestantism. Washington's usage of direct quotation from the Hebrew Bible alongside his denunciations of persecution and discrimination make the letter especially powerful.

In many ways, Longfellow's treatment of Judaism is quite sympathetic, even affirming, and it echoes the sentiments of Washington's famous letter to the community. This is not an entirely surprising dimension of Longfellow's poetry, as Longfellow belonged to one of the most theologically liberal and welcoming of Protestant denominations in the nineteenth-century United States, the Unitarian Church, and his tendency to be ecumenical in religious matters is characteristic of many nineteenth-century American literary figures. Longfellow shows considerable respect for the rich intellectual history of Judaism, and he deplores the bigotry that forced Jewish people from Spain and Portugal to leave their homes in Europe for the prospect of a new life in the Americas. Indeed, Longfellow's discussion of Christian bigotry against the Jewish people can be quite biting, and he leaves no doubt where his sympathies lie:

> How came they here? What burst of Christian hate,
>   What persecution, merciless and blind,
> Drove o'er the sea—that desert desolate—
>   These Ishmaels and Hagars of mankind?
>
> They lived in narrow streets and lanes obscure,
>   Ghetto and Judenstrass, in mirk and mire;
> Taught in the school of patience to endure
>   The life of anguish and the death of fire.
>
> All their lives long, with the unleavened bread
>   And bitter herbs of exile and its fears,
> The wasting famine of the heart they fed,
>   And slaked its thirst with marah of their tears.

Anathema maranatha! was the cry
   That rang from town to town, from street to street;
At every gate the accursed Mordecai
   Was mocked and jeered, and spurned by Christian feet.

(336, l. 29-43)

Longfellow dramatized precisely the intensity of anti-Semitic prejudice in Europe to which Lazarus would respond in her sonnet "1492." He forcefully rebukes "Christian hate" and "persecution, merciless and blind," and he makes clear that he sides with the "Ishmaels and Hagars of mankind," who have been driven from their native lands, against their persecutors. Moreover, he invokes the language of the Hebrew Bible and the practices of Jewish sacred observances as he catalogues the persecution that Jewish people had faced. Despite his sympathy, Longfellow's conclusion to the poem was grim.

But ah! what once has been shall be no more!
   The groaning earth in travail and in pain
Brings forth its races, but does not restore,
   And the dead nations never rise again. (337, l. 53-56)

Longfellow wrote with considerable sympathy for the Jewish victims of Christian anti-Semitism, but the sympathy he offered was compromised by the suggestion that Jewishness was a dying identity. This attenuated sympathy was precisely what led Lazarus to respond so forcefully.

Lazarus's response to Longfellow's seeming failure to acknowledge the flourishing of Jewish life in the United States was impassioned. In her poem "The Jewish Synagogue at Newport," Lazarus engaged many aspects of Longfellow's poem: its frank acknowledgment of the history of Christian anti-Semitism; its connection of the history of American Jewish people to the long history of Judaism around the world and in sacred texts; and, perhaps most importantly and contentiously, its implication that Jewish life was fading in the United States. This last premise Lazarus rejected forcefully. The concluding stanza of Lazarus's poem emphasizes that Judaism is a living tradition in the United States:

Nathless the sacred shrine is holy yet,
    With its lone floors where reverent feet once trod.
Take off your shoes as by the burning bush,
    Before the mystery of death and God. (10, l. 41-44)

Lazarus's conclusion represents a powerful reversal of Longfellow's image of Judaism as a vanishing religion. For Lazarus, as for Longfellow, the long historical past of Judaism is an important part of the story, but Lazarus emphasizes the ways in which this long past remains full of life in her own present time. As Esther Schor aptly notes, "Between this poem and Longfellow's lies the difference between an elegy for a 'dead nation' and a song of praise, an authentic legacy of devotion" (20). For Lazarus, the "burning bush" of Jewish religion and self-understanding remains as vital in her own lifetime as it had ever been. As a result, Jewish immigration to the United States becomes framed as part of the worldwide history of the Jewish diaspora, and Lazarus is able to identify in a profound way with her impoverished and oppressed coreligionists seeking refuge in the United States. Through this identification with Jewish refugees, exiles, and migrants around the globe, Lazarus is able to create a profound sense of communion with the immigrant experiences of the multi-religious, transnational tide of migration to the nineteenth and early twentieth-century United States.

    Notably, Lazarus's response to Longfellow was not a confrontation with nativism, an impulse that she certainly had to struggle against, given the fact that in the years surrounding Lazarus's birth in 1849, one of the most influential political parties in the United States was the virulently anti-immigrant Know-Nothing Party, and that in the years following her death, the Ku Klux Klan was reconstituted as an anti-immigrant organization that garnered widespread support among white Protestants (Bennett 105-117; 208-214). Lazarus's response to Longfellow is so fraught precisely because he was not a bigot, but rather a poet of broad sympathies who acknowledged the shameful history of Christian anti-Semitism and denounced it, as his most recent biographer, Charles Calhoun, has shown (200). Responding to the Know-Nothings and the Klan would have been pointless: given their bigotry, the only response possible to them was steadfast resistance. But Longfellow, as a sympathetic religious liberal, someone whose views on many issues and on the nature, value, and importance of art came quite close to those of Lazarus herself, required a response. If ecumenically-minded Unitarians like Longfellow viewed Jewish identity as a relic of the past and Judaism as a dying faith, then the task of defending Jewish immigrants in Lazarus's present would be undermined. Lazarus's response to Longfellow, then, is to emphasize that the Jewish community in the United States was alive, robust, and flourishing, and, therefore, not in need of elegies but of allies. As Lazarus's career continued, more and more of this robust lived Jewish experience in the United States would be as a result of Jewish immigration.

Lazarus thus bridged an important gap between new immigrants and Americans who had been in the country for generation but had not forgotten their immigrant ancestors. Lazarus was sufficiently ensconced in the Anglo-American literary elite that she could argue with Longfellow in print and maintain friendships with Ralph Waldo Emerson (to whom Lazarus dedicated a poem, "To R.W.E.") and James Russell Lowell in the United States and make connections with Robert Browning and William Morris in England (Young 24, 108, 234, 111). In some ways, her elite status constituted an obstacle to her sympathies with Russian Jewish immigrants who lacked her educational background, but it also meant that she was able to communicate her support for newer immigrants in ways that resonated across American society. Ultimately, her increasing support and advocacy for immigrants increased her appreciation for the complexities of Jewish history and of the lived community of Jewish people in the nineteenth-century United States, as illustrated in her response to Longfellow.

This emphasis on the living Jewish experience relates closely to Lazarus's understanding of the immigrant experience in the United States. Lazarus was not just a mournful chronicler of the challenges that immigrants faced, but rather a vigorous champion of their rights and their potential. Moreover, Lazarus did not imagine immigrants as simply fading into the background of American culture and society, but rather as helping to create a new picture of the society that they joined. As part of the Jewish minority in the United States, Lazarus vigorously defended, not just the rights of Jewish people, but the sense that the nation became morally and intellectually better and stronger by embracing its Jewish minority. As Schor argues in the concluding pages of her biography, Lazarus does not just defend the rights of immigrants to assimilate to the culture of their new country, she also insists on the ways in which the country can grow and prosper by assimilating itself to the values of its newest citizens.

Works Cited

Bennett, David Harry. *The Party of Fear: From Nativist Movements to the New Right in American History.* U of North Carolina P, 1988.

Calhoun, Charles. *Longfellow: A Rediscovered Life.* Beacon Press, 2006.

Lazarus, Emma. *Emma Lazarus: Selected Poems.* Edited by John Hollander. Library of America, 2005.

_____. "1492." *Emma Lazarus: Selected Poems*, edited by John Hollander, Library of America, 2005, p 87.

_____. "In Exile." *Emma Lazarus: Selected Poems*, edited by John Hollander, Library of America, 2005, pp. 77-78.

_____. "In the Jewish Synagogue at Newport." *Emma Lazarus: Selected Poems*, edited by John Hollander, Library of America, 2005, pp. 9-10.

_____. "The New Colossus." *Emma Lazarus: Selected Poems*, edited by John Hollander, Library of America, 2005, p. 58.

_____. "To R.W.E." *Emma Lazarus: Selected Poems*, edited by John Hollander, Library of America, 2005, p. 126.

Epes, Sargent. "A Life on the Ocean Wave." *American Melodies*, edited by George Pope Morris, Linen and Fennell, 1840, pp. 28-29.

Hollander, John. "Introduction." *Emma Lazarus: Selected Poems*, edited by John Hollander, Library of America, 2005, pp. xiii-xxiv.

Longfellow, Henry Wadsworth. "The Jewish Cemetery at Newport." *Longfellow: Selected Poems*, edited by J. D. McClatchy, Library of America, 2000, pp. 335-36.

Morris, George Pope. "Woodman, Spare that Tree!" *American Melodies*, edited by George Pope Morris, Linen and Fennell, 1840, pp. 93-94.

Poe, Edgar Allan. "Marginalia [part XIII]." *Southern Literary Messenger*, vol. XV, no. 4, Apr. 1849, pp. 217-222.

Schor, Esther. *Emma Lazarus.* Schocken, 2006.

Scott, Derek B. *The Singing Bourgeois: Songs of the Victorian Drawing Room and Parlor.* Routledge, 2017.

Washington, George. "To the Hebrew Congregation at Newport, Rhode Island." *Washington: Writings*, edited by John H. Rhodehamel, Library of America, 1997, pp. 766-67.

Young, Bette Roth. *Emma Lazarus in Her World: Life and Letters.* Jewish Publication Society, 1997.

Wing Sing and Edith Eaton: Their Great Adventures (Some Travel Writings by Sui Sin Far)

Robert C. Evans

Sui Sin Far (1865–1914), whose name at birth was Edith Maude Eaton, is one of the most intriguing of American immigrant writers, partly because she was one of the earliest Asian women on the American continent to make a successful living as an author. (Interestingly enough, her sister Winnifred Eaton, who wrote under the pen name Onoto Watanna, was another.) The biographical backgrounds of the Eaton sisters are themselves fascinating: they were born in Britain to an Englishman and his Chinese wife who had both lived in China for a time. While Edith was still a young girl, the ever-growing family moved to the United States, living in New Jersey while the father opened a business in New York City. After a brief trip back to England, they returned once more to the United States, then quickly relocated to Montreal, Canada. It was in Montreal that Edith began writing and publishing stories as well as working as a journalist. After a period in Northern Ontario, she visited New York City before relocating to Jamaica and then eventually returning to Montreal. In 1898, she moved to San Francisco, where she worked for a railway company with ties to Canada. She was living in Seattle by 1899 and living in Los Angeles by 1903, before she eventually returned to Seattle. By 1909, however, she had taken up residence in Boston; by the time of her death, she had returned to Montreal.

My reasons for outlining Eaton's life in such detail are several. First, by almost any standards, Eaton was a remarkably well-traveled person, and the sheer number of her residences seems especially unusual for a single woman of her era. Secondly, the fact that Eaton never married, and thus travelled both so widely and so independently, seems itself noteworthy. Furthermore, each place Eaton visited had its own distinct culture; differences between particular American cities, for instance, were significantly more pronounced then than they tend to be today, when a culture grounded in the mass media tends to make every place look and seem increasingly similar to every other place. Eaton, however, lived not only in a surprisingly large number of distinct cities; she was also very familiar with the Chinese subcultures of each of the places she visited or in which she resided. And those places, of course, were not only in the United States but also in Canada—and not only on the east coasts of both countries but also on the west coasts as well. Finally, Eaton's time in Jamaica gave her an even broader familiarity with different kinds of cultures and racial identities. She was, in short, an extraordinarily cosmopolitan person for her time. Half Asian, half English; sometimes a Canadian and sometimes an American; sometimes living in England and sometimes in Jamaica; and making full use of a lively, observant mind and real literary talent wherever she happened to visit or live—Eaton almost could not help but be an interesting multinational, multiethnic, multilingual immigrant writer.[1]

"Wing Sing" Enters the Picture

Among the most interesting—but until very recently very little known—writings by Edith Eaton are a series of articles she wrote for the *Los Angeles Express* newspaper from February to July 1904. These recount a cross-continental trip she herself made during these months, during which she traveled across Canada and then back, through the United States, to Los Angeles. She stopped in many different places along the way and described most of them, and she also met some memorable people—and had some memorable experiences—both on and off the various trains on which she traveled. Even if she had simply written up the trip in her own voice, Eaton would have produced an intriguing series of articles. But she did more than this: she created an entirely different persona, a Chinese American male businessman from Los Angeles whom she called "Wing Sing." Perhaps—or perhaps not—the name puns on her decision to "sing" while winging her way back and forth across the continent. In any case, Wing Sing has a mind and character all his own, and half the interest of reading "his" accounts of "his" journey involves the fact that he is a fictional male character created by a woman author. "He" encounters and comments on Canadians, Americans, Chinese, whites, Native Americans, African Americans, Irishmen, and so on, and he even brings in an anecdote about Jamaica. In short, Wing Sing both is and is not Edith Eaton/Sui Sin Far herself. Her decision to adopt the voice of a male persona adds extra interest to her tales.

These articles are not, to be sure, "great literature." Sometimes they are mundane and pedestrian. But often, they are intriguing both for their phrasing and for their content, both for their "plots" and for their characters, both for their varied settings and for their multiple glimpses of different kinds of local color. "Wing Sing's" accounts of his travels certainly deserve far more attention than they have received. They provide vivid, valuable insights into the experiences of Asian immigrants in North America that are not easily available elsewhere. They will, therefore, be the main focus of this essay.

"Wing Sing of Los Angeles on His Travels"

Each article in the fifteen-article series Eaton composed was titled "Wing Sing of Los Angeles on His Travels." The first article, which appeared on February 3, 1904, began with an immediate piece of fiction—an editor's note that read as follows:

> [Note—Wing Sing is the pen name of a well-known Americanized Chinese merchant of this city. He recently left Los Angeles to make a visit to his old home in China, going by way of Montreal. Before starting he promised The Express to write a series of articles in his own untrammeled style, telling of his travels. Appended is the first contribution.—Ed.] (Eaton 201)

Ironically, then, the series opened not with *one* lie but with several: "Wing Sing" was an invented name; the "well-known American Chinese merchant of this city" was not, in fact, the writer of the articles; and the invented merchant was not even a Chinese man but a half-Chinese woman! Moreover, Wing Sing never makes it to China, and why he would plan to do so by leaving from Montreal, of all places, is anyone's guess. Eaton seems to have enjoyed having fun with her readers, and with her characters, as the editor's note already suggests and as the ensuing articles amply demonstrate.

The fiction in this half-fake but half-true series of mixed-genre autobiographical pieces of partly fictional travel writing continues in the very next paragraph:

> I am a Chinaman. My name is Wing Sing. I got a wife and boy in China, but for ten years I live in America. I learn speak American. Some time white man laugh at my speaking and I say him, "Perhaps you not speak my Chinese talk so well I speak your talk. Perhaps I laugh more at you try to speak Chinese man's language." That American man not laugh any more. Los Angeles very nice place— like China some. I got big store opposite the Plaza. You know North Los Angeles Street? That where my store be. For ten year I work very hard. Then I say to me, "Wing Sing, not good work too hard. Perhaps you may take holiday." (Eaton 201)

Instantly, in almost her very first words, Eaton is already indicating several of the main themes, several of the major tones, and several of the key character traits Wing Sing establishes in the series as a whole. Wing Sing is not only a Chinese American; he is a Chinese American who is proud of his Chinese culture and language. Far from being intimidated when white people (usually men) make fun of him, he gives it right back to them. He is, throughout the series, anything but aggressive, but neither is he a shrinking violet. When challenged or insulted, he always responds effectively. Perhaps one reason Eaton adopted a male persona was that this decision made her alter ego's combative side more credible and acceptable than it would have been if the narrator were a woman. In any case, it is completely typical of Wing Sing that when he tries to pay a compliment to Los Angeles, he does so by comparing it to China. He is proud of his Asian heritage and is not afraid to say so, either to people within the articles or to the articles' readers, most of whom were probably *not* Asian.

Eaton's decision to have Wing Sing write in pidgin English was probably also designed to add credibility to the writing, and although some Asian readers may have disagreed with this tactic, it typifies her own pride in the Asian aspects of her heritage. Rather than having Wing Sing sound like a highly educated Anglo, she lets him speak in a voice that was probably very close to the actual voices of many Asian Americans (and Asian Canadians) at this time. Ways of speaking are often mentioned as the articles continue; such ways become an important theme of the series as a whole. And while Wing Sing sometimes talks in ways that may have contributed to comic stereotypes, his language is also often vivid, fresh, and poetic. Thus, when he explains that he decided to visit Montreal after a cousin living there invited him, he quotes his cousin as saying "that train fly fast with you to me" (Eaton 202). This is wonderfully inventive English. Eaton could easily have made her character's voice more conventionally "Anglo" and "educated," but she wisely chose not to do so.

Some of the key traits of Wing Sing's character (and some of both the humor and defiance of his and Eaton's own tones) come through almost immediately. For instance, he reports that on the train ride from Los Angeles to San Francisco, some people "in the car they look at me and old man say to his friend: 'See that Chinaman,' and his friend look at me and laugh at me. So I look at him and I laugh at him—plenty funny people in America" (Eaton 202). This is splendidly typical of the way Wing Sing acts throughout the trip whenever anyone tries to denigrate him. He immediately makes the denigration boomerang, and he almost always does so in a way that not only preserves his self-respect but makes fair-minded readers respect him all the more. That last comment ("pretty funny people in America") is typical of his wit. He manages to make an intended insult roll off of him as if he has just enjoyed a joke. He is rarely if ever at a loss for words.

At one point, a well-intentioned but ill-informed white woman speaks to him as follows:

"Mr. Chinaman, won't you please tell me all about Mr. Confucius?" I say to her: "I not teacher, I not scholar, I business man. Confucius to Chinaman same as Jesus to white man. I not go to white business man and ask him to tell me all about Jesus, for he not know. I go to American preacher to know all about your sage, Jesus. So you go

Chinese teacher and scholar to know about Confucius." Lady she go
back to her seat and I say to me that she was very nice American lady,
but too bad she have no sense. (Eaton 202)

Almost always, after an encounter with someone who is either
deliberately rude or foolishly ignorant, Wing Sing turns the whole
thing into a joke. His last six words here, for instance, will make
many readers laugh out loud. His jokes, however, are never mean-
spirited, and when he does joke at someone else's expense, he is
usually responding to another person's provocation.

Wing Sing, however, meets surprisingly few unfriendly people
along the way. If anyone imagined that nearly all whites treated all
Asians with disrespect in the very early twentieth century, Wing
Sing's reports do not support that assumption. Perhaps because
he is a well-dressed businessman, he is treated not only with good
manners but with genuine kindness in most cases and most places.
He even notes, for instance, in his first article, that before a voyage
from San Francisco to Seattle, a white man helped him get on the
right ship. And then, while on the ship, he reports that all the Anglo
sailors "make voyage pleasant to me." In a moment that might
have come from the pen of Whitman (if Whitman had written in
a Chinese American dialect), Wing Sing comments, concerning a
particular member of the crew, "I think sailor very good man, he
not drink, he have no girl and he look solemn at the sky and the
sea and think big thinks and talk big talks" (Eaton 203). Having
celebrated the nobility and thoughtfulness of a common man, Wing
Sing continues:

> I tell the captain I go visit Montreal, Canada. He go tell me my
> fortune and he say I marry when I go to Montreal. I put on face to
> believe, for it not polite not to believe the captain to his face, and
> I not tell him I got little wife in China. The engineer, he say he
> find Chinaman thumb in can of tomatoes. I say, "How you know
> Chinaman thumb?" (Eaton 203)

As always, Wing Sing turns what might have been interpreted as
a joking insult into a clever retort. One reason fair-minded readers

increasingly grow to admire Wing Sing is that he seems a good, simple, well-intentioned man, willing to be friends with anyone who shows him the slightest bit of friendship. Wing Sing is capable of letting unfortunate remarks slide right off his back, sometimes with a clever quip in response.

Having arrived in Seattle, Wing Sing notes the area's appeal, but he does so in his typical way—a way that often involves a compliment to China: "I say to me, 'Los Angeles fine sun, this country, fine air. In China, fine sun and fine air too'" (Eaton 203). It doesn't take long, however, before he meets another somewhat ignorant American, who asks him if he is married. "I say 'Yes.' He say, 'How many times?' I see that he think he have some fun so I think I have some fun too so I say 'Four time.'" The American thinks it scandalous that one man can have four wives. Wing Sing responds as follows, in a passage that concludes the first article:

> I say, "Now, my turn. I know American man, clerk in my store. One day I see him walking with a lady. I say to him, 'Who that lady?' He say, 'She my girl.' Another day I see him walking with another lady, and I ask him again, 'Who that lady?' and he say, 'She my girl.' 'That very funny,' I say. American man not think it right to have two wife. Chinaman not think it right to have two girl."
>
> But the train then come to Seattle and I go see my cousin. (Eaton 203)

The effectively abrupt ending is typical of Eaton's talent, while the fact that Wing Sing—an Asian—is wealthy enough to employ an Anglo clerk is mentioned in passing, never emphasized, but telling nonetheless. This is a "Chinaman" who is quite willing to respect others but who first of all respects himself.

Wing Sing Crosses Canada

In the second article, Wing Sing makes an Irish friend—whom he explicitly *calls* a friend—as his train begins moving east across Canada (Eaton 205). This Irishman is more than willing to make jokes at his own expense (206), but he also at one point inadvertently insults China. Wing Sing immediately sets him straight, and their friendship continues and even grows (206). Eaton, then, does not romanticize or sentimentalize the friendship between these two, and the fact that she does not makes the relationship more credible than it would have been otherwise. Soon they are back to admiring the landscape together. Seeing the Rocky Mountains, Wing Sing is stunned, and, in a wonderful bit of unintended irony, he expressively says, "I not can say nothing. My expression it not express me" (207). Actually, he could hardly have said it better than this. Anyone who has ever seen the Rockies or the Grand Canyon for the first time will know exactly how he feels. Later, when he sees some Canadian Mounted Police, he again expresses himself more vividly than he realizes: "All the people that I see wear big coat and plenty fur, their face red, and they look as if they had much blood. The Irishman tell me it is the climate make them so juicy" (209). The adjective "juicy" is exactly the kind of natural poetry we might expect from someone using a second language.

It is worth remembering that when Wing Sing comically comments on the talk of two women, the actual writer of his words was a woman herself: "The car go very fast, but I think six Canadian Pacific cars not near so fast as two lady tongue" (Eaton 210). But as we have already seen, Wing Sing is not only capable of cracking jokes but of admiring natural beauty, as when he praises "the beauty of the scenery that belongs to Lake Superior. We ride by the north shore in the morning, and in the evening we see the sun set over the big white lake. It is the sky of heaven then" (210). For a businessman, Wing Sing has a fairly poetic mind. By endowing her "Chinamen" with so many of the thoughts, feelings, and imaginative insights many Anglos took for granted in themselves, Eaton subtly helped humanize "Chinamen" in general. The more Wing Sing travels, the more he seems to have in common—mentally, emotionally, and spiritually—with the people who were reading about him. They probably *assumed* good qualities in themselves; Eaton helps them *see* good qualities in her alter-ego.

Part of the fun of reading Wing Sing's reports involves both their style and their frequent, often understated humor. At one point, for instance, Wing Sing explains the Chinese calendar: "The moon go round the earth thirteen times in the last Chinese year. One moon to a Chinaman same as one month to American. See!" (Eaton 212). That final word—"See!"—exemplifies the strongly oral nature of the narrative; it is as if Wing Sing is speaking to readers rather than writing for them. He comes across less as a remote, objective author than as a real personality—even a "character." For example, he explains that the Chinese, on the first day of a new year,

> have big ceremony call "Rounding the Year," and in the night we have another ceremony call "Keeping company with the gods during the night." Pardon me if not explain what that mean. There be some things to write about and some things to be quiet about. The American people not yet come to understand all the Chinese ceremony. (Eaton 212)

And that's where he leaves it. He raises an intriguing topic but then refuses to explain its significance. He arouses curiosity and then refuses to satisfy it, creating a sense of mystery but also showing, once more, that *he* is in control of what he will say or not say. He will not kowtow to his readers; in fact, he seems to enjoy having fun with them. But his humor is also often balanced by touches of more profound feelings, as when he reports that during the Chinese New Year ceremonies, "all the Chinese people are merry. They enjoy pleasant food, they get pleasure from music and they live comfortable," but then he continues "and not think of what make them mourn" (Eaton 212). Just when he perhaps leads us to think that the Chinese are an unusually happy people, he suddenly reminds us that they, like all people, know what it is to grieve. Their happiness is partly a way to cope with, or at least temporarily to forget, their grief. In touches like this one, Wing Sing creates a sense of the Chinese not as some "foreign," exotic people but as fellow human beings. Some of them have, for instance, many of the same subtle character flaws as their Anglo counterparts, such as an interest in showing off. Thus Wing Sing offers the following anecdote:

> My cousin he take me see many of his friend. Lee Chu very fine fellow. He bring his wife out from China last year, and he have one

fine boy. Lee Chu, he Chinaman, but he all same Canadian man. He wear fur coat and fur hat and he drink plenty beer. He interpreter in Montreal court. Sometime he talk English, sometime he talk Chinese and sometime he talk the French talk. When I go to bid him good-bye, he say "Au Revoir." I say to my cousin, "What he mean?" and my cousin he say, "I think he mean to tell you he know something you not know." (Eaton 212)

This story exemplifies much of the substance and tone of Wing Sing's narratives. He is less interested in making grand observations than in providing little character sketches that reveal more than Wing Sing himself makes explicit. In the sketch just described, however, Wing Sing lets his cousin suggest that Lee Chu is just a bit full of himself. Wing Sing reports his cousin's words and then immediately moves on to other topics, rather than commenting any further in his own voice.

Often Wing Sing suggests some of the interesting ways in which traditional Chinese culture was beginning to change in its new North American environment. The anecdote just cited, in fact, is one small instance of that recurring theme. But an especially fascinating example of this kind of change is revealed in the following story:

After I see Lee Chu I see Wong Chow. Wong Chow he look serious and he not drink no samshu. My cousin he tell me that Wong Chow, he brought his wife from China, five, six, seven years ago, and the American lady come see and talk much foolishness to her so that when Wong Chow tell his wife do this to do that, his wife, she ask question, "What for?" This make much trouble in Wong Chow's house, and one day, when Wong Chow away, his wife, she take the dog and the cat and she go live with the American lady, and she not come back to Wong Chow for a long time, and then she tell him she never not come back to him at all unless he make agreement that he not do one thing she not advise and he not want her to do one thing she not want to do. So Wong Chow make agreement; but that great shame to Chinaman. (Eaton 212)

Even North American Chinese culture, then, was beginning to be affected by the rise of the so-called "New Woman." When Wing

Sing suggests that it may not be a good idea to bring his own wife from China to America, his cousin reassures him but advises that he just not talk to his wife too much if he does so; too much talking to a wife can make the "woman lose her humility." Wing Sing, on the other hand, replies that too little conversation between a husband and wife can make her discontented. He concludes: "It is difficult to know how to behave toward a woman" (Eaton 213). The fact that these words were actually written *by* a woman makes the joke all the more amusing. Again, Wing Sing makes it clear that complexities in relations between the sexes are universal, not simply confined to Anglo culture.

Yet whatever Wing Sing describes, he describes in his memorable style, as when he reports, "I never see no city more better than Montreal." Citizens of that city make lots of money, but they also enjoy outdoor wintertime activities: "The cold, it is very cold, but the Canadian man and the Canadian woman they not like stay in the house too much. They sport like little child that is strong like man"—a splendidly paradoxical simile (Eaton 213).

Wherever Wing Sing happens to stop or stay, he makes intriguing observations. Commenting on New York City, for instance, he reports that most of the Chinese there "engage in the laundry work. That is, because it is a business that requires but little capital—beside it is a business that the Chinaman is allowed to go into. The white man he keep the Chinaman out of the millionaire business" (Eaton 215). Everything up to the point of the dash simply reaffirms common Anglo stereotypes about the Chinese. But everything after the dash puts an intriguing critical spin on standard assumptions. Wing Sing is often critical in just the same way: he makes one telling observation after another, never hectoring, never lecturing, and perhaps making his points all the more effectively for that reason. His satire is over with almost before one realizes the sting he has delivered. Consider, for example, the way he deals with the common charge that Chinese immigrants were addicted to drugs and illegal games of chance:

There is some gambling and some opium smoking in Chinatown, but not very much. The Chinaman gets fun out of life in other ways, too. The Canadian Chinaman he like very much to learn to speak the English and the French language and to learn the English and the French religions. Some Chinamen here [in Montreal] they be Protestant and Catholic both. Song Long he go to six Sunday schools—Episcopal, Presbyterian, Methodist, Baptist and Reformed Episcopal. He keep up the Chinese religion, too. I think he be what American people call very liberal man. (Eaton 215)

These comments are intriguing for several reasons. First, Wing Sing never tries to deny that *some* Chinese people in North America are indeed involved in drugs and gambling. Their involvement, however, stems only from a desire for "fun"—a desire to which most people can relate. But then he once more turns the tables on accusers: some Chinese enjoy the "fun" of learning new languages and even new religions—as many as possible, in fact! This is an entirely different kind of amusement, and Wing Sing leaves it unclear whether Song Long is devoted to amusement, to a desire for education, to a sincere interest in religious ideas, or to some combination of all of these possible motivations. Here, as so often elsewhere, Wing Sing's comments are more subtle and thought-provoking than they might on the surface seem.

Chinese Canadians and Chinese Americans
In one especially intriguing report, Wing Sing recounts how one of his cousins in Montreal, married but childless, was melancholy about having no children. Therefore, he and his wife decided to adopt a baby from New York City:

Well, the baby he come, he be white baby with eye the color of the blue China teacup, nose like a piece of jadestone that is carved, mouth same as the red vine leaf and hair all same silk worm make—the color all light and bright. The parent of the baby they not be proper parent and they be Irish. Some time I hear they be dead, but that not matter much to baby; only one thing sure, they love him. . . . Then my cousin, he say: "I will take that white baby and I will bring him up to be as a Chinaman. I will teach him the Chinese language and the

Chinese ways and the Chinese principles. Then one day I take him with me to China and find a little Chinese wife for him—and he will be to me as a son." (Eaton 218)

This is a kind of multiculturalism that probably would have astonished—or even shocked—some of Wing Sing's Anglo readers, but Wing Sing doesn't bat an eye when reporting it. Yet just when one might assume that Wing Sing is entirely at ease with the adoption, he ends his report by recounting how he walked in on his cousin and wife as they were bathing the child:

> The baby it be very happy, its hair twist all over its head, and so also its legs and arms. It laugh much, and my cousin and his wife they laugh too. Never have I seen them so forget the rules of propriety. "What do you think?" ask my cousin, and I reply, "I not say what I think." (Eaton 219)

And that's it: another ambiguous moment in a series of articles full of such moments. Wing Sing seems unbothered by the idea of his cousin adopting a non-Chinese baby, but he does seem disturbed by the idea of having so much fun bathing the child. In moments like this, we realize that even Wing Sing has his limits as an advocate for multiculturalism. Adopting a non-Chinese baby is one thing, but laughing while bathing the child seems to be crossing some important cultural line. Perhaps Eaton is here having fun at the expense of her own Chinese narrator.

On the whole, however, Wing Sing comes across as a man of cosmopolitan tastes and values—a man who has been broadened by his travels and whose narratives perhaps help broaden the mindsets of his readers. At one point, for instance, he recounts advice a cousin gave him about travelling:

> My cousin he go with me to station. He say pay little attention to those who talk much and to have not much to do with gamesters and chess players, also to keep myself from the seductions of beauty, music and pleasant food.

> I listen to all that I hear and I smile. I Chinaman that have travel
> much, and the suggestions my cousin make seem to me to savor of a
> small shrewdness. (Eaton 218)

That phrase—"small shrewdness"—can be interpreted in at least two ways: either his cousin shows very little shrewdness, or his cousin is shrewd in a small, limiting, and quite provincial or even petty way. Either way (or in both ways), the words imply Wing Sing's own confidence that he is wiser than his cousin. But, in his typically wise way, he never says so to his cousin. Wing Sing knows how to be tactful, letting others preserve their self-respect unless they blatantly threaten his own.

Conclusion

It would be easy to continue recounting various details of Wing Sing's narratives – easy if space were unlimited. Since space is not unlimited, however, suffice it to say that in creating Wing Sing, Eaton created one of her most memorable characters. And, in doing so, she revealed more of the wit, humor, wisdom, and complexity of her own personality. Everything Wing Sing says or does suggests something or other about Eaton herself. Surely she admired this figment of her own imagination: there is, after all, quite a bit to admire. He is intelligent, perceptive, sensible, wry, imaginative, diplomatic, and shrewd not only in his assessments of other people but also in his responses to the various cultures to which he is exposed and in his reactions to cultural changes. And, in all these ways, he reflects many traits of the woman who created him and set him on his journey.

Note

1. On Eaton's life, see (for instance) White-Parks. On her relations with her sister, see (for example) Ling. For early treatments of her fiction, Solberg and Ammons are good starting points, while Yin helps set her in various multicultural contexts. On works recently added to her canon, see Chapman. All quotations from Eaton are from the splendid edition compiled by Mary Chapman.

Works Cited

Ammons, Elizabeth. "Audacious Words: Sui Sin Far's Mrs. Spring Fragrance." *Conflicting Stories: American Women Writers at the Turn into the Twentieth Century*. Oxford UP, 1991, pp. 105-120.

Chapman, Mary. "Finding Edith Eaton." *Legacy*, vol. 29, no. 2, 2012, pp. 263–269.

Eaton, Edith Maude. *Becoming Sui Sin Far: Early Fiction, Journalism, and Travel Writing*. Edited by Mary Chapman, McGill-Queen's UP, 2016.

Ling, Amy. "Pioneers and Paradigms: The Eaton Sisters." *Between Worlds: Women Writers of Chinese Ancestry*. Pergamon, 1990, pp. 21-55.

Solberg, S. E. "Sui Sin Far/Edith Eaton: The First Chinese-American Fictionist." *MELUS*, vol. 8 no. 1, 1981, pp. 27–39.

White-Parks, Annette. *Sui Sin Far/Edith Maude Eaton: A Literary Biography*. U of Illinois P, 1995.

Yin, Xiao-huang. "The Voice of a Eurasian." *Chinese American Literature since the 1850s*. U of Illinois P, 2000, pp. 85-116.

Perpetual Foreigners, Settlers, and Sojourners: An Overview of a Century of South Asian Immigrant Writing in North America_____

Nalini Iyer

South Asian American immigration to North America began in the late nineteenth century. However, there is a common perception amongst scholars that this community's literary endeavors are relatively new and emerged only after the passing of the Immigration and Nationality Act of 1965, when the South Asian immigrant population increased significantly in the United States. Although immigration from South Asia had been subject to exclusions and quotas in the early twentieth century, South Asian American writing in English and in Indian languages did emerge in this period in the form of autobiography, revolutionary poetry, and journalism. This chapter, however, will focus on English-language writing by immigrants from South Asia in the United States.[1] "Immigrants" is used broadly here to refer to writers who have spent some significant time in the United States and have written about it. Although some writers identify as hyphenated Americans (Indo-American, Pakistani-American) and others as "Indian" or "Sri Lankan" while living and working in the US, and still others as transnational writers, for the purposes of this chapter, the focus is on the content of their writing and its engagement with the questions of citizenship and belonging for those who have voluntarily or involuntarily moved to the US. Additionally, the label "South Asia" is used here to encompass the contemporary nations of India, Pakistan, Bangladesh, Nepal, Sri Lanka, Bhutan, Afghanistan, and Maldives. These nations share cultures, religious practices, and histories and, at the same time, have conflicts within their national boundaries and also with one another. Furthermore, border issues and sovereignty questions in regions like Kashmir and Baluchistan complicate the question of national identity. The term South Asian American is one that emerged in the last two decades of the twentieth century in academic and activist circles to recognize that immigrants from this region experience the hostland through the lenses of immigration status, xenophobia, and racism. Activists and scholars use the term "South Asian American" to refer to the community that emigrated from South Asia either directly to the United States or through prior diasporas from Africa, the Caribbean, or Pacific Islands.

The 2010 census estimates that there were 3.4 million South Asians in the United States, with the majority of the immigrants coming from India. The Immigration and Nationality Act of 1965 changed the population flow from South Asia. Prior to this, South Asian countries were part of the Barred Zone of immigration, and very few individuals came to the United States each year; the 1965 Act shifted immigration criteria from nations of origin to skills-based immigration and paved the way for large numbers of people from South Asia with advanced degrees to emigrate. This growth in numbers also led to a cultural explosion in terms of South Asian American film and media, art, and literary works. Even as the numbers increased, South Asian immigrants found themselves challenged by cultural alienation and racism, and they grappled with questions of home and belonging. The attacks on the Twin Towers on 9/11 exacerbated the situation for South Asians, who became targets of an increasing number of violent and racist attacks, and many (particularly Sikhs) lost their lives.[2] South Asians were subjected to state surveillance and Islamophobia, and, following the economic crash of 2008, South Asians were also viewed as an economic threat because they were perceived as taking away jobs from "real" Americans due to their growing numbers in the tech industry. The rapid growth of the tech sector has also resulted in a large of number of South Asians who live and work in the US as H-1B (temporary worker) visa holders—they experience a precarity of visa status even as they contribute significantly to the economy and culture of the United States. As temporary workers, many H-1B visa holders live and work in the US for many years distanced from their home cultures but unable to build permanent lives in the US because of significant delays in moving to permanent residency (green card) status. The precarity of status, the increased surveillance, and incidents of violence against South Asians continue under the Trump Administration especially as there are debates in the public sphere about draconian travel bans and immigration reforms, about American sovereignty, and the need to ban or intern Muslims as national security threats.

South Asian American writing, therefore, is imbricated in the politics of American imperialism over the last century.[3] This chapter explores three phases in the development of South Asian American literatures: 1890s to the end of World War II, 1965 to 2000, and post 9/11 to identify major themes in writing by South Asians in the United States and to trace their evolution over this almost 100-year period. Although South Asians inhabit different immigrant identities, such as sojourner, settler, or transnational flexible citizen [4], they remain perpetual foreigners in North America. Their perceived foreignness structures their racialization through binaries, such as exotic/terrorist; insider/outsider; familiar/threatening. [5] The literature articulates this racialization as well as the resistance and strategies of survival embraced by the community.

1890s to World War II—the Pioneers

During the period that the British ruled the Indian subcontinent, many sailors, soldiers, and traders found their way to the United States. As Vivek Bald has written in *Bengali Harlem*, many of these people came as sojourners and eventually settled in various cities and established businesses. Many intermarried with the local black community and lived amongst communities of color in places like Harlem, New Orleans, and Baltimore. In the West Coast, people came first to British Columbia in Canada, and as immigration laws tightened and labor markets dried up there, they moved South across the border and down the West Coast of the United States. Although a majority of these migrants were Sikh and Muslim, they were often referred to as "Hindoos." Their numbers were not large, and they experienced racist backlash in towns like Bellingham, Washington, because of their willingness to work for lower wages. [6] Some of these immigrants formed the Ghadar (Revolution) Party in 1913 in Astoria, Oregon, and eventually established themselves in California. [7] Most of them were agriculturalists, and some were students who came to the major public universities on the West Coast and intermingled with the agricultural immigrants. Several of these immigrants married Mexican women because of the anti-miscegenation laws in place and a Punjabi-Mexican community formed in California. [8] These early immigrants sought to simultaneously fight racist immigration laws in the US and Canada that were exclusionary and also to resist British imperialism at home. They produced newspapers, radical tracts, and revolutionary poetry that focused on these twin goals. Important themes in the writing of this period include cultural alienation, racism and its impact on everyday life, and the depiction of India as a mystical space that offers spiritual renewal and refuge.

One of the earliest South Asian writers of this period was Dhan Gopal Mukerji, who was best known for his works of children's literature including *Gay Neck, the Story of a Pigeon*, which won a Newberry award in 1928. Mukerji also published an autobiography, *Caste and Outcast*, in which he describes his life both in India and in the United States. The second part of the autobiography describes in great detail how isolated Mukerji felt in the US, where he had arrived and had enrolled as a student at the University of California. He had no money and had to work to support himself. His upper caste upbringing in India had not provided him with the kind of skills (cooking, housekeeping, cleaning) necessary for the menial jobs he found near the university campus. He writes of his connections with other minorities, such as Jewish Americans and African Americans, who helped him along the way. Although there were several other Indian students in California, Mukerji avoided their company because he found their radical politics problematic. He connected with students and thinkers from different political and religious persuasions to debate philosophy and religion. Much of his energies were focused on Indian (Hindu) spirituality and explaining India's mysticism to the curious American. The autobiography speaks to Mukerji's exploration of his spiritual identity as a Hindu in America. He draws on an orientalist tradition of imagining India as a spiritual space in his writing and seeks to promulgate the glories of Indian civilization to an American audience, including children. His narrative also speaks to his profound alienation from both American culture and the fledgling Indian American community, and Mukerji's alienation eventually led to his suicide in 1936. [9]

Another person who writes about life in this early period of South Asian immigration is Kartar Dhillon (1915–2008). Dhillon was the daughter of Bakshish Singh Dhillon and Ratan Kaur, who had come to the West Coast in 1897 and 1910 respectively. Dhillon's autobiographical fragments published in the latter half of the twentieth century outline the rigors of the pioneers' lives. In "The Parrot's Beak" (www.saada.org/tides/article/20121004-1114), Dhillon recounts her mother's last days when she was dying in a hospital from a tumor. We learn that Ratan Kaur had been widowed young and had eight children. She had been harsh in her treatment of her daughters, particularly Kartar, and had managed to raise them through the family's sharecropping on West Coast farms. Dhillon speaks of the difficulties that she faced after her mother's death in caring for her younger siblings. Dhillon married another Punjabi revolutionary and also had children when still in her teens. Although the men in the Ghadar Party were fighting for social and political change, their treatment of their women reflected Punjabi patriarchal values. Dhillon recognizes that her mother's harshness came from her isolation in the United States. Since women were very few in number, her mother mostly lived amongst men, bereft of the support of women in her extended family, which would have been possible had she lived in India. Her female companionship came from her daughters as they grew older. Dhillon's recollection of her mother's life in the early days of South Asian immigration remains the only female-centered account of immigrant lives at this time. In her other work—such as the narrative for the film *Turbans* made by her granddaughter Erika Surat Andersen and an autobiographical fragment she wrote about her return to Astoria, Oregon, and still another piece in which she memorializes her brother, Bud Dhillon—Kartar Dhillon captures both the hardships of minority life as Sikhs and describes in great detail the resistance work undertaken by the early Punjabi migrants. [10]

The autobiographical narratives of this period are significant in the development of South Asian American writing because they capture the everyday experiences of the pioneering South Asians. These immigrants found their way in a culture that was significantly different from their own. They also experienced ambivalence in terms of citizenship and belonging in both the United States and in India under imperial control. The British considered them as inferior and subject peoples, and the Americans saw them as aliens whose only purpose was to work under harsh conditions. In these narratives, the authors assert their humanity and turn their gaze onto American life and offer critical insights. Although they dream of democracy for India, they are aware of the problematic place of minorities in American democracy.

1965–2000—the Immigration Boom and the Emergence of South Asian American Writing:

The passage of the Immigration and Nationality Act of 1965 (also known as the Hart-Cellar Act) transformed the demographics of the United States. By shifting away from nation-based quotas to skills-based immigration, the United States opened the doors for educated immigrants from Asia, including South Asia. [11] Immigration reform of the 1980s, which emphasized family reunification, added to the numbers of South Asian immigrants to the US, although not all of them were highly educated. Many South Asians came to the United States after 1965 as students, notably in the scientific fields. The majority of these immigrants were male, and they often stayed on in the United States for jobs.[12] However, several South Asians also came to the United States for graduate education in the humanities, including writers such as Bharati Mukherjee, Chitra Divakaruni, Meena Alexander, Agha Shahid Ali, and Tahira Naqvi. Although these new immigrants were fluent in English and college-educated, they experienced racism, cultural isolation, and a deep longing for the homes they had left behind. Jhumpa Lahiri, whose parents immigrated to New England via the UK, writes about these immigrants of the professional classes in her short stories in *The Interpreter of Maladies* and *Unaccustomed Earth* and also in her novels. In *The Namesake*, she traces how a Bengali student, Ashoke, arrives in the US for graduate education, marries Ashima on one of his trips home, and establishes a life in New England. In tracing Ashoke and Ashima's life over a couple of decades, the novel explores how immigrants who are professionals move up the economic ladder (home ownership, college education for the kids) and also build an ethnic community through informal gatherings and celebrations of milestones to capture a sense of home. The first generation yearns for the family and country left behind and seeks to recreate that culture in New England. Their children, however, are adrift. They share neither their parents' nostalgia for home nor do they feel completely at home in American culture. The novel examines how Gogol, the son of Ashoke and Ashima, understands his identity as a Bengali/Indian/American. He changes his name and uses an Americanized short version of his new name, Nikhil, and tries to assimilate in mainstream American culture through the women he dates. When his father dies suddenly, Gogol retreats into his parents' culture and marries the daughter of Bengali immigrants who shares his sense of alienation and hybridity. However, that shared sense of displacement is not enough for the marriage to succeed, and Gogol continues his search for home.

In her autobiography, *Fault Lines*, the poet Meena Alexander also writes about cultural identity and race. In one segment, she narrates how her biracial children map their identity fairly young. Whether it is her young son drawing an imaginary map of the world that shows where both sets of his grandparents live or her daughter, Svati Mariam, drawing a picture of her grandmother with a bone through her hair, thus confusing Indian American with American Indian because her school could not keep the cultural identities separate, these writers grappled with cultural, national, and racial identities in their writings.

Many of these writers also explore gender issues. In particular, Bharati Mukherjee, Chitra Divakaruni, and Jhumpa Lahiri among others write about the difficulties women experience with emigration.

As with Kartar Dhillon who preceded them, they are acutely aware of the struggles of women who are simultaneously navigating homeland values about family and marriage while also managing life in a new land with its own regime of gendered racialization. An early anthology of South Asian American writing *Our Feet Walk the Sky*, edited by a South Asian Women's Collective, articulates the complex and heterogeneous experiences of South Asian immigrant women. In this book, women share poems, narratives, essays, and critical analyses from a breathtaking variety of South Asian backgrounds. Their works signal different linguistic, religious, and class backgrounds. Some are first-generation immigrants and others are children and grandchildren of immigrants. Some had come directly from South Asia, and others had traversed the globe as part of earlier South Asian migrations to the Caribbean or Fiji. These women do not speak as one voice, and their powerful stories explode on the page. They challenge patriarchal authority, defy heteronormativity, and express sorrow, loss, nostalgia, anger, joy, and love. The book is divided into eight sections including "Lighting the Fire Beneath Our Homes;" "Surrounded By the Walls of Our Community;" "The Labourers of this War; "The Fear that Comes from their Eyes;" "She will not be Shamed"; "Fissures of the Past;" "The Strength that Mends her Soul;" and "My Feet Found Home." The titles and sequence of these sections tell the stories of women's struggle against family, community, and nation and also speaks to their resilience and courage. There are also critical essays by scholars like Samita Das Dasgupta and Inderpal Grewal that reflect the pioneering work done in articulating South Asian American studies as a field which had been marginalized in both postcolonial studies and Asian American studies.

A more recent anthology, *Good Girls Marry Doctors,* focuses on daughterhood and critically examines familial and cultural expectations of marriage and motherhood and the price of challenging cultural values. The authors of these essays come from different religious and national backgrounds in South Asia. Triveni Gandhi explores her religious practices through family taboos on meat and alcohol and how she arrives at a personal religious philosophy after reflecting on her own experiences of Indian culture outside her family's particular practices. Sayantani DasGupta's "Good Girls Become Doctors" explodes the idea that Indian families force their children into medicine as a profession. The daughter of a South Asian feminist and academic, DasGupta writes about growing up in a household where community-based activism for gender equality was part of the fabric of family life. When as a college student DasGupta is considering her own professional path, she understands that her father urges her to become a doctor not because he is a patriarch but because he wants his daughter to never be dependent on another for her livelihood. Ruksana Badruddoja's "The Fantasy of a Normative Motherhood" is a powerful essay on the author's growing realization that the ideals of Bangladeshi American expectations of marriage and motherhood shackled her to a world that furthered capitalistic and heteronormative expectations. She writes candidly of her discovery during a challenging pregnancy that she never felt the biological clock tick nor really wanted to be a mother. Motherhood isn't quite what she wants, and yet she continues her commitment to raise her now- teenaged daughter. In the "Politics of Being Political," Piyali Bhattacharya, the editor of this anthology, shares her experiences of navigating parental expectations—familiarity with Indian culture, fluency in the mother tongue, good grades—until she discovered feminism in college. While her parents supported her desire to be a writer, her career as a journalist who wrote on Black Lives Matter and the Indian presence in Kashmir caused conflict with her parents. Yet, when she receives the contract to publish this book, her parents respect her desire to speak her truth.

South Asians Americans also began writing about sexual identities and the challenges gay men and women experienced within traditional family structures as well as because of their racial identities within US gay culture. The anthology *A Lotus of Another Colour: An Unfolding of the South Asian Gay and Lesbian Experience* was a pioneering one. The novels of Sri Lankan Canadian writer Shyam Selvadurai; Indo-Trinidadian Canadian writer Shani Mootoo; transnational writer Sandip Roy; South Asian American writers Ginu Kamani and Minal Hajratwala; and the more recent narratives by Rakesh Satyal, S. J. Sindhu, and Rahul Mehta are among the many works that speak to the heterogeneity of the South Asian gay and lesbian experiences. In recent years, the poetry and performance of Alok Vaid-Menon and a children's book, *The Boy and the Bindi*, by Vivek Shraya focus on narratives of gender nonconformity. For these writers, the heteropatriarchal family is the site of psychic and physical violence, and these works question what constitutes assimilation and belonging if the family is the structure that facilitates that process.

The latter half of the twentieth century saw the emergence and establishment of South Asian American writing as a distinct genre in ethnic American literature. These literary works traced questions of national identity, cultural alienation, gender and sexuality, but they tended to be overwhelmingly produced by the professional class with many writers having advanced degrees or working in academia. Although this body of literature was referred to as South Asian American, it was also Indo-centric, and Pakistani, Bangladeshi, Sri Lankan, or Nepali voices were peripheral.

9/11 and after:

The attack on the Twin Towers on 9/11 had profound consequences for South Asian Americans. South Asians experienced increased state surveillance, harassment at airports, violent attacks, and Islamophobia, which exacerbated their marginalization and precarity but also sharpened religious differences between Hindus, Muslims, and Sikhs in the United States. Sikhs were often targets of violence because they were mistaken for Muslims, and Hindus sought to distance themselves from Muslims in an attempt to identify as the "good" South Asian immigrants.[13] Post-9/11 writing by South Asian immigrant authors has highlighted the complexities of identity. Among literary works that focus on South Asian racialization post-9/11 are Salman Rushdie's novel *Shalimar the Clown*, Mohsin Hamid's *The Reluctant Fundamentalist* and *Exit West*, Chitra Divakaruni's *Queen of Dreams* and *Oleander Girl*, and Ayad Akhtar's plays *Disgraced* and *The Who and the What*.

In his Pulitzer prize-winning play, *Disgraced*, Akhtar examines what it means to be Muslim in post-9/11 America. His protagonist, Amir Kapoor, is a prominent Pakistani American lawyer married to a liberal white woman artist. His nephew enjoins him to defend an Imam accused of terrorist activities and being tried under the Patriot Act. Amir is concerned that his involvement would jeopardize his place in his law firm where the partners are Jewish. As the play progresses, the audience learns that the growing prejudices against Muslim Americans fuel Amir's insecurities and impact his marriage as well as his professional relationships with colleagues in the law firm. In an explosive dinner party scene where Amir; his wife Emily; his African American colleague Jory; and her husband Isaac, an art dealer, discuss identity, race, and culture, Amir learns that Jory has been made partner over him and that his wife had an affair with Isaac. Amir falls apart and argues with Jory about their relative place in the law firm's racialized hierarchy. When Jory and Isaac leave the party, Amir confronts his wife about her fidelity, gets further enraged, and beats her. In this controversial and violent encounter, the play foregrounds gendered and racialized tensions within post-9/11 America. The characters' debate about anti-Black racism, anti-Semitism, Islamic values, and gender identities highlight how 9/11 has introduced new racial categories into American political and cultural life and that while different minority groups (white woman, black woman, Jewish man, Muslim man) fight about who is more oppressed, white supremacist structures remain intact.

If Akhtar explores the profound vulnerabilities of a Muslim male immigrant, a model minority from some perspectives, in post-9/11 America, then Chitra Divakaruni's focus in her novel *Queen of Dreams* is on the day itself and how it bred violence. In that novel, Rakhi, the protagonist, has established a tea house in an upscale Bay Area neighborhood with her best friend, Belle, who is Sikh, and with assistance from her father. The tea house is a gathering place for people of different immigrant backgrounds where, along with tea and snacks, the customers celebrate different cultures. When the planes crash into the Twin Towers and the Pentagon, a rash of violence occurs across the country as a backlash against those who look like the attackers. Belle's boyfriend, Jespal, is attacked in one such occurrence, and the white attackers do not care about his ethnic identity; they just want revenge against foreigners or those that they see as brown-skinned aliens.

These post-9/11 works depict the social, cultural, psychic, physical, and economic impact of racism and Islamophobia on South Asian Americans. These works counter the depiction in mainstream media and popular culture (thrillers, spy fiction, and police procedurals, for example) where brown-skinned men of West Asian or South Asian descent are stereotyped as terrorist threats and where West Asian and South Asian women are often depicted as victims of their patriarchal cultures who need to be rescued by white liberal Americans.

South Asian immigrant writing in the United States now has a substantial presence within Asian American literatures and is also recognized as distinct from postcolonial South Asian writing. However, the coalescing of an identity that centers common regional culture and common experiences within the racialized regime of American immigration law also tends to homogenize and erase distinctions within this group. Not only is this writing overwhelmingly representative of professional and middle-class immigrant experiences, it also becomes marketed as an exotic body of literature. There are also erasures of subaltern identities within this writing (caste identities, sexualities, religions, refugee, and undocumented experiences); any such overview, like this essay, must, ultimately, recognize this tension between the homogeneity and diversity within this literary canon.

Notes

1. Although the primary focus is on writers based in the United States, the experiences of South Asians in the US often cross the border into Canada and many of these writers—such as Bharati Mukherjee and M. G. Vassanji—have lived and worked in both countries.

2. For a discussion of 9/11 and its impact on South Asians, see Vijay Prashad and Aparajita De's books.

3. For a nuanced discussion of this, see Vivek Bald, et. al editors, *The Sun Never Sets: South Asian Migrants in an Age of U.S. Power.* NYU Press, 2013.

4. This is a term coined by Aihwa Ong in *Flexible Citizenship: The Cultural Logics of Transnationality.* Duke UP, 1999.

5. See Stanley Thangaraj. "Playing through differences: black-white racial logic and interrogating South Asian American Identity" *Ethnic and Racial Studies*, vol. 35, no. 6, June 2012, pp. 988-1006.

6. For a detailed discussion of the experiences of South Asians in the Pacific Northwest, see chapter 2 of Amy Bhatt and Nalini Iyer, *Roots and Reflections: South Asians in the Pacific Northwest.* U of Washington P, 2013.

7. For the development of Ghadar, see Maia Ramnath's *From Haj to Utopia: How the Ghadar Movement Charted Global Radicalism and Attempted to Overthrow the British Empire.* U of California P, 2011.

8. See Karen Isaksen Leonard's *Making Ethnic Choices: California's Punjabi Mexican Americans.* Temple UP, 1994.

9. For a longer discussion of Mukherji's autobiography, see Nalini Iyer's "Diasporic Subjectivity: Dhan Gopal Mukerji's *Caste and Outcast* and Sadhu Singh Dhami's *Maluka*" in *Crossing Borders: Essays on Literature, Culture, and Society in Honor of Amritjit Singh*, edited by Tapan Basu and Tasneem Shahnaz, Fairleigh Dickinson UP, 2016, pp. 109-118.

10. Dhillon's autobiographical narratives can be found in the digital archives of SAADA. For a greater discussion of her recollections of Astoria, Oregon, and of her narration for *Turbans*, see chapter 2 of Bhatt and Iyer's *Roots and Reflections.*

11. See Leti Volpp's "The Legal Mapping of U.S. Immigration, 1965–1996" for a discussion of the Hart-Cellar and subsequent immigration reform.

12. For a discussion of the Immigration and Nationality Act and its impact on education and employment, please see Bhatt and Iyer's *Roots and Reflections.*

13. See De and Prashad.

Works Cited

Akhtar, Ayad. *Disgraced.* Little, Brown, 2013.

Alexander, Meena. *Fault Lines*. 2nd ed., Feminist P, 2003.

Badruddoja, Roksana. "The Fantasy of Normative Motherhood." *Good Girls Marry Doctors: South Asian American Daughters on Obedience and Rebellion*, edited by Piyali Bhattacharya, Aunt Lute P, 2016, pp. 19-26.

Bald, Vivek. *Bengali Harlem and the Lost Histories of South Asian America*. Harvard UP, 2013.

_____. et al., editors. *The Sun Never Sets: South Asian Migrants in an Age of U.S. Power*. New York UP, 2013.

Bhatt, Amy, and Nalini Iyer. *Roots and Reflections: South Asians in the Pacific Northwest*. U of Washington P, 2013.

Bhatt, Sheela, et al., editors. *Our Feet Walk the Sky: Women of the South Asian Diaspora*. Aunt Lute, 1993.

Bhattacharya, Piyali, editor. *Good Girls Marry Doctors: South Asian American Daughters on Obedience and Rebellion*. Aunt Lute P, 2016.

Bhattacharya, Piyali. "The Politics of Being Political." *Good Girls Marry Doctors: South Asian American Daughters on Obedience and Rebellion*, edited by Piyali Bhattacharya, Aunt Lute P, 2016, pp. 33-40.

DasGupta, Sayantani. "Good Girls Become Doctors." *Good Girls Marry Doctors: South Asian American Daughters on Obedience and Rebellion*, edited by Piyali Bhattacharya, Aunt Lute P, 2016, pp. 55-58.

De, Aparajita, ed. *South Asian Racialization and Belonging after 9/11: Masks of Threat*. Lanham, MD: Lexington Books, 2016.

Dhillon, Kartar. *South Asian Digital Archives*, SAADA, 2017, www.saada.org/tides/author/kartar-dhillon/.

Divakaruni, Chitra Banerjee. *Queen of Dreams*. Anchor, 2004.

Gandhi, Triveni. "Good Girls Pray to Gods." *Good Girls Marry Doctors: South Asian American Daughters on Obedience and Rebellion*, edited by Piyali Bhattacharya, Aunt Lute P, 2016, pp. 65-72.

Lahiri, Jhumpa. *The Namesake*. Houghton Mifflin, 2003.

Iyer, Nalini. "Diasporic Subjectivity: Dhan Gopal Mukerji's *Caste and Outcast* and Sadhu Singh Dhami's *Maluka*." *Crossing Borders: Essays on Literature, Culture, and Society in Honor of Amritjit Singh*, edited by Tapan Basu and Tasneem Shahnaz. Fairleigh Dickinson UP, 2016, pp. 109-118.

Leonard, Karen Isaksen *Making Ethnic Choices: California's Punjabi Mexican Americans.* Temple UP, 1994.

Mehta, Rahul. *No Other World.* Harper Collins, 2017.

Mukerji, Dhan Gopal. *Caste and Outcast.* 1923. Stanford UP, 2002.

_____. *Gay Neck: The Story of A Pigeon.* 1926. Dutton 1968.

Ong, Aihwa. *Flexible Citizenship: The Cultural Logics of Transnationality.* Duke UP, 1999.

Prashad, Vijay. *Uncle Swami: South Asians in America Today.* New York: The New Press, 2012.

Ramnath, Maia. *From Haj to Utopia: How the Ghadar Movement Charted Global Radicalism and Attempted to Overthrow the British Empire.* U of California P, 2011.

Ratti, Rakesh, editor. *Lotus of Another Color: The Unfolding of South Asian Gay and Lesbian Experience.* Alyson Books, 1993.

Shraya, Vivek. *The Boy and the Bindi.* Illustrated by Rajini Perera, Arsenal Pulp P, 2016.

Sindu, S. J. *Marriage of a Thousand Lies.* Soho P, 2017.

Thangaraj, Stanley. "Playing through differences: black-white racial logic and interrogating South Asian American Identity" *Ethnic and Racial Studies,* vol.35, no.6, June 2012, pp. 988-1006.

Volpp, Leti. "The Legal Mapping of U.S. Immigration, 1965–1996." *Crossing into America: The New Literature of Immigration,* edited by Louis Mendoza and S. Shankar, New Press, 2003, pp. 257-269.

We Are Made to Leave, We Are Made to Return: Writing Movement in Contemporary Arab American Literature_____

Mejdulene B. Shomali

Introduction

In the poetry collection *I am Made to Leave I am Made to Return*, Marwa Helal troubles a linear and progressive narrative of Arab immigration to the United States. Rather than imagine that relocation to the United States is a singular, fixed act, or that it reaps positive rewards for the immigrant, Helal highlights the fraught relationship Arab immigrants have to their new country of residence. She does so by pointing toward the imperial violence that may have caused Arab departure from the Middle East and by articulating the many other kinds of violence Arabs may face in the United States. Helal's work also explores how Arab immigrants are in constant motion among multiple nations and locations, thereby muddying the permanence of immigration and the definition of the term itself. Helal's work is one lens into the treatment of immigration by writers of Arab descent, living in the United States. Drawing on the work of Helal and her contemporaries, this essay will explore the theme of immigration in Arab American literature. It will analyze how contemporary Arab American[1] writers engage questions of movement, space and time, and ancestry in their work. To do so, it is useful to first give an overview of the category Arab American, a brief history of Arab immigration to the United States, and an outline of Arab American literary periods in the United States.

Arab American Writers

It can be difficult to classify a category like "Arab American Literature" because the idea of "Arab Americans" is itself open to interpretation. The first term—Arab—refers neither to a singular country nor geographic region. Instead, Arab is often used to designate countries or populations that speak Arabic, national members of the Arab League, or communities with shared cultural and political histories. Each classification can back up against the next—Arabic is the language of the Koran and, as such, is used in Muslim communities that may or may not identify with Arab identity; regional differences in the spoken version of the Arabic language might render one Arabic speaker unintelligible to the next. The Arab League includes twenty two separate nations: Algeria, Bahrain, Comoros, Djibouti, Egypt, Iraq, Jordan, Kuwait, Lebanon, Libya, Mauritania, Morocco, Oman, Palestine, Qatar, Saudi Arabia, Somalia, Sudan, Syria, Tunisia, United Arab Emirates, and Yemen. Each has its own complex, individual history; how can the moniker "Arab" account for such heterogeneity? Moreover, the geopolitical region known as the Middle East contains countries and communities that are not included under the umbrella "Arab," though they share certain histories because of their geographic proximity, relationship to the West and colonial rule (e.g., Kurds, Iran).

As such, Arab can be an ambiguous and difficult term to apply to a community or body of literature even before immigration. When immigration is factored in, some of the regional, cultural, and historical specificities both advance and recede in significance. For example, recent immigrants seeking refuge from the Assad regime in Syria or fleeing amidst the Yemeni civil war may understand their nation of origin as central or significant to their presence in the United States in ways Saudi immigrants may or may not. Yet, all three groups may arrive and become understood in the United States context under a more generic, pan-Arab moniker. Or, alternately, many in the West are more aware of the Syrian humanitarian crisis than the Yemeni and may assume all new Arab immigrants come from the former and have no framework for understanding the latter. At the same time, Arab immigrants to the United States are subject to increased discrimination and profiling with regard to their Arab identities, yet on the United States census, Arabs are classified as white, thereby limiting their recourse to anti-discrimination protection and other resources occasionally allotted to minority ethnic groups in the United States. Like other immigrants, their path to citizenship can be unduly complicated by anti-Arab sentiment. In addition to legal hardship, these communities often face cultural and social exclusion in the United States. Finally, American could refer to not only immigrants in the United States, but to immigrants in the Americas, including Canada and countries in Central and South America. How then, do we understand the "American" in Arab American?

Here it is useful to turn to other scholars of Arab American literature who have organized critical analysis around the category and defined it with loose parameters that allow the nuances within the category to remain salient. In *Modern Arab American Fiction: A Reader's Guide* (2011), Steven Salaita uses the following: "Arab American literature consists of creative work produced by American authors of Arab origin and that participates, in a conscious way or through its critical reception, in a category that has come to be known as 'Arab American Literature'" (4). Salaita addresses the problem of ambiguous identity classification by attribution of intentionality to the author or to reception of the texts by an audience. So, the writer and the reader together understand a category. In his analyses, Salaita emphasizes the writer's ethnic origin and thematic content in helping materialize the literature as Arab American. In *Immigrant Narratives: Orientalism and Cultural Translation in Arab American and Arab British Literature* (2011), Wail S. Hassan focuses on first-generation Arab immigrants to the United States and Britain, who despite fluency in Arabic, write in English. For Hassan, then, Arab refers to country of origin and American refers to the language of the text (4-5). In *Contemporary Arab-American Literature: Transnational Reconfigurations of Citizenship in Belonging* (2014), Carol Fadda-Conrey uses Arab American to "[denote] a minority collective whose members are connected not only through a shared cultural and linguistic Arab heritage but more importantly through common investment in shaping and performing a revisionary form of US citizenship" (10-11). Like Salaita and Hassan, she locates Arab via the authors' cultural histories. Unlike the others, Fadda-Conrey understands American to be a conscious reckoning on behalf of those authors, who seek to transform the category of American via its coupling with Arab. Drawing from each of the preceding definitions, in this essay we will consider Arab American literature as Anglophone texts published in North, Central, and South America by authors of Arab origin, whose works invoke a linguistic and cultural connection to the Arabic language or Arab nations.

Arab American Immigration Histories

Historians of Arab America outline three waves of Arab immigration to the United States: the 1800s–1925, 1945–1967, and 1965–the current period. Immigrants during the first period were commonly Christian from the Ottoman-ruled provinces of Syria, Mt. Lebanon, and Palestine; immigration records place their numbers in the region of one hundred thirty thousand (Suleiman 2). The first wave's end is marked by the passing of the Immigration Act of 1924, also known as the Johnson-Reed Act, which limited immigrants to the United States by limiting new immigration based on nation of origin and capping new arrivals at 2% per year of the then- population in the United States. Despite the emphasis on nation of origin, immigrants in the first wave often identified through religious or familial affiliations, rather than through a pan-Arab, national, or racial affiliation (Hassan 15; Suleiman 4). Indeed, Arabs experienced uneven racialization in early records of immigration, sometimes being counted as white and awarded citizenship, and other times not. Often the racial status assigned to Arabs by white America reflected other kinds of identity markers, including religion and socioeconomic status (Saliba 312-3; Gualtieri 7-8).

The second wave is bookended by two wars: the end of World War II in 1945 and the Six Day Arab Israeli War in 1967. Notably, this period marked a spike in immigrants exiled from Palestine. It also saw renewed immigration from previously noted Arab regions as well as a growing Yemeni population. The immigrant population in this time period was both more affluent than previous generations and expressed more religious diversity. This period also witnessed an increase of Arab immigrants traveling to the United States on student visas, many of whom remained in the United States after graduation (Suleiman 9; Arab American National Museum, "Arab American Immigration").

Immigration of Arabs to the United States resumed in 1965 after the passing of the Immigration and Nationality Act, or the Hart-Cellar Act. This act attempted to redress the discrimination of the Johnson-Reed Act by eliminating nation-of-origin quotas and substantiating instead a categories system that preferred immigrants with kin already in the United States and immigrants with specialized skills. As before, wars in the Middle East, notably in Iraq and Lebanon, contributed to large influxes to the United States from these nations (Ludescher 94; Arab American National Museum, "Arab American Immigration").

Scholars of the latter two periods suggest that the politicization of Arabs in the 1950s and 60s and the increased anti-Arab and anti-Muslim sentiment in American culture with regard to Middle East politics (e.g., the Arab Oil Embargo, the Gulf Wars, and 9/11) changed the tenor of immigrants to the United States; rather than seeking status via assimilation or identification with whiteness, many later immigrants exalted or maintained cultural proximity to their countries of origin. Similarly, those who arrived in the United States as exiles or as refugees had a different orientation than those who might have arrived to seek education or other career opportunities (Saliba 310-1; Fadda 13).

Though it is difficult to narrate proximate history from the present moment, we can hypothesize that the ongoing Syrian and Yemeni civil wars will impact Arab immigration to the United States. One can also imagine how the 2017 sanctions on travel under the Trump Administration in the form of Executive Order 13780 will impact immigration from the Arab countries under heightened scrutiny. Current records from international student enrollment suggest that immigration to the United States is waning on the whole (Redden par. 2). When we revisit this period down the line, we might understand the 2000s as a distinct wave of Arab immigration.

Immigration in Arab American Literature

As Arab immigration to the United States proceeded in waves, so too did the production of Arab American literature. Critic Evelyn Shakir sees Arab American literature in three movements—early

(1900s–1920s), middle (1930s–1960s), and late (1970s–present) (Majaj, "Arab-American Literature" 3). These movements correspond roughly to the waves of immigration delineated above (Ludescher 93-4). The work of the first wave of immigrant writing in the early1900s shares a political motivation toward acts of translation and bridging the East/West (Shakir, "Coming of Age" 67; Majaj, "Arab-American Literature" 1; Ludescher 95-6). In the second and briefest, Arab writers distanced themselves and their work from an Arab American classification, and instead understood themselves as mainstream creative producers (Shakir, "Coming of Age" 67; Ludescher 100-101; Majaj, "Arab-American Literature" 2). In the last movement, however, the writing reflects the tonal shift in immigration suggested above: it, too, became more politicized about its Arab identity, was critical of its new American surroundings, and imagined an Arab American identity that existed within and against both ends of the identity (Majaj, "Two Worlds Emerging" 75; Hassan 35; Salaita 7-8; Fadda 24-5). This section will briefly cover the first two phases, suggest an end cap for the third, and turn toward texts from the contemporary moment to articulate new modes of engaging immigration.

Mahjar Writers: 1900–1920s
Many critics consider *The Book of Khalid* (1911) by Ameen Rihani as the first Arab American novel. Rihani was a prolific writer and was part of a collective of Arab writers known as Al Rabita al Qalamaiyya (the Pen League). The Pen League included Khalil Gibran as the first Arab American writer to be taken up by a mainstream audience. Rihani, Gibran, and the other members of the Pen League were active producers of Arab American literature in the 1920s in the form of novels, plays, poetry collections, and literary journals. These writers and their work are collectively referred to as the Mahjar school of Arab American literature. Mahjar is the Arab émigré and the writing of the group was strongly influenced by the status of its members as Arab immigrants in the United States.

Evelyn Shakir noted in her 1993 essay "Coming of Age: Arab American Literature" that much of the Mahjar work was concerned with substantiating Arab writers' facility with the English language and thereby underscoring their American identity. Following this critique, Lisa Suhair Majaj argued that "they [the Mahjar group] actively sought to establish philosophical meeting points between Arab and American ideologies . . . not only in an attempt to bridge worlds . . . literature of this period often reflected a strong need to prove oneself worthy in the U.S. context" ("Arab-American Literature" 1-2). Hassan takes up this critique in *Immigrant Narratives* as well, noting that the work of Rihani and others should be considered, in its form and aims, as influenced by Orientalism—the repertory of images and ideologies from which Arab identities and cultures are viewed and interpreted in the West (3). Mahjar writers navigated this Orientalism in multiple ways—primarily, Hassan argues, through the mode of translation—interpreting their originary countries to their countries of residence (28-9).

"Regular Americans": 1930s–1960s

If the Mahjar writers were conscious of their dual identities and attempted to create work that bridged their lives and experiences, their descendants in the mid-to-late 1900s were instead "costumed . . . as 'regular Americans,' and hoped to pass" (Shakir 67). Majaj classifies the literature of this period as quiet in comparison to the flourishing of literary production in the Mahjar and states that it "reflects a hesitancy to engage with Arab-American identity as something of contemporary relevance" ("Arab-American Literature" 2). Vance Bourjaily, William Peter Blatty, and Eugene Paul Nassar, the major Arab American writers of this time, were in turn indifferent, embarrassed and overwhelmed, and highly sentimental about their ethnic backgrounds (Ludescher 102). Two other writers worked during this period, Salom Rizk and George Hamid, but Shakir, Ludescher, and Hassan delineate their work as more thematically aligned with the Mahjar and the late period. In either case, however, this relatively sparse period of Arab American literature corresponds with slower immigration patterns to the United States.

The Multicultural Boom: 1970s–early 2000s

It is difficult to locate a unifying theme or concept that can adequately capture the heterogeneity of work and ideologies represented in contemporary Arab American literature, especially if one dates the category as early as the late 1960s. Instead, I suggest a useful periodization might consider the 1970s–the early 2000s as one moment of Arab American literary production that focuses on canon building. Several critical texts engage how Arab American literature changed in the latter half of the twentieth century. The engagements of the United States with the Middle East (e.g., oil embargo and Gulf War) as well as the progression of the women's, civil rights, and lesbian and gay liberation movements in the US created a political climate wherein minority communities were vocal and active in their critiques of their nation of residence (Majaj, "Arab-American Literature" 2-3; Fadda 21-2). This climate also facilitated the rise of ethnic literature canons in the US, wherein narration of one's history and experiences were one mode of consciousness-raising and resistance to discrimination. Specifically, the 1980s and 90s witnessed a flourishing of the Arab American literary scene in the form of numerous collections. Anthologies like *Grape Leaves: A Century of Arab-American Poetry* (1988), *Food for Our Grandmothers: Writings by Arab-American and Arab-Canadian Feminists* (1994), *Post-Gibran: Anthology of New Arab American Writing* (1999), attempted to situate Arabs alongside other minority groups in the United States as one means of inclusion in American citizenship (Hartman 172-3; Shomali 4). Rather than wax nostalgic about home, or attempt to be read as or assimilate into whiteness, Arab American writers, like other minority ethnics, became legible through the marketing of themselves as hyphenated Americans.

Critical Reconfigurations: After 9/11

Though Arab American writers had been critical of their relationship to the United States and their countries of origin well before the events of September 11, 2001, the climate and response to Arabs in the United States became explicitly hostile in its wake. Though Arabs had been long subject to Orientalism and anti-Arab racism, the virulent Islamophobia that flourished during this time period has had a broad and sustained impact on Arab American lives and their creative output (Naber, "Introduction" 39-40). Scholars refer to this period as one of heightened visibility and simultaneous invisibility—wherein Arab and Muslim life in the United States is highly scrutinized and, at the same time, seemingly invisible (Cainkar, "The Arab American Experience" 9; Jarmakani, "Arab American Feminisms" 234; Naber, "Ambiguous Insiders" 55). It is invisible because stereotypes and tropes cloud representations of Arab Americans and often obscure the narrative Arab American writers and artists attempt to circulate. It is within this moment of always-already politicization that contemporary writers must navigate the production and circulation of their work. Here I would like to turn to Helal's work to capture some of the dominant preoccupations and themes in Arab American literature today.

In the front matter of *I am Made to Leave I am Made to Return*, Helal identifies some of the central conceits of contemporary Arab American literature: translation, memory, ancestry, and movement. The front matter consists of an Egyptian proverb translated into English and a quote from contemporary Arab American poet Fady Joudah about translation and memory. The reference to Egyptian colloquialism and Arab American literature, both Anglophone and in translation via Joudah's quote, outlines the three literary genealogies that shape Helal's work: Egyptian, American, and Arab American. Another moment of this hailing occurs later in the collection with the piece ")[[;".'.,:]](REMIXED," which simultaneously references Arab American poet Philip Metres's *abu ghraib arias* in *Sand Opera* (2015) and African American rapper Kanye West's track "Runaway" off *My Beautiful Dark Twisted Fantasy* (2010). The poem combines references to contemporary American politics and its transnational interventions with a staccato delivery that resonates not only with West's music, but call-and-response rhythms that populate Arab oral histories.

Through the sleight of hand of presenting an Egyptian quote in translation and then commenting immediately after on the process of translation, Helal signifies to her reader that language and its manipulation will be the dominant mode of interaction between these three legacies. Later in the collection, Helal coins a new poetic form called the Arabic—a poem written in English and read from right to left, as in the Arabic language. The form further calls for an Arabic letter, numeral, and footnote to appear without translation. The poem was originally published in *Winter Tangerine*, and included the author's comment:

> The Arabic . . . vehemently rejects you if you try to read it left to right. To vehemently reject, in this case, means to transfer the feeling of every time the poet has heard an English as Only Language speaker patronizingly utter in some variation the following phrase: "Oh, [so-and-so] is English as a Second Language. . . ." As if it was a kind of weakness, nah" (Helal, "poem to be read from right to left").

Both the poem and the comment articulate a politics of refusal—the refusal to appear in a singular capacity or language, the refusal to capitulate to English as the only or most significant language an Arab immigrant would speak, and the refusal to accept anti-immigrant or racist depictions of the poet as less than the hypothetical speaker. Helal's sustained code switching throughout the collection underscores that her duality, or even unquantifiability, while potentially a kind of displacement, is simultaneously a strength in her interaction with the world. In the writer's words from "generation of feeling," "[she] is trying to tell you something about how/rearranging words/rearranges the universe" (*I am Made* 7-9).

The dedication, "for absence, for presence" emphasizes the ephemeral nature of memory from Joudah's passage: "Memory is . . . translation's muse and taxonomy. Memory is sometimes unconscious cognition, other times absence." How memory works in tandem with language, legacy, and movement is another central preoccupation of the work that speaks to Arab American literature writ large. In the prose poem "involuntary memory" the speaker narrates the experience of driving through a tunnel on a US street and imagining it exits into Cairo. The reference—a memory activated by the fluorescent lighting—comes unbidden but certain. The disorientation of the speaker and the poem's stream-of-consciousness narration muddle the geography of here or there. The final line "im almost home," suggests that the reader, and perhaps the speaker, is uncertain (Helal, "involuntary" 34). Where, finally, is home? In the short "returning note no. 6" Helal writes, "when you know youre walking into a memory before youve made it" (1). The play on location and dislocation renders memory the most stable home in the collection, but memory itself is unreliably presented. I would suggest these doubled ambiguities reflect a kind of response to the nostalgia of previous immigrant generations (Ludescher 107) and at the same time reject the impetus to supplant one location with the next.

The dedication thus also alludes to the work the collection will do around movement: across language, across space, and across time. Within the collection are poems titled as numbered leaving notes and returning notes—but the collection does not include a sequential or complete set. The notes are brief, numbered missives from the speaker, which could be about the processes of leaving and returning or are notes left when one leaves or returns. These fragmentary, short notes echo the first poem in the collection "made" which repeats the chapbook's title as the first two lines: "i am made to leave, i am made to return" (Helal, *I am Made* 1-2). The collection does not speak to arrival or departure so much as the constant shuffle of leaving and returning, going and coming. In the endnotes, Helal credits the title of the collection to graffiti artist ESPO, who painted a mural titled "Love Letter to Brooklyn" on the side of Macy's parking garage. The complete work includes references to the NYC train system. The mural's location on a garage and reference to travel emphasizes Helal's transitory focus. But perhaps most tellingly, the complete two lines of ESPO's original piece are "I AM MADE TO LEAVE/I AM MADE TO RETURN HOME." Helal absents home from the arc of her travels; she deemphasizes a stable or clear location in favor of the time and space between.

In "poem for palm pressed upon pane" the speaker is once again in a car and later a bus. These transitory spaces bookend the poem, while the palm of the title turns out to be a plant 5,000 miles away, stretching toward a window, toward light. As in "involuntary memory," the speaker eludes a singular location; mansurah, cairo, delta, desert, heliopolis, ohio, new mexico, and masr all make appearances in the fifteen lines of the piece, leaving the reader to wonder where the speaker is in the car; where the bus is taking a character named hatem; which living room a mother stares from; and, finally, where the palm tree lives. The poem "if this was a different kind of story id tell you about the sea" repeats the title forty-three times on forty-three separate lines, each time using italics to emphasize some, all, or none of the words. At first glance, the reader might attempt to decode the italicization pattern, but no discernable pattern emerges. Sometimes the italicization begins or ends mid-word; the line appears entirely italicized five times, and not italicized at all twenty-one times. The poem functions as the first line to a story that is never told: we are in a different story, and in it, we will not hear about the sea. But the story that is not about the sea never gets started; we, instead, repeatedly hear about what we will not hear about. The uneven italics cause the lines to dance on the page like waves or water. The sea and its story are told by reference to their absence. Movement here is figured through the page and against, while the reader navigates the sea of the story untold in the writer's refusal to tell it. A few poems later, in "leaving note no. 3" Helal writes "i ocean you" (1). Bodies of water materialize as spaces of action and movement, which occur frequently in immigrant literatures; Helal goes further by dwelling on the water and making its meaning ambiguous—what is the story of the sea? What does it mean to "ocean" another? It ceases to be the passage, or a means from one location to the next, but becomes the focus and meaning itself.

Conclusion

Perhaps the attention to ephemerality and constant movement characterizes contemporary Arab American literature most accurately. While early immigrant writers imagined their work bridging divides, and others attempted to move toward whiteness and away from Arab identity or again back toward Arabness and away from whiteness, the constant evocation of Arab American

---

writing is its dedication to travel—the suspension between locales as location, the articulation of change over difference itself, and an anticipatory echo of clocks ticking in every time zone. Movement, with its emphasis on process—the act after leaving and before arrival—supplants immigration in the Arab American imaginary.

Note

1. I use Arab American rather than Arab-American or other versions. This is consistent with nomenclature for other ethnic minorities in the US as well as both the current preference in Arab American studies and the Chicago Manual of Style.

Works Cited

Arab American National Museum. "Arab American Immigration." *Reclaiming Identity: Dismantling Arab Stereotypes*, April 2011, www.arabamericanmuseum.org/Coming-to-America.id.18.htm/. Accessed 30 Nov. 2017.

Cainkar, Louse. "The Arab American Experience: From Invisibility to Heightened Visibility." *The Routledge Handbook of Asian American Studies*, edited by Cindy I-Fen Cheng, Taylor and Francis, 2016, pp. 1-19.

Fadda-Conrey, Carol. *Contemporary Arab American Literature: Transnational Reconfigurations of Citizenship and Belonging*. New York UP, 2014.

Gualtieri, Sarah. *Between Arab and White: Race and Ethnicity in the Early Syrian American Diaspora*. U of California P, 2009.

Hassan, Wail. *Immigrant Narratives: Orientalism and Cultural Translation in Arab American and Arab British Literature*. Oxford UP, 2011.

Hartman, Michelle. "Grandmothers, Grape Leaves, and Khalil Gibran: Writing Race in Anthologies of Arab American Literature." *Race and Arab Americans Before and After 9/11: From Invisible Citizens to Visible Subjects*, edited by Amaney Jamal and Nadine Naber, Syracuse UP, 2008, pp. 170-203.

Helal, Marwa. ")[[;".'.,:]](REMIXED."*I am Made to Leave I am Made to Return*. No Dear and Small Anchor Press, 2017.

_____. "generation of feeling." *I am Made to Leave I am Made to Return*. No Dear and Small Anchor Press, 2017.

_____. *I am Made to Leave I am Made to Return*. No Dear and Small Anchor Press, 2017.

_____. "if this was a different kind of story id tell you about the sea." *I am Made to Leave I am Made to Return*. No Dear and Small Anchor Press, 2017.

_____. "involuntary memory." *I am Made to Leave I am Made to Return*. No Dear and Small Anchor Press, 2017.

_____. "leaving note no. 3." *I am Made to Leave I am Made to Return*. No Dear and Small Anchor Press, 2017.

_____. "leaving note no. 6." *I am Made to Leave I am Made to Return*. No Dear and Small Anchor Press, 2017.

_____. "Made." *I am Made to Leave I am Made to Return*. No Dear and Small Anchor Press, 2017.

_____. "poem for palm pressed upon pane." *I am Made to Leave I am Made to Return*. No Dear and Small Anchor Press, 2017.

_____. "poem to be read from/ right/ to left." *I am Made to Leave I am Made to Return*. No Dear and Small Anchor Press, 2017.

_____. "poem to be read from right to left." *Winter Tangerine*, n.d., www.wintertangerine.com/helal-poem-to-be-read/. Accessed 30 Nov. 2017.

Jarmakani, Amira. "Arab American Feminisms: Mobilizing the Politics of Invisibility." *Arab and Arab American Feminisms: Gender, Violence, and Belonging*, edited by Rabab Abdulhadi, Evelyn Alsultany, and Nadine Naber. Syracuse UP, 2011, pp. 227-241.

Ludescher, Tanyss. "From Nostalgia to Critique: An Overview of Arab American Literature." *MELUS*, vol. 31, no. 4, Winter 2006, pp. 93-114.

Majaj, Lisa Suheir. "Arab-American Literature: Origins and Developments." *American Studies Journal*, vol. 52, no.2, 2008, pp.1-14.

_____. "Two Worlds Emerging: Arab-American Writing at the Crossroads." *Forkroads*, Spring 1996, pp. 64-80.

Naber, Nadine. "Ambiguous Insiders: An Investigation of Arab American Invisibility." *Ethnic and Racial Studies*, vol. 23, no.1, 2000, pp. 37-61.

_____. "Introduction: Arab Americans and U.S. Racial Formations." *Race and Arab Americans Before and After 9/11: From Invisible Citizens to Visible Subjects*, edited by Amaney Jamal and Nadine Naber, Syracuse UP, 2008, pp.1-45.

Redden, Elizabeth. "International Enrollments: From Flat to Way Down." *Inside Higher Ed.*, 5 Sept. 2017, www.insidehighered. com/news/2017/09/05/some-universities-are-reporting-declines-international-enrollments-ranging-modest/. Accessed 30 Nov. 2017.

Salaita, Steven. *Modern Arab American Fiction: A Reader's Guide.* Syracuse UP, 2011.

Saliba, Therese. "Resisting Invisibility: Arab Americans in Academia and Activism." *Arabs in America: Building a New Future*, edited by Michael Suleiman, Syracuse UP, 1999, pp. 304-319.

Shakir, Evelyn. "Coming of Age: Arab American Literature." *Ethnic Forum*, vol. 13-14, 1993–1994, pp. 63-80.

Shomali, Mejdulene. "Scheherazade and the Limits of Inclusive Politics in Arab American Literature." *MELUS*, spring 2017.

Suleiman, Michal. "Introduction: The Arab Immigrant Experience." *Arabs in America: Building a New Future*, edited by Michael Suleiman, Temple UP, 1999, pp. 1-21.

West, Kanye. "Runaway." *My Beautiful Dark Twisted Fantasy.* Roc-A-Fella Records, 2010.

"Create Dangerously":[1] Immigration as Radical Hope in Edwidge Danticat's Fiction and Creative Nonfiction

Marion Christina Rohrleitner

> All immigrants are artists, because they create a life, a future, from nothing but a dream.
>
> (Patricia Engel)

In a 2013 interview with *The Atlantic*, the award-winning Haitian American writer Edwidge Danticat describes her strong reaction to reading the passage from *It's Not Love, It's Paris*, cited in the epigraph above:

> And this is a fascinating notion: that re-creating yourself this way, re-creating your entire life is a form of reinvention on par with the greatest works of literature. This brings art into the realm of what ordinary people do in order to survive. . . . I've never seen anyone connect being an artist and an immigrant so explicitly, and for me it was a revelation. (Fassler and Danticat)

In her own fiction and creative nonfiction, Danticat, too, has dedicated ample space to the connection between the experience of immigration as an artistic act and between emigration and the creation and consumption of art. Art allows immigrants to creatively express individual survival and resilience and helps to establish and maintain cultural continuity and community in the diaspora. In this essay, I focus on the complex engagements with immigration as art in fiction and creative nonfiction by Edwidge Danticat to demonstrate the critical importance of radical hope—a utopian, creative imagination—to the immigrant experience in the twentieth and twenty-first centuries.

According to Danticat, the process of immigration "requires everything great art requires—risk-tasking, hope, a great deal of imagination, all the qualities that are the building blocks of art. You must be able to dream something nearly impossible and toil to bring it into existence" (Fassler and Danticat). Danticat's emphasis on the intimate connection between immigration and a creative imagination that allows us to think the beyond is in tandem with Ernst Bloch's famous definition of hope as an "expectation . . . [and] intention towards possibility that has still not become" (7). This emphasis on a utopian impulse, of imagining beyond what is immediately possible, as a powerful force rather than a tool of deception seems, at first sight, to stand in contrast to what Lauren Berlant has called "cruel optimism" (3)—a hegemonic belief that serves to entrench the status quo rather than challenge it. Drawing on James Baldwin's critique of an alleged national "innocence" (3), Ta-Nehisi Coates similarly develops a harsh indictment of what he calls "The Dream" (50) as one of the main reasons for the ongoing second-class status of African Americans and other minorities in the United States. While I agree with Berlant's and Coates' incisive critiques of the media-produced and reproduced reifications of a forever-unattainable American Dream that denies the existence of a complex system of socio-economic and legal injustices underlying US-American race relations, I find Danticat's simultaneous emphasis on the power of a utopian vision inspiring in its embrace of "radical hope."

Radical hope, a term popularized by philosopher Jonathan Lear, is far removed from uncritical naiveté or blind hope; instead, it "anticipates a good for which those who have the hope as yet lack the appropriate concepts with which to understand it" (103). It is utopian and futuristic, but never escapist because it is grounded in practice and political action.

In US-American fiction, immigrant narratives are often used as vehicles to represent the promises and pitfalls of the American Dream. In her 1923 autobiographical essay "America and I," Anzia Yezierska, for example, celebrates the freedom of mobility and access to higher education the United States offers her, a Yiddish-speaking immigrant and victim of both Russian pogroms and a strictly patriarchal society that severely limits her life choices. At the same time, Yezierska is keenly aware of racialized and gendered power hierarchies and of the greed that dominates American society, including immigrant communities.

What allows Yezierska to make it in her new home is her ability to imagine the as-of-yet impossible, and the vehicle that allows her to do so is her creative use and mastery of the English language. Writing and telling the many stories of immigration are major manifestations of radical hope in Edwidge Danticat's work as well.

Edwidge Danticat arrived in New York City in 1981, at the age of twelve, to join her parents who had left Haiti for economic reasons and to escape the dictatorial regimes of François and Jean-Claude Duvalier in the early 1970s. Bilingual in Haitian Kreyol and French, a beginning student of English, and a hardworking and dedicated writer, Danticat thrived in the bilingual school she attended in Brooklyn. Only two years after her arrival in New York, she published a story on her experiences as a Haitian immigrant in *New Youth Connections*. At sixteen, Danticat published "A New World Full of Strangers," which became the foundation of her 1994 debut novel *Breath, Eyes, Memory*. She won a scholarship to Barnard College, where she graduated in 1990 with a BA in French; three years later Danticat graduated with an MFA in Creative Writing from Brown University, and the accolades have not ceased since. To date, Danticat has published four novels, a collection of short stories, three works of nonfiction, four young adult novels, served as an editor on five volumes of fiction and nonfiction, and collaborated on two screenplays. She has won an American Book Award; a National Book Critics Circle Award; and, most recently, a Neustadt International Prize for Literature. She was a finalist for two National Book Awards and has honorary degrees from Smith College and Yale University. In 2009, Danticat was awarded a MacArthur fellowship. In many ways, Danticat embodies the upwardly mobile immigrant, who, through enormous talent and hard work, "makes it" in her newly-chosen home. And yet, Danticat, in her fiction and nonfiction, never loses sight of the plight most immigrants face in their daily lives and never forgets that immigration is always, also, a story of loss and of leaving behind.

In *Breath, Eyes, Memory*, Danticat merges the personal challenges she faced as a young Haitian girl immigrating to the United States with a larger comment on the tensions between tradition and modernity in an immigrant's life and the gains and losses immigration to the United States brings to Haitian women and girls in the diaspora and on the island in the 1970s and 1980s. Sophie Caco, the novel's main protagonist, is raised by her Tante Atie in rural Haiti before joining her mother Martine in New York City at the age of twelve. Martine is the survivor of rape committed by marauding *tontons macoutes* who terrorized Haitian civilians with impunity during the Duvalier regime, and Sophie is the product of this sexual violence. Martine is ever concerned with Sophie's virginity and her academic success to ensure a "good marriage" for her daughter. Deeply steeped in traditional Haitian gender roles and traumatized by the sexual violence she endured, Martine is unable to be open to her daughter's artistic inclinations. Sophie longs to leave this restrictive environment and falls in love with her older, African American neighbor Joseph, a jazz musician whose sensuality stands in stark contrast to her strict upbringing, which is hostile to all physical and artistic pleasures.

The inspirational role of music is central to Sophie's decision to stand up against her mother's ossified beliefs and to resist the invasive virginity "testing" she is submitted to every month. Music allows her to both face her family's tragedies, to confront her own desires and goals, and to link her Haitian cultural heritage with that of African diasporic communities in the United States. It is hardly a coincidence that Joseph is from New Orleans, that US-American city most intimately connected to the Caribbean, and Haiti in particular. During their first conversation, Joseph comments, "We have something in common. *Mwin aussi.* I speak a form of Creole, too" (Danticat, *Breath* 70). Joseph's playing allows Sophie to escape the narrow confines of her life as laid out by her mother: "I spent the whole week with my ear pressed against the wall, listening to him rehearse. . . . Sometimes at night, the saxophone was like a soothing lullaby" (71). Joseph's soothing music calms Sophie and invites her to dream of a different future.

Joseph also encourages Sophie to think about and act on her own desires, rather than succumb to and comply with her mother's wishes. When Sophie, citing her mother, comments that "there's a difference between what a person wants and what's good for them," Joseph suggests, "It is ok not to have your future on a map. . . . That way you can flow wherever life takes you" (Danticat, *Breath* 72). Joseph's approach to life mirrors his approach to music. Inspired by his music and their conversations, Sophie begins to imagine a life beyond the limitations laid out for her and makes a decision that will impact her life and her relationship with her mother for good—she destroys her own hymen with a pestle to prevent her mother from ever testing her again. Crucially, Sophie precedes this violent act of self-harming with a story about a woman who suffers from excessive bleeding and thus no longer wants to be a woman. Instead, she asks the Vodun loa, or Goddess, Erzulie to transform her into a butterfly, a wish that is granted. Sophie links her own transformation to that of the woman in the folktale; she changes who she is, which allows her freedom of choice and mobility. To Sophie, storytelling is the art form she comes to embrace the most and which allows her to face the most difficult challenges in her life. Like the woman in the Haitian folktale, she rejects the suffering that comes with her culture's obsession with female sexual purity and thus transforms herself into a virgin whose virginity can no longer be tested. At the end of the novel, Sophie proudly asserts, "I come from a place where breath, eyes and memory are one, a place where you carry your past like the hair on your head. Where women return to their children as butterflies or as tears in the eyes of the statues that their daughters pray to" (Danticat, *Breath* 234). Sophie embraces storytelling, physical transformation, and psychological change as necessary stepping stones towards a self-actualized life. Immigration affects her cultural identity as a Haitian woman.

In *Create Dangerously: The Immigrant Artist at Work*, Danticat asserts, "the nomad or immigrant who learns something rightly must always ponder travel and movement" (16). This emphasis on the importance of movement and change embodies Stuart Hall's definition of cultural identity in the diaspora, when he argues,

We cannot speak for very long with any exactness about one's experience, one's identity without acknowledging its other sides—the ruptures and discontinuities, which constitute, precisely, the Caribbean's uniqueness. Cultural identity . . . is a matter of becoming as well as being. It belongs to a future as well as to a past. . . . Cultural identities come from somewhere, have histories. But, like everything which is historical, they undergo constant transformation. (225)

Rather than reiterating a simplistic and one-directional immigrant myth of reinvention, Sophie chooses to be ever conscious of her country's and her own painful past when negotiating her becoming sense of self.

Sophie's concluding comments in *Breath, Eyes, Memory* set the stage for Danticat's 1995 collection of short stories, *Krik? Krak!*, in which the protagonists are forever leaving Haiti, arriving in the Dominican Republic and in the United States, or are suspended in the multiple phases in between leaving one's country of origin and truly becoming part of a new one. Danticat's display of radical hope in her short fiction is seen in the resilience of characters who venture to imagine the impossible, even and especially in the face of utter violence and extinction. "Children of the Sea," the short story that opens the collection, features two star-crossed lovers in a setting that denies them any humanity. Set during the anarchic chaos in the aftermath of the first coup d'état against President Jean-Bertrand Aristide in September 1991, the story unfolds in a series of letters written and never sent, or merely imagined, by a young woman and a young man separated by political strife; the young woman is locked up in her parents' home for fear of rape and murder by the *tontons macoutes*, while her lover is on a boat in the Mona Strait, desperately hoping to make it to Puerto Rico or Florida. What sustains the loving couple is a suspension of disbelief and the power of their imagination. Danticat gives these two young people the voices they never had; it becomes abundantly clear that the young man, along with his fellow refugees, will drown, and the young woman's fate is equally hopeless. And yet, their words sustain them and the readers, and force us to acknowledge the humanity, resilience, and artistry of the victims of military dictatorship who are silenced not only by their torturers, but also by an indifferent global community. As Robert Houston asserts in his review of the collection in the *New York Times Book Review*, "The best of these stories humanize, particularize, [and] give poignancy to the lives of people we may have come to think of as faceless emblems of misery, poverty, and brutality." The imagining beyond the possible, here, is not an act of vain hope, but rather of radical hope in the face of extinction. As Junot Díaz, Edwidge Danticat's close friend and frequent collaborator, puts it, "radical hope is not so much something you have but something you practice; it demands flexibility, openness, and what Lear describes as 'imaginative excellence'"(Díaz, 'Under').

This imaginative excellence is displayed in the letters the lovers compose for each other in the face of impending death. After relaying a particularly gruesome episode of the devious ways in which the *tontons macoutes* taunt a mother whose son they just beheaded, the young woman reassures her absent lover and herself by stating, "yes, i will. i will keep writing like we promised to do. i hate it, but i will keep writing. you keep writing, too, okay? and when we see each other again, it will seem like we lost no time" (Danticat, *Krik?* 8). The young woman's letters are offset via bold font and her idiosyncratic spelling and punctuation choices, which defy regular grammar, highlight her turn to creative expression.

The young man, in turn, shares the tragedies unfolding aboard the refugee barge, where suicide and death from exposure are a daily occurrence. And still, the survivors prevail by resorting to music and storytelling:

> We spent most of yesterday telling stories. Someone says, Krik? You answer Krak! And then they say, I have many stories I could tell you, and then they go on and tell these stories to you, but mostly to themselves. Sometimes it feels like we have been at sea longer than the many years I have been on this earth. . . . I feel like we are sailing for Africa. Maybe we will go to Guinin, to live with the spirits, to be with everyone who has come and has died before us. (Danticat, *Krik?* 14)

In this passage, the young man connects his fate as a Haitian refugee in the 1990s to the plight of his ancestors on the Middle Passage. And yet, true to radical hope, he conveys the idea of a return to the motherland, offering a contemporary commentary on the African American folktale of "The Flying Africans" who, rather than submitting to slavery, chose to fly back to Africa.

In her historical novel *The Farming of Bones* (1999) Danticat further heartbreakingly illustrates this imaginative excellence by lyrically writing about the ultimate price many immigrants have paid in the face of rampant xenophobia and racist nationalist rage. In this collection, Danticat highlights that immigration, in a Haitian context, is steeped in a longstanding tradition of transnational movements not only from the Haiti to North America, but also within the Caribbean.

The majority of Haitian immigrants came to the Dominican Republic in one of three waves. The first wave occurred in the second decade of the twentieth century, when the Dominican Republic promised work and a steady income in the cane fields to Haitian guest workers. In 1912, just four years prior to the eight-year long occupation of the Dominican Republic by the United States, the mostly US-owned sugarcane companies in the Dominican Republic were in need of cheap labor and invited Haitian guest workers to move across the border. The second wave of emigrants left Haiti after François "Papa Doc" Duvalier came to power in 1957 and began a regime of terror. The third wave of immigrants arrived in the Dominican Republic in the aftermath of the devastating earthquake that shook Haiti on January 12, 2010, claimed between 160,000 and 200,000 lives, and destroyed the country's infrastructure. In the face of such political and natural catastrophes, hope is a difficult thing to muster; and yet, Danticat's protagonists, like her real-life models, display radical hope in their decision to leave their country of origin and imagine a different, better life beyond the familiar.

Set shortly before, during, and in the aftermath of El Corte, the notorious massacre of some 20,000 Haitian migrant workers in the Dominican Republic in October 1937, the narrative focuses on Amabelle Desir, a migrant who left Haiti for the Dominican Republic in search of economic betterment. Amabelle works as a maid in the household of Valencia and Pico Duarte, wealthy Dominicans who own the sugarcane plantations where the majority of laborers are migrants from nearby Haiti. Similar to Martine in *Breath, Eyes, Memory*, the novel's main female protagonist is a survivor who persevered in the state-sponsored massacre against Haitian migrant workers on the Dominican-Haitian border and witnessed the brutal murder of her lover Sebastién and many close friends at the hands of Trujillo's henchmen. Deeply scarred in body and mind, Amabelle dedicates her life to commemorating the dead. She is both nourished and consumed by her memories of the massacre and suffers from survivor's guilt; yet, her commitment to go on living as a memorial to the victims of the massacre demonstrates her ability to imagine life beyond the horrors of the past. Her very survival is an act of radical hope, and her lyrically-phrased memories are a testimony to the lives lost. Early on in the novel, Amabelle recalls intimate moments with Sebastién:

> I can still feel his presence there, in the small square of my room. I can smell his sweat, which is as thick as sugarcane juice when he's worked too much. I can still feel his lips, the eggplant-violet gums that taste of greasy goat milk boiled to candied sweetness with mustard-colored potatoes. I feel my cheeks rising to his dense-as-toenails fingernails, the hollow beneath my cheek-bones, where the bracelet nicked me and left a perfectly crescent-moon-shaped drop of dried blood. I feel the wet lines in my back where his tongue gently traced the life-giving veins to the chine, the faint handprints on my waist where he held on too tight, perhaps during some moment when he felt me slipping. And I can still count his breaths and how sometimes they raced much faster than the beating of his heart. (Danticat, *Farming* 3)

In this moving passage, Amabelle's visceral memories of Sebastién evoke Audre Lorde's emphasis on the 'erotic as power' (88). In Lorde's definition, the erotic goes beyond the sensual and sexual, as she associates the erotic with the very power of creation: 'When I speak of the erotic, then, I speak of it as an assertion of the lifeforce of women; of that creative energy empowered, the knowledge and use of which we are now reclaiming in our language, our history, our dancing, our loving, our work, our lives" (89). Sebastién, and her memories of their strong physical and emotional bond, sustain Amabelle in her life after the massacre.

Even in her utmost despair, Amabelle manages to muster one ray of hope in her own lyrical language: "Two mountains can never meet but perhaps you and I can meet again. I am coming to your waterfall" (Danticat, *Farming* 283). The aptly named Massacre River, which both connects and divides Haiti and the Dominican Republic, was the site of a 1728 massacre between warring French buccaneers and Spanish colonial forces, of the death of Amabelle's parents by drowning in the aftermath of a devastating hurricane in the 1920s, and of the notorious El Corte. At the end of the novel, Amabelle returns to the place of her parents' and her lover's and friends' demise and, merging with the life-giving force of the water and her ability to dream, is reborn:

> The water was warm for October, warm ad shallow, so shallow that I could lie on my back in it with my shoulders only half-submerged...I looked to my dreams for softness, for a gentler embrace, for relief from fear of mudslides and blood bubbling out of the riverbed, where it is said the dead add their tears to the river flow. (Danticat, *Farming* 310)

She then joins the professor, an acquaintance from her past in the Dominican Republic, in "looking for the dawn" (Danticat, *Farming* 310), a clear indication of radical hope for a new day and a less violent future.

In *The Dew Breaker*, Danticat's novel about a Haitian immigrant father who was a member of the notorious *tontons macoutes* and a torturer in Duvalier's regime, the dew breaker's daughter is a sculptor whose work is inspired by her relationship to her immigrant father. In *Create Dangerously* Danticat claims, "all artists, writers among them, have several stories—one might call them creation myths—that haunt and obsess them" (5). The story that obsesses the second-generation-immigrant sculptor in *The Dew Breaker* is her father's enigmatic past in Haiti. Ka, the main narrator of the novel, travels to the home of the Haitian-born television celebrity Gabrielle Fonteneau in Miami to deliver a sculpture, and comments: "I'm really not an artist, not in the way I'd like to be. I'm more of an obsessive wood carver with a single subject thus far—my father" (Danticat, *Dew* 4). Artistic expression is the only way Ka knows how to engage with her father's silence surrounding his and her mother's lives in Haiti before their emigration to the United States. When she reflects on her artistic choices before starting work on her sculpture, Ka's thwarted relationship with her father emerges in the raw material she chooses:

> I'd used a piece of mahogany that was naturally flawed, with a few superficial cracks along what was now the back. I'd thought these cracks beautiful and had made no effort to sand or polish them away, as they seemed like the wood's own scars, like the one my father had on his face. (Danticat, *Dew* 7)

The cracks in the wood come to embody the cracks in the story of her father, who, Ka learns in the opening chapter, was "the hunter, . . . not the prey" (Danticat, *Dew* 20). The dew breaker subsequently submerges the sculpture in a bayou because, as he says, he does not "deserve a statue" (Danticat, *Dew* 19).

In the last chapter of the novel, the infamous dew breaker himself takes on the narrative voice and testifies to his crimes as a torturer in Duvalier's regime. The utopian impulse in *The Dew Breaker* looms large over the novel's central question of forgiveness and transformation—can a member of the *tontons macoutes*, a torturer and murderer, ever be forgiven by those he hurt and be redeemed by a new life in the diaspora, or must his life forever be spent in atonement for his crimes? The final chapter does not absolve the father from his crimes, which, in true fascist form, he describes as diligent performances of duty; instead, a possibility for renewal and reconciliation opens up in the birth of Ka, the artist, "their good angel" (Danticat, *Dew* 241). The scarred wood is, to Ka, an ideal material to represent the scars her father left on the bodies of his victims, and the scars the Duvalier regime left on the Haitian people at large. Rather than rejecting and condemning the flawed piece of wood, Ka comes to embrace it as a representation of Haiti's painful and violent history, and of the thwarted relationship between the country of origin of her parents and the nation Ka calls home.

After Danticat moved far away from the autobiographical mode in *The Dew Breaker*, she began to turn to creative nonfiction in her next two works. In 2008, Danticat won both a National Book Critics Circle Award and the Dayton Literary Peace Prize for nonfiction for her memoir *Brother, I'm Dying*, her most personal work to date. The Dayton Literary Peace Prize is an award that acknowledges "the power of literature to promote peace and non-violent conflict resolution" ("Mission"). Danticat dedicates this work of creative nonfiction to "the next generation of 'cats,'" hinting at the way US-immigration has misread and changed her family's last name from the Kreyol Dantica to the Anglicized Danticat, one of many acts of violence her immigrant family endured in the United States. Edwidge Danticat's beloved Uncle Joseph, her father's brother, who helped raise Edwidge after both of her parents had left Haiti for the United States by 1973, died a detainee of the United States Customs and Border Protection Agency at the Krome Service Processing Center outside of Miami because he was cruelly denied the medical treatment he desperately needed.

In painstaking detail, Danticat reconstructs her uncle's slow and painful death at the hands of a bureaucratic and inhumane immigration institution. Instead of assisting the immigrants and asylum seekers in their care, the INS systematically failed to ensure Joseph Danticat's survival and safe entry into the United States. Danticat juxtaposes this utterly bleak scenario of death by bureaucracy with the resilience of her family in Haiti.

After meticulously piecing together the series of careless, xenophobic, and outright racist decisions that led to her uncle's death in custody, Danticat concludes:

> Still, I suspect that my uncle was treated according to a biased immigration policy dating back from the early 1980s when Haitians began arriving in Florida in large numbers by boat. In Florida, where Cuban refugees are, as long as they're able to step foot on dry

land, immediately processed and released to their families, Haitian asylum seekers are disproportionately detained, then deported. While Hondurans and Nicaraguans have continued to receive protected status for nearly ten years since Hurricane Mitch struck their homelands, Haitians were deported to the flood zones weeks after Tropical Storm Jeanne blanketed an entire city in water the way Hurricane Katrina did parts of New Orleans. Was my uncle going to jail because he was Haitian? (*Brother* 222)

In this memoir, Danticat highlights the radically different treatment immigrants and refugees from Haiti and the Dominican Republic received in the US in contrast to Cuban immigrants. The "dry foot wet foot policy," which automatically granted residency to all Cuban refugees and emigrants who reach US American soil and which had been instituted under the Clinton administration in 1995, was kept in place until January 12, 2017. Haitian refugees and immigrants, on the other hand, have historically been treated abysmally by the American immigration system. In the wake of the devastating earthquake in January 2010, tens of thousands of Haitian immigrants were given Temporary Protective Status; however, Elaine Duke, Acting Secretary of Homeland Security in the Trump administration, has since "determined that those extraordinary but temporary conditions caused by the 2010 earthquake no longer exist," and ended the protective status for Haitians with a deadline of July 2019 on November 20, 2017 (Tatum).

The impact of Danticat's memoir as a critique of existing immigration policy in the United States thus gains further momentum after the devastating earthquake that hit Haiti on January 12, 2010. In addition to the earthquake, Haiti's thwarted relationship with the Dominican Republic reached a new low point on September 23, 2013, when the Dominican Supreme Court issued ruling TC 0168/13, which effectively rendered an estimated 250,000 Dominicans of Haitian descent who were born to undocumented migrants between 1929 and 2007 stateless; the ruling decreed that Dominicans of Haitian descent will no longer be eligible for citizenship unless they could prove that their parents had been legal residents of the Dominican Republic at the time of their birth. This effectively equals a retroactive withdrawal of access to Dominican citizenship for those born between 1929 and 2007. Because the majority of immigrants who left Haiti for the Dominican Republic were illiterate and poor, and as a result of political instability and corruption in both Haiti and the Dominican Republic, they had never been issued a birth certificate in Haiti, nor had they been able to register themselves or their Dominican-born children in the Dominican Republic. The ruling created outrage in the Dominican Republic, in Haiti, and in the diasporic communities in the United States. The case was also brought before the Inter-American Court, which concluded, on October 22, 2014, that "the criteria used by the Dominican Supreme Court are discriminatory and contrary to the principle of equality before the law, since it ignores the characteristics of the person born in the DR and focuses on the lack of documentation of their parents, without justifying this distinction" (Quintana). The last day to prove that at least one parent was a Dominican citizen at the time of birth was June 17, 2015. A mere 300 people were able to get their papers in by that time. The perfidy of ruling TC 0168/13 is not only in its rather obvious racist targeting of the Haitian Dominican community, but how this overt racism is veiled in a disinterested legal language that will, in effect, be difficult to challenge in an international court.

In an editorial in *The Los Angeles Times* of November 10, 2013, Dominican American authors Junot Díaz and Julia Alvarez—whose historical novel *In the Name of Salomé* engages with the roots of anti-haitianismo in the intellectual elites of the Dominican Republic in the nineteenth century—along with Edwidge Danticat and American journalist Mark Kurlansky have drawn attention to the plight of impending statelessness of Dominicans of Haitian descent. Junot Díaz has gone so far as to state that "the last time something like this happened was in Nazi Germany, yet people are shrugging about it" (Kurlansky et al.). The Dominican Republic has since opened seven detention centers on the border and relabeled them, in an Orwellian doublespeak, "centros de bienvenido," welcoming centers. As in the case of the parsley massacre, language manipulation and linguistic adaptability may decide over life and death. Edwidge Danticat participates in this very public debate by connecting the plight of Dominicans of Haitian descent to a larger global phenomenon. She suggests,

> What's going on in the D.R. is a nightmare in its own right, but has to be understood as part of a larger global movement to demonize and marginalize immigrants—and as part of the U.S.'s post-9/11 push to "strengthen borders"—which is really to militarize them. (André, Danticat, and Díaz)

In her efforts to highlight the global dimensions of anti-immigrant sentiments in the first two decades of the twenty-first century, Danticat, in her fiction and nonfiction, relentlessly draws attention to the resilience and creative power of migrants, immigrants, and refugees alike. She lyrically describes the radical hope that underlies the emigrants' decision to move to another country and confront a new language and a different culture, in view and in spite of xenophobia and racism in a powerfully imagined place that benefits both host country and immigrants.

Note

1. The title of my essay is taken from the title of Danticat's collection of essays *Create Dangerously: The Immigrant Artist at Work* (2010), which, in turn, is inspired by the English translation of a lecture given by Albert Camus on December 14, 1957, at the University of Uppsala in Sweden.

Works Cited

Alvarez, Julia. *In the Name of Salomé: A Novel.* Plume, 2000.

André, Richard, Edwidge Danticat, and Junot Díaz. "The Dominican Republic and Haiti: A Shared View from the Diaspora." *The Americans Quarterly*, Summer 2014, americasquarterly.org/content/dominican-republic-and-haiti-shared-view-diaspora/. Accessed 19 Oct. 2017.

Baldwin, James. *The Fire Next Time.* 1963. Vintage, 1992.

Berlant, Lauren. *Cruel Optimism.* Duke UP, 2011.

Bloch, Ernst. *The Principle of Hope*. Translated by Neville Plaice, Stephen Plaice, and Paul Knight, The MIT Press, 1995.

Camus, Albert. "Create Dangerously." *Resistance, Rebellion and Death: Essays*. 1960. Translated by Justin O'Brian, Vintage, 1995, pp. 249-285.

Coates, Ta-Nehisi. *Between the World and Me*. Spiegel & Grau, 2015.

Danticat, Edwidge. *After the Dance: A Walk through Jacmel, Haiti*. Vintage, 2002.

_____. *The Art of Death: Writing the Final Story*. Graywood, 2017.

_____. *Breath, Eyes, Memory*. Vintage, 1994.

_____. *Brother, I'm Dying*. Knopf, 2007.

_____. *Claire of the Sea Light*. Knopf, 2013.

_____. *Create Dangerously: The Immigrant Artist at Work*. Vintage, 2010.

_____. *The Dew Breaker*. Knopf, 2004.

_____. *The Farming of Bones*. Vintage, 1999.

_____. *Krik? Krak!* Vintage, 1995.

De Robertis, Carolina. *Radical Hope: Letters of Love and Dissent in Dangerous Times*. Vintage, 2017.

Díaz, Junot. "Radical Hope." *Radical Hope: Letters of Love and Dissent in Dangerous Times*, edited by Carolina De Robertis, Vintage, 2017, pp. 11-14.

_____. *The Brief Wondrous Life of Oscar Wao*. Riverhead, 2007.

_____. "Under President Trump, Radical Hope is Our Best Weapon." *New Yorker*, 21 Nov. 2016, www.newyorker.com/magazine/2016/11/21/under-president-trump-radical-hope-is-our-best-weapon/. Accessed 2 Jan. 2016.

Engel, Patricia. *It's Not Love, It's Paris*. Grove Press, 2014.

Fassler, Joe, and Edwidge Danticat. "All Immigrants Are Artists." *The Atlantic*, 27 Aug. 2013, www.theatlantic.com/entertainment/archive/2013/08/all-immigrants-are-artists/279087/. Accessed 30 Sept. 2017.

Hall, Stuart. "Cultural Identity and Diaspora." *Identity: Community, Culture, Difference*, edited by Jonathan Rutherford. Lawrence and Wishart, 1990, pp. 222-237.

Houston, Robert. "Expecting Angels." *New York Times Book Review*, 23 April 1995.

Kurlansky, Mark, Julia Alvarez, Edwidge Danticat and Junot Díaz. "In the Dominican Republic, suddenly stateless." *LA Times*, 10 Nov. 2013, articles.latimes.com/2013/nov/10/opinion/la-oe-kurlansky-haiti-dominican-republic-citizensh-20131110/. Accessed 2 Jan. 2018.

Lear, Jonathan. *Radical Hope: Ethics in the Face of Cultural Devastation.* Harvard UP, 2006.

Lorde, Audre. "The Uses of the Erotic: The Erotic as Power." *Sexualities and Communication in Everyday Life*, edited by Karen E. Lovaas and Mercilee Jenkins, Sage Publications, 2007, pp. 87-91.

"The Mission of the Dayton Literary Peace Prize." *Dayton Literary Peace Prize*, n.d., daytonliterarypeaceprize.org/mission.htm/. Accessed 2 Feb. 2018.

Quintana, Francisco. "Inter-American Court Condemns Unprecedented Situation of Statelessness in the Dominican Republic." *European Network on Statelenessness*, 27 Oct. 2014, www.statelessness.eu/blog/inter-american-court-condemns-unprecedented-situation-statelessness-dominican-republic. Accessed 18 Oct. 2017.

Tatum, Sophie. "Trump Administration to end Protective Status for Haiti." *CNN*,edition.cnn.com/2017/11/20/politics/dhs-temporary-protected-status-haiti/index.html/. Accessed 20 Dec. 2017.

Walker, Alice. *In Search of Our Mothers' Gardens.* Harcourt, 1983.

Yezierska, Anzia. "America and I." *Children of Loneliness: Stories of Immigrant Life in America.* Funk & Wagalls, 1923.

Writing, Freedom, and the Immigrant Experience: A Reading of Ha Jin's *A Free Life*

Te-hsing Shan

1. The Sea Change and the Challenge of *Dr. Zhivago*

As a first-generation Chinese American writer, Ha Jin has been best known for his stories of mainland China, which he left behind. It was not until 2007, twenty-two years after he had moved to the United States, that he published his first novel about the diasporic Chinese-American community. In *A Free Life*, Ha Jin tells a moving story about how Wu Nan,[1] a Chinese immigrant in the US, decides to pursue his writer's dream despite his realization of the American dream in terms of material gains. Since writing, freedom, and the immigrant experience are tightly interwoven in this novel, we might as well call it "a portrait of the artist as a middle-aged immigrant."

In comparison with Ha Jin's previous novels, *A Free Life* involves a sea change and is distinguished from earlier works in two major respects. In terms of content, Ha Jin's attention shifts from China to the US, focusing on the Chinese-American community to which he belongs. So far as the structure is concerned, unlike his previous novels, which are presented in the form of long, consistent narratives, *A Free Life* is divided into two sections. The first section (Jin, *Free* 1-621), a long narrative in seven parts, is about Nan's struggle to fulfill his American dream and, after its fulfillment, his further aspiration to achieve his ideal as a poet. The second section (623-60) is an "Epilogue," consisting of the aspiring poet's thirteen journal extracts (625-29) and twenty-five poems (633-60), which serves to substantiate the previous narrative and conclude the novel.

This structural arrangement reminds us of Boris Pasternak's *Dr. Zhivago*. To Nan, "Pasternak wrote as if no novels had existed before. The loose structure of the book seemed improvident, yet after finishing the last page, Nan felt everything hung together, uncannily unified. What an amazing book!" (Jin, *Free* 517). "Amazing" as it might be, Nan is puzzled by the connection, or rather, non-connection between the story and the poems attached at the end of *Dr. Zhivago*. Moreover, a little bit to his disappointment, this literary masterpiece hardly mentions "how the protagonist struggled to write poetry" (517). Seen in this light, *Dr. Zhivago* is an important intertext from which Ha Jin draws inspiration, but which he also strives to challenge. This is proven by my interview with the novelist:

> Shan: What's special about *A Free Life* is that Wu Nan's poems are attached at the end of the story so as to complement the narrative text coming before them. What effects do you intend to achieve? Does this arrangement have anything to do with *Dr. Zhivago* you mention earlier in the text?
>
> Jin: I knew that the poetry would remind people of *Dr. Zhivago*, but there was no way for me to cut corners. I had to show that Wu Nan was talented and that his talent was stunted and frustrated by the immigrant process. Yes, coming to the end of the story, he has reached some kind of spiritual ascendance, which cannot but be expressed in his art. That was why I had to add the poems. (Shan, "In" 150-51).

In other words, the novelist knowingly attaches those poems and runs the risk of reminding people of the artistic affinity with, or even artistic flaw of, *Dr. Zhivago*. However, Ha Jin is willing to accept this challenge to demonstrate the protagonist's talent and frustration with the process of his literary creation due to his status as "the writer as migrant," to borrow the title of Ha Jin's collection of critical essays. In addition, he also seeks to emphasize Nan's determination to become a poet in his adopted country so as to achieve "some kind of spiritual ascendance."

2. Homeland and Loyalty

Although Ha Jin is reluctant to admit to the autobiographical elements in *A Free Life*, a careful reader will not fail to detect similarities between the author and the protagonist. For instance, both pursued advanced studies at Brandeis University, decided to stay on in the US after the Tiananmen Massacre in 1989, and were determined to fulfill their dream of being a writer in English rather than in their Chinese mother tongue. Moreover, this novel functions to flesh out some of the crucial ideas presented in *The Writer as Migrant*, which draws heavily from Ha Jin's own writing experience. One of the main arguments in this collection of essays is the idea of "homeland."

In his famous essay on diaspora, James Clifford distinguishes between "roots" and "routes," arguing that the former has to do with the past, history, native land, and nostalgia, whereas the latter, the future, innovation, alien country, and prospects. In their introduction to *Indigenous Diasporas and Dislocations*, Graham Harvey and Charles D. Thompson Jr. contrast "indigenous" with "diaspora," associating the latter with "dispersed, separated, spread, strange, alien, alienated, disconnected, outgoing, other, rootless, uprooted and so on" (Harvey and Thompson, *Indigenous* 1).[2] However, as Yu-cheng Lee rightly points out, diaspora can also serve as a positive and productive space, where what was previously prohibited could be expressed freely (Lee, *Diaspora* 26). In addition, people might just take roots and make themselves at home in a non-native land. Based on his own experience, Ha Jin has this to say about "homeland":

> By definition, the word "homeland" has two meanings—one meaning refers to one's native land, and the other to the land where one's home is at present. In the past, the two meanings were easy to reconcile because "home" also signified "origin" and the past and the present were inseparable. In our time, however, the two meanings tend to form a dichotomy. Thus, we hear the expressions "my new homeland," "my second homeland," "my newly adopted homeland," or "homeland security." . . . In other words, homeland is no longer a place that exists in one's past but a place also relevant to one's present and future. (Jin, *Writer* 65)

After giving some literary examples, Ha Jin concludes, "for most migrants, especially migrant artists and writers, the issue of homeland involves arrival more than return. . . . Its meaning can no longer be separated from home, which is something the migrant should be able to build away from his native land. Therefore, it is logical to say that *your homeland is where you build your home*" (Jin, *Writer* 84, emphasis added). This very same expression also appears in *A Free Life* (635), providing further proof of the close relationship between these two books.

Intimately related to the idea of homeland is that of loyalty. At the end of Part One, bitterly disappointed with China, Nan says to his friend Danning, who has decided to go back to China to teach at the People's University, "*I spit at China, because it treats its people like gullible children and always prevents them from growing up into real individuals. It demands nothing but obedience*" (Jin, *Free* 96).[3] He even claims, with tears in his eyes, "*I've wrenched China out of my heart*" (96). However, his previous homeland does not allow its native son to get away so easily. One afternoon while Nan is at the Gold Wok, the restaurant he and his wife, Pingping, acquire after years of hard work, he is approached by a man and a woman connected with the Georgia Tech Chinese Student Association who ask for "a donation for the flood victims in mainland China" (232). At first Nan refuses to donate, saying, "*We've separated ourselves from China long ago, and for good. We don't owe it anything*" (233). After some heated conversation between the solicitors and Nan, his wife finally writes a check, much to the protagonist's reluctance. Whereas Nan wishes, "*If only we could squeeze the old country out of our blood,*" this incident reminds the immigrant couple that "China would never leave them alone. Wherever they went, the old land seemed to follow them" (235). Therefore, as Chinese American immigrants affected by both "old" and "new" lands, the Wu's find themselves living under what L. Ling-chi Wang calls "the structure of dual domination."[4]

If in the previous episode the "old land" comes to him, Nan voluntarily approaches it in the following one, which occurs while he is still in the process of applying for US citizenship, since his Chinese passport has already been revoked for political reasons. Attending a meeting to discuss *China Can Say No*, a controversial book by two mainland China journalists, at the community center of local Chinatown, the protagonist finds his in-between status under severe attack. Before he attends the meeting, he comes up with "a pair of metaphors" to describe his relationship with his native and adopted countries, "comparing China to his mother and the United States to the woman he loved" (Jin, *Free* 489).[5] Trite though they appear, these metaphors could help him "sort out his emotions" (490). As the discussion of the book becomes more and more vehement, Nan cannot help jumping in, expressing that as Chinese Americans, their position and interest differ from the authors'. To him, *"China is our native land, while America is the land of our children—that's to say, a place of our future"* (495). After he reveals that he is going to be an American citizen before long, he is called a *"shameless American!"* and several persons demand *"Americans out!"* (495). What is more, his choice to write poetry in English, which he regards as an expression of his freedom of speech, makes him appear to fellow Chinese Americans like *"a madman"* and *"a banana"* (496). What to him is *"my personal choice"* to be *"a real individual"* only makes him *"a lone wolf"* (496) in the eyes of the audience. Consequently, the whole meeting becomes a farce and ends "in a tumult" (496). This incident shows that even among Chinese living in the US, the strong attachment to the native land is sometimes more powerful than expected, and capable of putting people like Nan, who tries to negotiate past and present, in a complicated situation.

3. The American Dream and Its Discontent

Geographically and psychologically unable to go back and settle down in China, their native land, Nan and Pingping strive to provide a decent life for their son, Taotao, for "[b]y any means, the boy must live a life different from his parents' and take this land to be his country!" (Jin, *Free* 9). Ha Jin gives a detailed description of the couple's struggle in this new land of opportunity, which could be seen as a small part of the collective history of immigrants to the US. After years of hard work, they finally own a restaurant and a mansion by the lake, something far beyond their reach in China. To an ordinary immigrant, or to be more exact, to Nan as an FOJ, "fresh off the jet" (10), this would be the realization of the American dream. Indeed, when he wants to buy the mansion, his lawyer tells him, "This is a major step toward realizing your American dream"

(219). Pingping's former employer in America is glad to find this Chinese couple is doing well, for "in less than a decade you already have your own business, a house, and two cars" (390). She continues, "Amazing. This can happen only in America. I'm very moved by the fact that you and Nan have actualized your American dream so quickly. I'm proud of this country" (390). Obviously, Nan and Pingping seem to offer another example of Chinese Americans as a model minority.

However, the protagonist is somewhat disappointed with material success and laments that "[t]he struggle had ended so soon that he felt as though the whole notion of the American dream was shoddy, a hoax" (Jin, *Free* 418). Characterized as a "dreamer" and "idealist" several times in the story (43, 55, 588), Nan has been nicknamed "Mr. Wagon Man" by his fellow Chinese students in the US because he once quoted the Ur-transcendentalist Ralph Waldo Emerson's famous saying, "Hitch your wagon to a star" (55). At last, legally a naturalized citizen and yet mentally an exile, Nan demonstrates characteristics which Edward W. Said ascribes to the life of an exile: "Exile is life led outside habitual order. It is nomadic, decentered, contrapuntal; but no sooner does one get accustomed to it than its unsettling force erupts anew" (Said, "Reflections" 186). As a result, even if Nan gets used to the kind of material comfort his adopted country offers, something deep inside remains unsettled and unsettling. Therefore, after Nan returns from his frustrating visit to China and finally decides that the US would be his home for the rest of his life, his dissatisfaction with his current situation increases, with one of the main reasons being "[h]e couldn't make any progress in his writing" (604).

This sense of dissatisfaction and frustration grows day by day. Finally, there comes the moment for explosion. One afternoon after busy hours, Nan sits down to read *Good Advice on Writing* and comes across a remark by William Faulkner: "The writer must teach himself that the basest of all things is to be afraid; and, teaching himself that, forget it forever, leaving no room in his workshop for anything but the old verities and truths of the heart" (qtd. in Jin, *Free* 604).[6] As if struck by lightning, the protagonist suddenly realizes that the reason why he has been procrastinating and endlessly delaying his dream of writing is due to his fear of leaving his comfort zone and of undertaking a soul-searching task. This shock of recognition ignites his long-hidden discontent. What follows is the climax of the whole novel:

> Tears were rolling down his cheeks. How he hated himself! . . . The more he thought about his true situation, the more he loathed himself, especially for his devotion to making money, which had consumed so many of his prime years and dissolved his will to follow his own heart. A paroxysm of aversion seized him and he turned to the cash register, took all the banknotes out of the tray, and went to the alcove occupied by the God of Wealth, for whom they had always made weekly offerings. With a swipe he sent flying the wine cups, the joss sticks, and the bowls of fruit and almond cookies. . . . He thrust a five-dollar bill on the flame of a candle and instantly the cash curled, ablaze. (Jin, *Free* 605)

Symbolizing his strong dissatisfaction with the material side of the American dream, this violent act shocks Pingping and other witnesses. After this incident, Pingping's health problem and the terrible cost of treatment enable him to understand that external material conditions do not necessarily guarantee inner peace nor a sense of security. Consequently, he decides to sell their hard-won restaurant and find a job at a motel, which provides medical insurance, though he has to spend one-third of his income to pay for the insurance. In exchange, he has time to follow his literary dream, take care of his family, and not worry about the tremendous costs of medical treatment if a family member falls ill. Just as Ha Jin says in my interview with him,

> As for the American dream, I am not satisfied with the popular version of it, because some immigrants did not come to this country just for a house and two cars. There is always something metaphysical in my understanding of the American dream, which ought to have something spiritual in it. (Shan, "In" 143)

This sudden change shatters the stereotype of Chinese Americans as being hardworking merely in pursuit of material prosperity. Nan's friend Shubo tries to dissuade him from his "impatient" attempt and "impractical" dream of writing poetry in English as a first-generation Chinese American: *"We're new here and cannot go a million miles in one life. Writing poetry can be a profession only for your grandchildren'"* (Jin, *Free* 420). As Shubo observes, *"Nan, you're too impatient. In your life span you want to go through the course of three generations"* (421). In fact, Nan is not unaware of the situation of ordinary immigrants, for "[u]sually the first generation drudged to feed and shelter themselves and their families," so that the second generation might "go to college and become professionals and 'real Americans'" (418-19). Consequently, it is for the third generation to pursue literary and artistic ideals. He compares first-generation immigrants to "manure used to enrich the soil so that new seeds could sprout and grow" (419). As for himself, however, he wants to be both manure and new seed, and, hopefully, to flower by achieving both his secular and spiritual goals.

4. Poetic Ideals and Practices

With this vision in mind and "at peace with himself" (Jin, *Free* 616), Nan is "determined to follow his own heart" (618) and find a home in his adopted language by writing poetry. Composed of thirteen journal entries and twenty-five poems (one more than *Dr. Zhivago*) by the fledgling poet, "Epilogue" shows his effort to think through the significance of writing poetry, the hardships encountered during the writing process, as well as the results of his poetic endeavor. In contrast with the consistent and linear narrative, this section is relatively loose and fragmentary in structure, with an aim of complementing and reinforcing the narrative, something that Pasternak fails to do in *Dr. Zhivago*. Written between January 3 and October 30, 1998, these journal extracts—"a traditional practice of ancient Chinese poets"—articulate the aspiring poet's thoughts and feelings in daily life and offer the "material for his poems" (616). Presented in journal form, they allow readers a glimpse into the protagonist's inner state, and have a unique claim to privacy and authenticity.

Many people who dream of being writers aim at fame and fortune. However, the very first extract shatters this rosy picture, when Nan finds in a used bookstore a remarkable collection of poetry published in 1969, which is "fresh, elegant, intimate, and full of mysterious lines" (Jin, *Free* 625). And yet, there is no information about the poet, and no big chain store carries any book by the poet. This crude fact makes Nan realize "how fragile and ephemeral a poet's reputation can be" and that the result of writing poetry "may be only failure" (625). Still, this shock of recognition does not prevent him from writing poetry. On the contrary, it shows that Nan writes with full knowledge of inevitable oblivion; nonetheless he cherishes poetry as a means of self-exploration and self-expression, rather than as a route to fame or fortune.

Fully committed to his chosen path, Nan submits a number of his poems to poetry journals. Some are accepted, others rejected. Among the editors, one lady is especially harsh, warning in their first correspondence, "English is too hard for you" and criticizing the way he uses the language as being "too clumsy" (Jin, *Free* 626). On another occasion, she quotes William Butler Yeats, "no poet who doesn't write in his mother tongue can write with music and strength" (628) and questions, "Can you imagine your work becoming part of our language?" (628). These remarks are disheartening for the poet at the beginning of his literary career. However, with no intention of seeking fame or fortune, Nan already regards himself "as a loser who has nothing to lose anymore." To him, writing poetry is of existential significance, for "[t]o write poetry is to exist" (626). In a sense, writing poetry has become his calling, in that he feels "I write only because I have to" (628). His determination is strengthened by famous lines from the preeminent Chinese poet Tu Fu (712–770 CE): "Writing is a matter of a thousand years; / My heart knows the gain and the loss" (627).

With regard to writing in a language other than one's mother tongue, Ha Jin deals with this issue in *The Writer as Migrant*. As the holder of a PhD in English literature, a prolific writer in English with a number of prestigious literary awards to his credit, and a man of letters versed in Chinese and Russian literature, Ha Jin has much to offer concerning this topic. In my opinion, *The Writer as Migrant* aims at two ends at once: (1) to establish a tradition of migrant writers using their adopted English language, with Joseph Conrad and Vladimir Nabokov as two maestros writing in different styles but making significant contributions to English language and literature, and (2) to find Ha Jin's own place in this literary tradition by highlighting, not downgrading, his unique cultural resources as well as linguistic and literary "foreignness."[7] As Nan asserts in his journal, "the vitality of English has partly resulted from its ability to assimilate all kinds of alien energies" (Jin, *Free* 628).

With this in mind, Nan embarks on his poetic journey. Closely related to the dichotomy between roots and routes, the aspiring poet decides to sever his ties to his native land and make the US his homeland. Moreover, he attempts to go beyond the material side of the American dream by pursuing something more spiritual and transcendental. His situation is in perfect accord with Theodor Adorno's statement: "In his text, the writer sets up house. . . . For a man who no longer has a homeland, writing becomes a place to live" (87). Nan's feelings and thoughts find their best expression in his poems.

For instance, the speaker in "An Admonition" (Jin, *Free* 653) offers a contrast between his native land and his new homeland. The first stanza lists a number of things that "you used to see" (653) back in China. In contrast, "Here in America you can speak and shout, / though you have to find your voice and the right ears" (653). Therefore, as a Chinese immigrant in the US, the Promised Land, "All your sufferings are imaginary," "all your misfortunes are imaginary," and "Your hardship is just commonplace" (653). Whatever difficulty and complaint the immigrant might encounter in his adopted country, his is still "a fortune many are dying to seize" in his old homeland (653). In other words, in contrasting his land of arrival with that of his departure, the speaker in the poem urges acceptance of a sense of appreciation and satisfaction in his new homeland.

The poem that immediately follows, "Immigrant Dreams" (Jin, *Free* 654), tells a different story concerning the attractions and pitfalls of material achievement in the US. For the two persons in the poem, probably husband and wife, the female immigrant's "dream has evolved into a house / on two acres of land with a pool" by "[giving] up art school" and "sell[ing] her hours in America" (654). Here in a capitalist society, "dollars can equalize most lives" (654). On the other hand, the male immigrant wishes that he could return to "twenty again" or "stop patching his dream / with diffident feet and rhymes" (654). Propelled by his creative urge, the male immigrant is still filled with youthful ideals of creative writing. Short as it is, this poem serves to complement the long narrative by showing the achievement of the American dream in terms of material gains on the one hand, and the unflinching devotion to the art of poetry writing on the other. It can be read as an alternative version of "An Admonition," reminding immigrants to the US about the attraction and pitfalls of the American dream, and the significance of youthful ideals.

Whatever variations might be found in immigrant dreams, at least one thing remains certain: how to redefine "homeland" is a theme that constantly haunts immigrants. The three stanzas in the poem "Homeland" (Jin, *Free* 635) appear like a syllogism. In the first stanza, the one going abroad assures his/her friend that he/she will return in a few years "like a lion" and "[t]here is no other place I can call home" (635). The following stanza presents a different picture, for somehow he/she is not allowed to go back and becomes "expendable to / a country never short of citizens" (635). The third stanza thus concludes: "Eventually you will learn: / your country is where you raise your children, / *your homeland is where you build your home*" (653, emphasis added). This conclusion not only supports the protagonist's stance in the narrative, but also echoes one of the main themes of *The Writer as Migrant*.

In brief, whereas these poems are the embodiment of Nan's poetic practices, the journal extracts represent his feelings, ideas, and the story behind his creative writing. Moreover, extracts and poems not only illuminate each other, but also showcase the results of the protagonist's dedication to his ideal. In his interview with Ming Di, the Chinese translator of Ha Jin's poems and *The Writer as Migrant*, Ha Jin thus comments on the quality and function of these poems: "The poems in *A Free Life* are personalized poems, written solely for Nan. They are not as good as those in *Dr. Zhivago* because Nan is not a successful poet. But as a whole, *A Free Life* may stand side by side with *Dr. Zhivago*" (Ming, "Interview" 225). The reason for Ha Jin's confidence comes mainly from the recognition that, structurally speaking, the poems in this novel are organically intertwined with the whole narrative and enhance its main theme, characterization, and the development of the plot. All these work together to give a vivid representation of the writer as a migrant, writing in a language other than his mother tongue.

5. "Garlands of Words" and "A Path of Flowers"

The difficult situation of a migrant writer can best be observed in "An Exchange" (Jin, *Free* 658-59). This five-stanza poem forms a dialogue, or rather, a debate between the poet and a collective "we" from his native land. In fact, the first stanza creates a species of ambiguity, for the reader does not know exactly who the speaker is. It remains unclear whether the poet or someone else is blaming him(self) for his "folly" or wishful thinking for having "determined to follow the footsteps of Conrad / and Nabokov" and for having believed "you can write verse in English, / whose music is not natural to you?" (658). The second stanza makes it clear that it is actually "our people" in the native land who condemn the poet for betraying them and "our ancient words" by choosing to write in "gibberish" (658). The third stanza delves even deeper by invoking racism to further discourage the poet from his artistic pursuit in a foreign language, for even if he is accepted "in the temple housing those high-nosed ghosts," he will still be regarded merely as "a clever Chinaman" (658).

In the next two stanzas, the poet refutes these accusations and formulates his own idea of loyalty. To him, "Loyalty is a two-way street" (Jin, *Free* 658). In return, he accuses the nation of having betrayed its people and condemns "those who have hammered / our mother tongue into a chain / to bind all the different dialects / to the governing machine?" (658-59). In other words, a nation is not entitled to demand loyalty from its people unilaterally. Instead, the nation and its people should be loyal to each other. Furthermore, those who diminish the diversity and heterogeneity of different dialects in order to serve the state machine are being disloyal to their mother tongue. Confirming the poet's determination, the final stanza brings the whole debate to an abrupt end: "To write in this language is to be alone, / to live on the margin where / loneliness ripens into solitude" (659). The longest poem in the book, "An Exchange" expresses in a nutshell both the poetics and politics of the freedom of writing in an adopted language in an adopted country. Faced with various accusations from his native land and severe challenges from his new homeland, Nan embraces his task as a poet and embarks on his journey.

After "An Exchange" comes the last poem, which concludes not only Nan's collection of poems but also the whole novel. Written in a serene mode, "Another Country" (Jin, *Free* 660) readily reminds the reader of Yeats's famous poem "The Lake Isle of Innisfree." A utopian state for the poet, it is "a country without borders, / where you can build your home / out of garlands of words" (660). It seems that after his journey from his native land to the US as his new homeland, after his material success as a new immigrant in the land of opportunity, and after his determination to accept his calling as a poet writing in another language in another country, Nan finally wins entry into a truly free life in his promised land:

> You must go there, quietly.
> Leave behind what you still cherish.
> Once you enter that domain,
> a path of flowers will open before your feet. (Jin, *Free* 660)

Notes

1. According to the Chinese translation of the novel, for which Ha Jin writes a preface, Wu is the surname. In the novel, he is referred to as "Nan." A literal translation of the Chinese name Wu Nan is "Martial

Man." The irony or tension between Nan's name and his ideal is noteworthy.

2.   I want to thank Hsinya Huang for providing this reference.

3.   A stylistic characteristic of *A Free Life* should be noted here. Conversations in Chinese are italicized throughout the novel, in contrast to those in English.

4.   For a detailed discussion of how Chinese Americans are simultaneously under the influence of China and the US, see L. Ling-chi Wang, "The Structure of Dual Domination: Toward a Paradigm for the Study of the Chinese Diaspora in the United States."

5.   Edward W. Said's distinction between filiation and affiliation is of use here. Whereas filiation has to do with birth, life, and nature, affiliation, with choice, society, and culture (Said, "Introduction" 16-20).

6.   This passage comes from Faulkner's Nobel Prize acceptance speech in 1950.

7.   Ha Jin elaborates on this issue in "In Defense of Foreignness."

Works Cited

Adorno, Theodor. *Minima Moralia: Reflections from Damaged Life.* Translated by E. F. N. Jephcott, Verso, 1978.

Clifford, James. *Routes: Travel and Translation in the Late Twentieth Century.* Harvard UP, 1997.

Jin, Ha. *A Free Life.* Pantheon, 2007.

_____. "In Defense of Foreignness." *The Routledge Handbook of World Englishes*, edited by Andy Kirkpatrick, Routledge, 2010, pp. 461–70.

_____. *The Writer as Migrant.* U of Chicago P, 2008.

Harvey, Graham, and Charles D. Thompson Jr. "Introduction." *Indigenous Diasporas and Dislocations*, edited by Graham Harvey and Charles D. Thompson Jr., Ashgate, 2005.

Lee, Yu-cheng. *Diaspora.* Asian Culture, 2013.

Ming, Di. "An Interview with Ha Jin on Poetry Writing." *Time Missed: Selected Poems by Ha Jin.* Linking Books, 2011.

Said, Edward W. "Introduction: Secular Criticism." *The World, the Text, and the Critic.* Harvard UP, 1983, pp. 1-30.

_____. "Reflections on Exile." *Reflections on Exile and Other Essays*. Harvard UP, 2000, pp. 173-86.

Shan, Te-hsing. "In the Ocean of Words: An Interview with Ha Jin." *Tamkang Review* vol. 38, no. 2, 2008, pp. 135–57.

Wang, L. Ling-chi. "The Structure of Dual Domination: Toward a Paradigm for the Study of the Chinese Diaspora in the United States." *Amerasia Journal* vol. 21, no. 1-2, 1995, pp. 149-69.

Making a Place: Life Narratives of Undocumented Youth_____

Marta Caminero-Santangelo

During the first decade of the 2000s, the life stories of undocumented youth began to emerge in the media as a form of political activism, rhetorically crafted to move politicians to pass a DREAM Act (Development, Relief, and Education for Alien Minors) that would have provided a path to eventual legalization for young people who had either entered the United States illegally with their parents or had overstayed legal visas and fallen out of status. Such stories shared some common elements and patterns. Chief among these was a focus on the United States as "home"—the nation of memory, experience, culture, and deep loyalty (Caminero-Santangelo, *Documenting*). Undocumented youth—they came to call themselves DREAMers—emphasized in their stories that they saw themselves as fully American, although this emphasis came at the expense of discussing continuing transnational ties or affinities with a culture of origin (Caminero-Santangelo, *Documenting* and "DREAMers").

Another standard narrative trope involved the meritorious, deserving immigrant who was pursuing the "American Dream." The stories that gained the most media attention were the stories of high-achieving individuals. As Roberto G. Gonzales explains in his book *Lives in Limbo*,

> In the early stages of advocacy for undocumented students, educators, legislators, and lobbyists tried to paint a portrait of undocumented students that would appeal to all who love the American dream. . . . [Advocates] depicted undocumented youth as innocent of the 'criminal' decision to break US laws by crossing the border. . . . Images of valedictorians, class presidents, and model citizens . . . multiplied in the media. (26-27)

Indeed, politicians who supported the DREAM Act argued that "we" shouldn't punish the children for the crimes of the parents; some DREAM narratives and creative work echoed and reinforced this sentiment (see, for instance, "Undocumented and Unafraid" 2011; Kalma, "The Undocumented"). These representations painted undocumented youth as "good" immigrants who had high potential to contribute to their communities and to the economy—as opposed to the trope of the "bad" immigrant who "takes things from us" (jobs, social services) without contributing meaningfully (Honig 74, 96).

With the implementation of DACA (Deferred Action for Childhood Arrivals, instituted as a stop-gap measure in the failure of DREAM Act passage) in 2012 under President Barack Obama, DREAMer storytelling as activism died down. While DACA was not a DREAM Act—not law but policy—it apparently gave young undocumented people *enough* of a sense of security that pressure to pass a DREAM Act was relieved. But with DACA, some alternative DREAMer narratives began, also, to emerge. DREAMers began to note that the term "DREAMer" as a synonym for all young people without legal status was highly exclusionary. The "good immigrant" narrative was itself problematic:

> Increasingly, immigrant integration proposals and legislation have exacerbated divisions between high achievers and other undocumented youth, rewarding the meritorious with an easier pathway to access while leaving others further behind. . . . By framing the issue around school, they moved the discussion away from immigrant rights to one that distinguishes "worthy" immigrants from "unworthy ones," "innocent" and "deserving" immigrants from felons and gang members. (Gonzales 26-27)

Most significantly, some challenges to the "deserving immigrant" narrative began to be posed by DREAMers themselves.

One challenge was to the assumptions of high academic performance that "representative" DREAM narratives implicitly advanced. Every DREAM Act proposal since 2001 (but prior to 2017) had required at least two years of attendance at an institution of higher education, or two years of service in the military, in order to be eligible to complete the path to legalization as a permanent resident. This proposal left out of the equation—until the 2017 version—students who did not go to college (which was, in any case, priced out of reach for many because of the lack of eligibility for any form of federal financial aid); it made the "dream" unattainable for those students who never graduated from high school. (In 2014, the dropout rate for all Latinx high school students reached a new low of 12%, but in 2000, it was 32% [Krogstad].) Emerging voices began to point out that, by using academic credentials (or military service) as a condition of legalization, the DREAM Act was exclusionary in more ways than just its focus on youth. (The 2017 version of proposed DREAM Act legislation offered a work/employment route as an alternative to higher education or the military.) Further, a most often unremarked aspect of both DACA and the Dream Act had to do with "good moral character" (in the words of the 2010 DREAM Act proposal). While this criterion may seem completely logical on its face, some scholars and critics, as well as undocumented youth themselves, began to point out that teenagers often engage in risky behaviors (speeding, light shoplifting, underage drinking, or drug use) that do not necessarily reveal anything enduring about moral character and do not make these young people less worthy of a path to residency in the country in which they were raised (see Golash-Boza).

The life narratives that DREAMers had disseminated leading up to DACA's implementation in 2012 (*Underground Undergrads*, *Papers*) had, by and large, reinforced the "good immigrant" narrative and been told in sound-bites (short prose narratives) rather than fully fleshed-out stories of a complicated life. But some life narratives by so-called DREAMers also began to emerge in the DACA era, and these significantly complicated and challenged the stock DREAMer narrative by presenting their prior selves as less than always "meritorious" or "innocent." Stories also drew a far more complicated picture of "place"; while, ironically, earlier DREAMer narratives, in their insistence on the right to stay, emphasized staying put (in the United States), some of the more recent narratives attend not just to a singular emplacement but to a multiplicity of places, marking mobility (either between the US and the country of origin or among sites in the US) and a continuous crossing of geographical and psychological borders as an expanded experience of place.

Perhaps the two most prominent book-length life narratives of undocumented youth in the new millennium are *Undocumented: A Dominican Boy's Odyssey from a Homeless Shelter to the Ivy League* (2015) by Dan-el Padilla Peralta and *The Distance Between Us* (2012) by novelist Reyna Grande. Notably, both of these authors were eventually able to fully legalize their status, making them the exception rather than the norm among DREAMers and giving them the safety and security to publish their stories without fear of deportation. Both narratives trace a path from poverty to a prestigious education and "success" as defined by US norms; thus, in some ways, both retrace the narrative pattern of the "good immigrant" who makes a substantial contribution to society, as well as of the "meritorious" DREAMers who "deserve" to be legalized because they have proven themselves to excel academically. In other ways, however, both life stories resist these narrative patterns, eschewing notions of "innocence" in favor of more fully fleshed-out individuals with agency over their own lives. Further, both narratives complicate static notions of bounded place (e.g., a US with borders that must be crossed to be "entered" and that therefore exists apart from other places); instead, emplacement in the US becomes a matter of links to multiple "places" and to entangled networks of belonging, exclusion, and *movement*. Place is encoded in the body, and the body leaves its traces in places.

Doreen Massey, in her introduction to the book *Space, Place, and Gender* proposes that if we imagine our understanding of space as always of necessity "formed out of social relations at all scales," then place can be conceived of as

> a particular articulation of those relations, a particular moment in those networks of social relations and understandings . . . . [Place] includes relations which stretch beyond [the geographical place itself] . . . . [T]he particularity of any place is, in these terms, constructed not by placing boundaries around it . . . but precisely (in part) through the specificity of the mix of links and interconnections *to* that "beyond." (5)

This understanding of place is a useful lens for reading the full-length life narratives of undocumented youth, who understand "place" precisely in these terms—always as constituted through their relations to other places. Thus, as we will see, the meanings of "el otro lado" (the United States) and Mexico for Reyna Grande are inextricable from the economic and social forces which draw her parents north and leave her behind, deeply imbricated in a larger network of relations of labor, capital, and cultural representations that link the United States and Mexico closely together. And the meanings of places for Dan-el Padilla Peralta are even more finely grained, taking account of economic and social distinctions between the different places he inhabits within the United States (homeless shelter, tenement, elite private school, ivy league college) and even to the geographical routes by which he physically moves from one place to another.

"El Otro Lado"

Grande's life story begins with what, for the young child protagonist, amounts to an abandonment: her parents migrate north to the United States in order to raise the family's standard of living and send money back to Mexico. As I have written elsewhere ("DREAMers"), this initial act of migration casts the United States in a far different light than it appears in most previous undocumented narratives, where the United States still potentially offers some version of "the American Dream." Rather, in young Reyna's mind, the US is linked to the Mexican folklore bogeywoman figure of "La Llorona" (the crying woman). This figure, widely known in Mexican culture, is a woman who weeps through the night—often near rivers—in search of her lost children and is also threatening and scary to young children who are told the story by their parents to warn them from straying too far at night because she will take children to replace her own. But in author Grande's retelling, "La Llorona" is reimagined as the United States, and in a reversal, it is scary because it "takes away parents, not children"; "What I knew back then was that El Otro Lado ["The Other Side"] had already taken my father away. What I knew was that prayers didn't work, because if they did, El Otro Lado wouldn't be taking my mother away, too" (3-4). Reyna's early imaginings about the United States already suggests that the meanings of place are a product of complex social relations, since the initial meaning of the United States for the young Reyna is derived not from US culture but from *Mexican* culture. It is through the myth of La Llorona that Reyna understands and processes the dynamics of migration.

Repeatedly throughout her childhood and in her parents' absence, Reyna internalizes the lesson that the United States has drawn her parents away and that it therefore must hold more appeal for them than their own children do. All things "American," by logical extension, are to be preferred to things Mexican: "El Otro Lado is a beautiful place. Every street is paved with concrete. You don't see any dirt roads there. No mosquitoes sucking the blood out of you . . . . There's no trash in the streets like here in Mexico. Trucks there pick up the trash every week" (Grande 45). Eventually, this one-upmanship of the US over Mexico includes her own siblings, who are born in the United States. Early in the memoir, Reyna's young friend Élida warns her and her sister Mago, "Your mother is not coming back for you . . . . Now that she's got a job and is making dollars, she won't want to come back, believe me." Mago responds, "Speak for yourself. It's your mother who's not coming back . . . . Doesn't she have another child, over there in El Otro Lado?" (24-25). But this taunt comes back to bite Mago and Reyna when their own mother announces, from the United States, that she, too, is pregnant. Reyna wonders, "Why would she come back to Mexico . . . when she could stay on that side of the border and give birth to an American Citizen?" (33). The unspoken assumption is clearly that an American Citizen child is preferable to a Mexican Citizen child.

This impulse and preference works its way into Reyna's psyche as well, but always in an anxiety-ridden fashion, since Reyna has to *learn* to look down at her Mexican home and culture. This is a lesson her Tía Emperatriz reinforces:

"From what I've heard, El Otro Lado is a very beautiful place. But here . . . " She waved her hand for me to look outside the cab window.

I know now what she had wanted me to see back then: the banks of the canal lined with trash and debris floating in the water, the crumbling adobe houses, the shacks made of sticks . . . . But what I saw back then I saw through the eyes of a child . . . velvety mountains around us, the clear blue sky, the beautiful jacaranda trees covered in purple flowers . . . . "Don't you think there's beauty here, too?" I asked Tía Emperatriz. (Grande 64-65)

The beauty endemic to Mexico is something that Reyna must be taught to unsee, in favor of the imagined beauty of the US. Even the young Reyna, who still sees the beauty of her birthplace, internalizes the "lesson" that the US is better, that it is the desired destination. When her younger brother Carlos plays in a car and pretends to drive, asking "Where are we off to today?" Reyna's automatic response is, "To El Otro Lado" (Grande 31).

It is within this highly ambivalent framework that young Reyna begs her father to take her and her siblings back with him to the United States. (By this point, Reyna's parents' marriage has fallen apart.) Even Reyna's deliberations about how she and her siblings— including her American-born sister Betty—will manage the trip north provokes her inculcated sense of Mexican inferiority and resentment of the US: "Betty could fly back . . . since she was a U.S. citizen. For a brief moment, I felt the familiar jealousy I'd felt when I had first heard of my American sister. Being born in the U.S. was a privilege I wished I had had. That way, I wouldn't need to sneak across the border like a thief" (Grande 150). Reyna's conflicted emotions about the United States, as the desirable and enviable destination to which she does not fully have access and simultaneously as the monstrous thief of her own parents, vastly complicate simplistic narratives of aspiration to a reductive "American Dream."

But Grande's narrative also challenges the construction of the DREAMers as having "no choice," since it is *Reyna herself* who pushes an initially unwilling father: "Papi, you have to take me back to El Otro Lado with you" (149). Reyna's father reluctantly brings her to the United States; she subsequently has cause to remind herself of this decision when life with her abusive father fails to live up to the "Dream": "I *begged* him to bring me. I got what I wanted, after all. How could I complain now, simply because things weren't all that we had hoped for?" (256). Reyna's agency, even as a child, in the decision to come north poses a significant wrinkle to the story pattern in which undocumented youth are represented as unwilling or unknowing participants in their own migration.

Reyna Grande's story in many ways concludes by paralleling the model narrative of the meritorious DREAMer: she graduates from the University of California, Santa Cruz, goes on to earn an MFA, becomes a published novelist (who meets other famous Latina novelists including Sandra Cisneros, Julia Alvarez, and Helena María Viramontes)—and, along the way, becomes a US citizen, a legalization of status that is today unavailable to the vast majority of undocumented youth living in the United States. In some ways, the language of Grande's memoir echoes and reinforces the cliché of the deserving immigrant: "I had gotten this far, despite everything. Now, all I had to do was focus on why I was there—to make my dreams a reality" (Grande 318). Nonetheless, the American Dream plotline does not convey the complexity of the places that hold significance for Grande, and in which she feels rooted.

While the immigrant version of the American Dream hypothesizes an imagined immigrant who leaves every tie and loyalty behind to "make good" in the US, Grande clearly continues to feel a strong psychological attachment to the places of her childhood. On the one hand, her responses to place mark her distance from where she grew up, as becomes evident when she and her sister return to Mexico for a visit: "I knew that I had been in the U.S. for too long when the sight of my grandmother's shack, with its bamboo sticks, corrugated metal roof, and tar-soaked cardboard, shocked me. *Had I really lived in this place?*" And yet, her powerful visceral responses to places and the ways in which they have changed simultaneously confirm that she *had* lived there, and that she is still fundamentally attached to these sites. Reyna notes with sadness the way the places she knew have changed:

. . . a year before, the Mexican government had privatized the railroad system, and the service to Iguala was suspended. There were no more passengers coming through every day. There were no more vendors who sold their wares and food. . . . I turned to look at the train station, feeling my eyes burn with tears. It was no longer one of the most important places in Iguala. Now, it was just a relic, an open wound . . . . [Today's children] would never hear the whistle of the evening train or taste the wonderful chicken quesadillas that Mago had once sold at the train station. (Grande 277)

Although the place as Reyna knew it has changed almost beyond recognition, she is still able to vividly conjure all the senses she attached to the place, in such a way that not only her memory but also her *body* recalls the place; thereby she is (re)emplaced. While Reyna's older sister Mago "[tries] to erase Mexico completely" from the traces of her life, Reyna violently resists this impulse: "I didn't know why I was so angry at my sister. *How could she just sever the ties that bind us to this place* [?] . . . How could I stop myself from feeling sad that Mago no longer cared about Mexico, that she didn't think of this place as special because it was once our home?" (Grande 282). To recall Massey, Iguala for Reyna signifies not just a geographically bounded locale, but "a particular articulation of . . . [social] relations, a particular moment in those networks of social relations and understandings . . . . [Place] includes relations which stretch beyond" the specific location to insert it into a complicated network of all the places Reyna has, to that point, experienced. Reyna understands through her body the ways in which her homeland continues to be a formative part of her.

"Beyond Resurrection, Beyond Harlem"
From the beginning of his memoir *Undocumented*, Dan-el Padilla Peralta, too, displays a heightened awareness of place. In his case, this is not the home country, the Dominican Republic (which he left at age four), but very specific places to which he belongs *within* the United States and where he is "emplaced." His prologue begins with a description of place: "Every weekday morning of my high school years, I left my apartment building in Spanish Harlem and took the subway or bus to Manhattan's Upper West Side, where I

attended private school" (Padilla Peralta 1). Pictures of Dan-el and other family members, strewn throughout the memoir, are most often labeled by place: "Yando on the playground slides, Jackson Heights, Queens, spring 1993" (21); "Dan-el attired in his finest while Jeff looks on, the Bradhurst apartment, fall 1995" (78); "Yando and Dan-el dancing at the Princeton Senior Prom, spring 2006" (189). The specificity of place locates concretely what Dan-el has called the "contradictions" of his life; he belongs in a multitude of different places that do not fit easily next to each other. Though he longs to go "Beyond Resurrection" (his family church) and "beyond Harlem" (97) both in a literal sense and in a more metaphorical one, "beyond" does not mean to "leave behind."

Dan-el is hyper-aware of his movement among the different spaces that mark his life—describing, for instance, the route that his family takes, literally, to travel from the homeless shelter to their new low-income tenement apartment building on Bradhurst Avenue: "We rode the subway from Bushwick into Manhattan, switched to the red line at Fulton Street, and rode the 3 train to 148th Street in Harlem. . . . At the corner of 149th and Eighth, as we waited for the light to change, I looked around and noticed an abandoned building on my right. Up and down Eighth, up and down 149th, I saw boarded-up apartment buildings" (Padilla Peralta 54). The route that Dan-el takes is not just a description of geographic place (as on a map) but of socio-economic place: Dan-el takes note of the surroundings of his new apartment and the impoverishment and lack of economic investment that they suggest, and these signs "locate" him. Later, he is once again hyper-aware of the social meanings of his route back and forth between his tenement building and Collegiate, the private school he attends thanks to a scholarship, as he describes his battles with his mother over wearing his school uniform: "I didn't want to wear my blazer and tie on the walk to and from the subway every morning. . . . I wanted to shout, "I WILL GET JUMPED if I walk around Bradhurst in a blazer and tie!" (107). Dan-el understands that the different contexts will interpret and receive his school uniform attire quite differently; whereas in one place they signal his belonging, in the other they potentially mark him as an outsider and a target. Further, he is aware that even though he is undocumented, he paradoxically in some ways has access to more of these spaces— more mobility—than many of the children he grew up with: "I had my safe white-boy school, my safe white-boy friends, my safe Upper West Side. For my Resurrection friends, on the other hand, Harlem was the world. They had to live there, go to school there, grow up there" (151). Though he lacks "*papeles*" (papers), in his day-to-day existence, he can move fairly easily from one location to another, thanks to the "luck" (as he puts it) that gave him a mentor who helped him navigate the process of getting scholarships to attend elite schools, as well as to his academic abilities that grant him institutional access to those schools. For others who do not have this combination of luck and ability, but who share his poverty, the spaces in which they can move freely are more confined.

In the end, Dan-el's argument about why he belongs in the US is, in large part, a spatial one. In a direct challenge to the anti-immigration "account" in which "immigrant invaders . . . are bodies to be rounded up, detained, and deported by the full apparatus of the surveillance state," Dan-el notes the ways in which he is embedded in specific American landscapes and inseparable from them:

> Every time I walk around New York, I think of how it is mine not only because I was raised there but also because my traces are all over its landscape. . . . On a street in Queens, I cut my foot as a seven-year-old and bled on the pavement . . . . On a street on the Upper West Side, my pranking eight-grade classmates wrote my home phone number in hardening concrete. . . So I lay claim to New York City as my city because my life has been staged on it, because I am embedded in it. (Padilla Peralta 298)

The specifics of place are important to Padilla Peralta because the physical space is marked by his existence—thus place, socially constructed and with social meanings, *includes him*. This argument enriches and deepens the standard refrain of shorter, more abbreviated DREAMer narratives that *they belong here.*

Dan-el's life narrative also complicates the standard "meritorious DREAMer" story by showing us a more fully fleshed-out individual

---

than this storyline suggests in isolation—one who certainly had accomplishments but could also potentially have been excluded from qualification for a DREAM Act based on the stupidities of young teenagers who don't know any better. Dan-el's intelligence and studiousness earn him spots and scholarships to a prestigious private high school, then to Princeton, then to Oxford for graduate school—in this way, like Reyna, he conforms to the storyline of academic achievement. But Dan-el extends this narrative; he is not *just* a student getting good grades. As he notes in his prologue, "It was so played out, this whole hood-boy-in-richy-rich-school saga; my story was just a variation on a familiar theme" (Padilla Peralta 4). It is a stock narrative, however, that he actively resists.

In one episode, he describes planning a shoplifting of headphones and other music paraphernalia from Tower Records with his friends from Resurrection Church. Even though, by this point in his career, he is attending Collegiate School and planning to apply to ivy league universities, he is the planner and organizer of the shoplifting endeavor, taking the "blame" retrospectively squarely upon himself: "I'd been fucking stupid to get caught up in this mess in the first place" (Padilla Peralta 155). But, although this incident would seem to place Dan-el within the "bad immigrant" model, this single experiment with crime hardly rules out Dan-el's potential for contribution to society, as his later accomplishments indicate; rather, it is much more in line with the countless numbers of *citizen* teenagers who do stupid (and illegal) things in their youth, when the awareness of consequences is not yet fully developed, and go on to be accomplished adults.

As Dan-el notes in his epilogue, he has been forced "to confront the stories that could and would be told about me if I did not take charge of their telling. . . . I had and have no intention of ever being only a Dominican, or a minority, or an undocumented immigrant, or a Spanish Harlem resident; or a Collegiate man, a Princeton man, an Oxford man" (Padilla Peralta 294-95). Dominant racist and anti-immigrant stereotypes shape the "stories that could and would be told" about the first four categories such that they easily fit within the "bad immigrant" mold; conversely, equally reductive stereotypes about the last three categories fit them within the story of a "good immigrant" or meritorious DREAMer. Dan-el's retrospective narrative, as well as his crafting of the "plot" of his memoir, insists on his intersectionality—he is not any one of these things but all of them, even though they might complicate the stories told for strategic political purposes.

Conclusion: The Gilded Cage

On September 5, 2017, President Donald Trump—who had been elected the previous November with a campaign platform that included the deportation of all undocumented immigrants—announced the end of DACA. One documentary compilation of the stories of DREAMers from San Francisco State University, posted to YouTube in December 2016, bears witness to the tremendous fears of students who already had some sense of the changes in immigration policy and enforcement that were soon to come ("Undocumented and Unafraid 'In Loving Memory'"). While an earlier era of DREAMer testimonies available on YouTube and in anthologies spoke of what it was like as teenagers to live in the shadows, the emerging post-DACA era testimonies might well prove to be notably different. DREAMers who became eligible for DACA when it was implemented in 2012 have had the experience of not needing to live entirely underground lives. The suddenness of change in policy, which threatens to drive DREAMers back into the shadows, has also stimulated a striking new production of testimonies about the psychological effects of living in a post-DACA era.

Recently, stories have also emerged in the media of DREAMers who returned to their home countries—either through deportation, or through voluntary relocation. While some of these stories attest to a sense of displacement and disorientation in their "home" country, some also bear witness, retrospectively, to the severe restrictions in the United States that stymied fulfillment. One of these stories is of Orlando Lopez, who came to the US at age three and grew up in Fort Worth, Texas, but was deported back to Mexico when he was twenty-four years old (after being released from prison, where criminal activity had landed him as a teenager). He is now married and supervises over eighty employees in Mexico. He says, "Being deported was the best thing that's happened to me. . . . The rhythm of the life I was living, I would have been a statistic. . . . Being here in Mexico, I found my wife and we have a beautiful baby daughter together—those are huge blessings." To DREAMers still in the US, he has this message to pass on: "Though your cage may be gilded, it doesn't stop being a prison. . . . In Mexico, at least you'd be free" (Blanco). Narratives of DREAMers in this new post-DACA age are likely continue to complicate and contest both prevailing stereotypes about undocumented immigrants and the paradigmatic DREAMer narratives, shaped for strategic political purposes, that circulated in the first decade of the new millennium.

Works Cited

Blanco, Octavio. "Getting Deported Was the Best Thing that Ever Happened To Me." *CNN Money*, 24 Jun. 2017, money.cnn.com/2017/06/24/news/economy/deported-mexico-immigrant/index.html/. Accessed 15 Oct. 2017.

Caminero-Santangelo, Marta. *Documenting the Undocumented: Latino/a Narrative and Social Justice in the Era of Operation Gatekeeper.* U of Florida P, 2016.

_____. "DREAMers: Youth and Migration / American DREAMers and Mexico." *Modern Mexican Culture*, edited by Stuart A. Day, U of Arizona P, 2017.

Doreen, Massey, editor. *Space, Place, and Gender.* Polity P, 1994.

Golash-Boza, Tanya. "Racism, Citizenship, and Deportation in the United States." *Open Democracy*, 23 Jun. 2015, www.opendemocracy.net/beyondslavery/tanya-golashboza/racism-citizenship-and-deportation-in-united-states/. Accessed 26 Nov. 2017.

Gonzales, Roberto G. *Lives in Limbo: Undocumented and Coming of Age in America.* U of California P, 2015.

Grande, Reyna. *The Distance Between Us.* Washington Square P, 2012.

Honig, Bonnie. *Democracy and the Foreigner.* Princeton UP, 2001.

Kalma. "The Undocumented." *Papers: Stories by Undocumented Youth*, edited by José Manuel, et al. Graham Street Productions, 2012, p. 34.

Krogstad, Jens Manuel. "5 Facts about Latinos and Education." *Pew Research Center*, 28 Jul. 2016, www.pewresearch.org/fact-tank/2016/07/28/5-facts-about-latinos-and-education/. Accessed 26 Nov. 2017.

Padilla Peralta, Dan-el. *Undocumented: A Dominican Boy's Odyssey from a Homeless Shelter to the Ivy League*. Penguin, 2015.

"Undocumented and Unafraid." *YouTube*, Shatteredverve, 28 Feb. 2011, www.youtube.com/watch?v=xdOrxLLHo0U/. Accessed 11 June 2016.

"Undocumented and Unafraid 'In Loving Memory of Gaby'." *YouTube*, Guerra Production, 7 Dec. 2016, www.youtube.com/watch?v=VLnLC7Xv6S4/. Accessed 1 Nov. 2017.

Reading about the Migrant and Immigrant Experiences in Latina and Latino Young Adult (YA) Literatures: Identities and Voices of Youth and Families

R. Joseph Rodríguez

Oh, America, can you see and notice us, standing before you?
On your lands and shores we arrive: tossed into detention
for a place at your table and in your pages of history.
Who's a pioneer or settler now? We migrate to your door
for inalienable rights and truths so self-evident.
Stories you cover and hide like our face and labor.
See us now and be the liberty that enlightens the world.
R. Joseph Rodríguez, from "Oh, America, Can You See?"
(Rodríguez, "Oh, America, Can You See Us?")

Immigrants who come to the United States are by nature optimists—
they leave everything they know and love in hopes of a better life.
(Sonia Nazario, *Enrique's Journey, Adapted for Young People* 15)

Introduction
Many migrants who travel in search of labor as well as immigrants who leave their place of birth to live permanently in a new country arrive daily to the lands and shores of the United States. They seek entry for a new life filled with hope and equal opportunity. Their reasons for immigrating vary, but often they have been driven out of their native countries due to instability and strife, caused by factors such as discrimination, persecution, poverty, violence, and war. The new arrivals range in status from naturalized citizens, legal permanent residents, refugees, asylum seekers, and international students to those on long-term temporary visas and others designated as unauthorized immigrants. With new policies enacted by the US Congress each year, categories and opportunities vary and change, leading to challenges in gaining access to equal opportunity and a better life in the United States.

The US Census Bureau reported that, as of July 1, 2016, people of Hispanic origin are the nation's largest ethnic or racial minority. Overall, Latinos constitute 17.8 percent of the nation's total population. Of the Latino population, youth are a significant group. More specifically, for Latino-origin youth, as Eileen Patten has explained, "Hispanics are the youngest major racial or ethnic group in the United States. About one-third, or 17.9 million, of the nation's Hispanic population is younger than 18, and about a quarter, or 14.6 million, of all Hispanics are Millennials (ages 18 to 33 in 2014)" (3). Latino-origin adolescents comprise a large segment of the adolescent population in the United States.

In *Tell Me How It Ends: An Essay in Forty Questions*, Valeria Luiselli chronicles the North American refugee experiences of youth and their families and the interrogations they face on paper and in person in their pursuit of residency and citizenship. "Why did you come to the United States?" the children are often asked (Luiselli 12). The answer is often about reunification with their families. The stories of migration and immigration appear in American literature as nonfiction, fiction, poetry, and drama and are written by authors from diverse backgrounds, cultures, nationalities, and religions. Their narratives are connected to the pluralism and histories shaping what has become our union to the present day and include youth seeking to name their identities as scribes, residents, and citizens of a new country they now call home (Rodríguez, *Enacting Adolescent Literacies*).

In the making of the United States, indigenous communities faced persecution and extermination due to European immigration and policies enacted to create displacement and land theft in the name of progress to the detriment of many (Zinn and Stefoff). Today, recent arrivals must navigate bureaucracies and endure harsh treatment through policies that often lead to detention and expulsion.

Defining Our Changing Identities

To define the terms Latina and Latino can become a challenge, with varied meanings influenced by geography and multiracial categories. For this chapter, the definition and explanation provided

---

by Suzanne Bost and Frances R. Aparicio are fitting for a discussion of both immigration and young adult (YA) literature. With an inclusive interpretation of histories and a hemispheric vision, Bost and Aparicio explain,

> The history and politics of US Latino/a literature are distinct. "Latino/a" identity is a product of layers of conquest, colonialism, and cultural mixture—beginning with Western European territorial battles upon indigenous lands of the "New World," from the sixteenth through the nineteenth centuries, and, after most Latin American nations achieved independence, continuing through the US imperialist expansions of the nineteenth century to the present. (2)

This definition, which is interconnected with diverse influences—from colonization to sociopolitical encounters—informs the chapter, and thus the term Latina/o will be favored to reflect the hemispheric diversity and US diversity of Latino-origin adolescents and their families.

Culture, like identity, can be fluid and ever-changing, and this also applies to self-affirmation, self-identification, and self-membership of both migrants and immigrants coming of age in the United States. Alma Flor Ada and F. Isabel Campoy describe the Latina/o ethnic group as follows: "Most Latinos and Latinas have mixed origins: whether by blood or by culture. Their heritage includes roots from indigenous, African, and Spanish people, as well as the many others who have settled in Latin America over centuries" (7). Thus, histories, policies, and migration affect how Americans view newly-arrived immigrants and their place in US education and labor as well as the greater civic society.

In *Lives in Limbo: Undocumented and Coming of Age in America*, Roberto Gonzales notes, "[A] complex web of polarizing rhetoric regarding the place of immigrants in American society entangles the lives of these young undocumented Mexican immigrants. Descriptions such as 'innocent' and 'deserving' vie with ones such as 'illegal' that conflate nationality, immigration status, and outsiderness" (Gonzales 4). In the "web of polarizing" binaries, young immigrants' voices tend to remain unheard or are relegated to the margin and away from the larger picture of telling their story as they come of age as immigrants in American society.

Young Adult (YA) literature provides avenues to express experiences and possibilities of hope for newcomers and new Americans. In *Young Adult Literature in the 21ˢᵗ Century*, Pam B. Cole identified the following as characteristics that have historically defined YA literature as a genre:

1. The protagonist is a teenager.
2. Events revolve around the protagonist and his/her struggle to resolve conflict.
3. The story is told from the viewpoint and in the voice of a young adult.
4. Literature is written by and for young adults.
5. Literature is marketed to the young adult audience.
6. Story doesn't have a "storybook" or "happily-ever-after" ending—a characteristic of children's books.
7. Parents are noticeably absent or at odds with young adults.
8. Themes address coming-of-age issues (e.g., maturity, sexuality, relationships, drugs).
9. Books contain under 300 pages, closer to 200. (49)

These characteristics position YA literature as being simultaneously distinct and accessible to both adolescents and adult populations. As a genre, YA literature continues to appeal to many readers, with bestselling and award-winning titles coming out each year.

Nilda Flores-González argues that immigrant Latina and Latino youths' narratives "capture their feeling of exclusion from the imagined American community along three dimensions—racial categorization, racial hierarchy, and national inclusion" (2). She adds, "Racialized along these three dimensions, these youths find themselves outside of the boundaries of how 'American' is defined. Yet their narratives challenge their exclusion and push for their recognition as Americans" (2). In the face of exclusion, youth are claiming their selfhood and identities in the making of their own journey in a new land.

In the essay titled "What Good Is Literature in Our Time?," Rudolfo A. Anaya reflects on the purpose of literature at the turn of the century. He explains, "Literature and art have always provided direction. The great myths of the past teach that the eternal return is possible for the individual and for the community" (Anaya 472). At the same time, forces of both exclusion and inclusion appear in literature as human migrations change demographics and societal participation. Moreover, whether voices are valued by canon keepers can often determine whether works are regarded as possessing literary merit and are studied in literature classrooms. However, this is changing as teachers' text selections now include the hemispheric Américas.

How are definitions and identities of Latinas/os shaping what we read, examine, and nationalize? John Morán González notes,

> Latina/o literature renders in aesthetically powerful ways the dynamics of life-in-diaspora that has become characteristic of the contemporary world, in which migrant flows continually disturb the boundaries of the nationalisms they exceed, whether that of the sending nation or that of the receiving one. Simultaneously, Latina/o literature indexes the historical development of life-in-diaspora through the specific stages of its unfolding in the Américas over more than two centuries. (xxiii)

The indexing that González describes mirrors the experiences of many migrants and immigrants whose stories also appear in YA literature. However, in the building of a literary canon about the migrant and immigrant experience, issues concerning belonging and non-belonging, inclusion and exclusion, and native and non-native status of both migrant and immigrant readership are evident. For instance, the exclusion and inclusion do not rest solely on the editors and the adopted texts in digital and nondigital forms, but on educators and readers who decide whose voices merit literary analysis and have value. In the article "A Postcolonial Primer with Multicultural YA Literature," Victor Malvo-Juvera argues, "By connecting fictive texts and real-world examples, students can begin to understand how immigrants are often Othered through debasement in political discourse" (47). Thus, in the selected extracts from YA literature that follow, the youth and their families presented are humanized via literary works that tell their stories of struggle, survival, and triumph as they come of age in a country divided by their presence, contributions, and future.

Meet Enrique and the Journey

Pulitzer Prize-winner Sonia Nazario's journalism addresses some of this country's on-going challenges that include hunger, drug addiction, and immigration. Her reporting and writing about social issues affecting US life and thought span more than twenty years. A fluent Spanish speaker and of Jewish ancestry, Nazario's personal history includes living in Argentina during the *Guerra Sucia*, Dirty War, which the Argentine government named during state-sanctioned terrorism from 1974 through 1983.

In 2000, a sixteen-year-old boy named Enrique left his home village in Honduras in search of his mother, who had immigrated years earlier to the United States. Nazario retraced the journey that both Lourdes, Enrique's mother, and Enrique braved through Central America and México to reach the United States. Nazario, in *Enrique's Journey; The True Story of a Boy Determined to Reunite with His Mother, Adapted for Young People*, tells their story of separation and homecoming to shine a light for Americans, who are often shielded from the fact-based stories of struggle to reach a new country. In fact, she notes six guiding questions that informed her migrant journey as a journalist in order to narrate the odyssey of Latina and Latino immigrants:

1. What's the exact route migrants take?
2. What are the best and worst things that can happen at each step of the way?
3. The places where migrants face the greatest cruelty? And the greatest kindness?

4. Where are the places along the [train] tracks where the gangs rob, where the bandits kill people?
5. Where do Mexican immigration authorities stop the train?
6. Might I be the only woman on the train? (Nazario 15)

Enrique is young, resilient, and determined to reach his mother in the United States. He leaves Honduras on a perilous journey riddled with danger and violence; during his numerous attempts to arrive in the United States and reunite with his mother, he often encounters law enforcement officers and vigilantes, who send him back to Honduras. Nazario paints the picture of his circumstances and journeys as follows:

> Enrique wades chest-deep across the Río Suchiate. The river forms a border. Behind him is Guatemala. Before him is México's southernmost state, Chiapas. *"Ahora nos enfrentamos a la bestia.* Now we face the beast," migrants say when they enter Chiapas. Enrique will risk "the beast" again because he needs to find his mother. This is his eighth attempt to reach *el Norte.* (65)

Nazario, like Enrique, rides *El Tren de la Muerte*—The Train of Death—as it traverses the length of México for a nearly 1,450-mile journey. The freight train line is also known as *La Bestia*—The Beast— and *El Tren de los Desconocidos*—The Train of the Unknowns—by its riders, who endure hardship and even face death as they ride atop the trains and hold on to make the journey North. The journey is treacherous and risks include death, which riders face along the thousand-mile stretch through the continent.

In a reflection, Nazario explains, "Enrique and the migrants I spent time with gave me a priceless gift. They reminded me of the value of what I have. They taught me that people are willing to die in their quest to obtain what I often take for granted" (14). Nazario's reflection reveals the perils migrants face daily and the comfort and safety many Americans take for granted. She argues that immigrants "become our neighbors, children in our schools, [and] workers in our homes" to form a 'greater fabric' of the United States" (15).

Meet Julia Reyes in Chicago

Erika L. Sánchez describes herself as "a poet, feminist, and cheerleader for young women everywhere." Moreover, she is an essayist, journalist, and novelist who grew up in the mostly working-class town of Cicero, Illinois, which borders Chicago's southwest side. As a daughter of undocumented Mexicans from the state of Durango, Sánchez possesses the determination to defy borders of any kind in her life and art. While growing up, her role model was—and continues to be—Lisa Simpson from the animated sitcom *The Simpsons*. She explained that since she was twelve years old, she dreamed of becoming a successful writer. Moreover, she dreamed of writing complex, empowering narratives about girls of color and, especially, stories that she yearned to read then as a young adult.

In Sánchez's YA novel *I Am Not Your Perfect Mexican Daughter*, readers meet the protagonist Julia Reyes, who is US-born and a daughter of Mexican-origin, immigrant parents living in Chicago, Illinois. Partly autofictive and loosely based on Sánchez's experiences, Julia is coming of age as an adolescent in a changing, conflicting world. Julia has already had to deal with the accidental death of her older sister Olga, who was killed as she entered a crosswalk. Known as the least favorite daughter, Julia must face conflicts within her family and also define herself in her own terms as an adolescent. Julia's mother has plans for her daughter's development and future that are not Julia's choices. The plans include a *quinceañera*, adherence to cultural norms, and acceptance of family responsibilities that are often in conflict with practices in the United States. In an empowering, first-person point of view, Julia explains,

> I've done the calculations and have figured out that from the ages of thirteen to fifteen, I've spent about forty-five percent of my life grounded. Seriously, what kind of life is that? I know I mess up sometimes, I know I can be a sarcastic jerk, I know I'm not the daughter my parents wanted, but Amá treats me like I'm a degenerate. (Sánchez 116)

Julia's analysis is the story of cultural change and shifts that many adolescent children of immigrants can face in the United States. This may be due to cultural expectations and pressures as well as generational change affected by families immigrating to a new country. Julia's perspectives shed light on becoming and being an independent, female adolescent, but also succumbing to the expectations and norms as a first-generation immigrant who is influenced by two cultures, identities, and ways of seeing the world.

Julia's perception of the border conflicts with the enforcement and policies that were enacted for control and authority. She points out to her boyfriend Esteban on a trip in central México: "[The border's] nothing by a giant wound, a big gash between two countries. Why does it have to be like that? I don't understand. It's just some random, stupid line. How can anyone tell people where they can and can't go?" (Sánchez 280). Julia's interpretations of the border are marked by alienation, frustration, and even anger faced by many who traverse borders seeking a better life.

We read about Julia's ways of seeing and reading the world that includes the following six essential experiences and trials: (1) developing and maintaining friendships as an adolescent who is coming of age, (2) facing verbal and sexual harassment as well as low expectations, (3) coming to sexuality on her own terms as an adolescent girl, (4) accepting her identity as a writer in the face of obstacles and indifference, (5) meeting a boyfriend who cares and listens with mindfulness, and (6) pursuing higher education with the support of a teacher and her own family.

Julia's visit to her parents' native land permits her to meet more of her extended family members. She witnesses their ways of coping and surviving, which make the migrant and immigrant journeys more complex, relevant, and vivid for Julia far from her native Chicago. She learns about her parents' traumatic journey across the Río Grande into El Paso, Texas, and their migration thereafter to the Midwestern United States. Lastly, Julia faces emotional, family, and social conflicts, which include mistreatment and self-harm. She learns to understand change in the quest to become human and loved.

Looking Homeward or Coming Home Again

The poet Diana García was born in the San Joaquín Valley of California, in a migrant farm labor camp owned by the California Packing Corporation. She pursued university studies in creative writing and remains committed to social action by documenting the stories of migrant-worker life in the United States. Her poems humanize the lives of laborers and their families as she constructs narratives that are both simple and complex with sensory detail that reflect sociopolitical realities. García's poems capture the everyday affairs of children, men, and women who are in constant movement to live, work, and survive with dignity.

García examines the point of view of people living outside of the United States as well as those who have chosen the United States for a better life. In fact, many choices and circumstances are faced by people who become desperate in the search for employment and safety for themselves and their families. García's poems humanize the story of leaving home and coming home again for both the migrant and immigrant in a changing, global world shaped by competing economies.

Like in Nazario's account about Enrique, the human movement northward via El Tren de la Muerte, The Train of Death, appears as a North Star to a life with opportunities for poor and working-class families. For instance, in the narrative poem "On Staying Behind," García provides the perspective of a mother regarding her daughter's imminent migration:

> She thinks I don't know why she runs. Not to catch the trains
> or escape *la migra* or outrun packs of wild dogs. I listened
> to the advice her cousins sent, the older girl cousins, married,
> hard-working girls who left our village with their husbands.
> The journey is harsh, more than two weeks if she's lucky.
> So many dangers, only two younger male cousins to protect her.
> My daughter has no husband. She cannot stay with me. I will
> not have her stay with me to starve. She leaves with no wealth.
> She and her cousins are their own wealth. I see the strength
> in their arms and shoulders, blood that pumps through heart and lungs.
> No water, no beans or corn. Today, the woman studying our village,

---

una profe de los Estados Unidos, spilled our pot of beans.
This woman has never known hunger. I saw her shock when I sifted
beans from dirt, placed beans, dirt, the bit of water I had planned to use
for grinding the last dried corn. What is a little dirt, I thought, the same dirt
in which I grew these beans. A child should not see a mother starve to death.
A mother should not hear that her last daughter has disappeared.
I bless this last child, daughter of my heart, the one I hoped
would wrap my body in a *serape* and lay me next to her father
at the edge of the church yard. I bless her journey, wishing
her safe passage, fleet journey. I have said my prayers
to the village saints. I have eaten my small meal. I will lay
myself alongside her dog tonight. Perhaps tomorrow, more food
will come my way. Again, I stay behind. I will wait and hope. (11-12)

The speaker in the poem is a survivor and possesses intuition about
the generational journeys even while "stay[ing] behind." Sacrifice
and selflessness appear in the poem with a love for family and
understanding of human migrations. The poem communicates how
humans must make decisions for sustenance and everyday essentials
known as the "hierarchy of needs" in the 1943 study titled *A Theory
of Human Motivation* by Abraham H. Maslow (9). According to
Maslow's theory, humans possess "needs [that] arrange themselves
in hierarchies of pre-potency" (6). Moreover, Maslow explains:

> [T]he appearance of one need usually rests on the prior satisfaction
> of another, more pre-potent need. Man [*sic*] is a perpetually wanting
> animal. Also[,] no need or drive can be treated as if it were isolated
> or discrete; every drive is related to the state of satisfaction or
> dissatisfaction of other drives. (6)

The poem communicates the roles of a provider for others who
depend on water, beans, and corn, among other essentials. The
migrant and immigrant must remember the purpose of leaving the
homeland to undertake a journey that is also made for the sake of
those who stayed behind in bleak, challenging circumstances.

As a counterpart to the previous poem, García presents the
poem "On Leaving" in support of a dialogue on migration and
immigration. The speaker here seems to be the young adult daughter

of the speaker from the previous poem, who believes that she is ready for the journey to the North. The readers learn about the conditions that lead to flight in countries far from the United States. The journey is driven by economic and social injustices that dominate the lives of many humans seeking a better way to live and survive. García begins the poem with a description about human flight and speed to reach a destination:

> I can run five times around the village, my dog beside me. I have tested
> myself against her speed, my younger cousins' endurance. I win.
> My cousins go with me this morning, their dark hair glossy, so young
> their shoulders. Their mothers tell me to watch over them.
> I have said goodbye to all who remain, grayed village elders,
> wooden statues of saints in our small church, my mother.
> I go with the blessings of my mother and her sisters. I am the youngest
> of the girl cousins, no great beauty, no wealth to keep me here.
> I wear only what I have. I carry a blouse one aunt gave me,
> a friend's old sandals for days when heat persists into the night.
> My cousins who have made the journey send this advice: travel early
> in the morning and at night. When you reach the trains, gain a space
> in the middle; don't move. Don't let anyone steal your space. When we
> reach México, we are to look for coyotes wearing yellow bandanas,
> not red or green. Those wearing yellow come from our region,
> they speak our language, they are known to our village.
> If no one waits at the border wearing yellow, we wait or take
> our chances. I have waited two years for this chance. No more.
> If the coyotes separate me from my two cousins, *mis primas*
> instruct me to let them take what they will, but not my life, never my life.
> They think I don't know what they mean. I know what a man
> can take from a woman. I know my younger cousins' pride.
> I will protect them from their pride, our family honor. I will scream
> or fight if I can. I will run if I can. I know now how fast I can run. (12-13)

The poem presents the endangered lives of migrants and immigrants who, in the quest for a better life, are then beset by danger, stress, and violence, much like an odyssey with tribulations and tragedies. Speed on foot as a hiker or runner can save a life, but danger lurks for all and that includes physical and sexual assaults. Specific codes, rules, and messengers appear in the journey and can either help or hinder the traveler seeking to arrive safely at the destination in México and the United States. Overall, the journey is treacherous and imperiled by many difficult circumstances and possibilities.

García's two corresponding poems chronicle the odysseys of migrants and immigrants seeking a better life. This often means that people must leave their native lands to survive elsewhere, far from familiar spaces with extended family members.

The circumstances immigrants face are depicted by García in a humanizing manner to bring voice to their plight in flight. In a complementary approach, the anthropologist Jason De León chronicles the "lives and bodies of undocumented people" who face "complicated life histories that reflect an intimate relationship with transnational migration and global economic inequality" (4-5).

Future Migrations and Immigrants

Families immigrate to the United States due to the instabilities created by an international superpower along with other countries in the parts of the world that they currently inhabit (Mignolo). The journalist José Antonio Vargas describes his immigrant journey as follows:

> I struggled with conflicting realities of belonging and exclusion and still do. My mother and I have not seen each other in person for over twenty years, not from deportation, but from an equally unyielding U.S. immigration policy that prevented her, a single parent with limited means, from legally joining me in California when my grandfather smuggled me over from the Philippines at age twelve. I weathered the transition as best I could. (xi-xii)

Vargas's perspectives about belonging, inclusion, and exclusion are prevalent in YA literature. The experiences articulated by characters in YA literature emphasize the challenges faced by young immigrants across the country in their families, schools, and civic communities.

As shown in the narratives that feature Enrique and Julia, and the speakers in the two poems, immigrants face tribulations and hardships that they must overcome to make a new life in a new country. The experiences presented are fraught with chaos, indifference, and uncertainty as immigrants attempt to claim a home, identity, and voice. To gain their selfhood, these individuals seek a community of hope and inclusion that values their humanity and dignity.

Works Cited

Ada, Alma Flor, and F. Isabel Campoy. *Yes! We Are Latinos: Poems and Prose about the Latino Experience.* Charlesbridge, 2013.

Anaya, Rudolfo A. "What Good Is Literature in Our Time?" *American Literary History*, vol. 100, no. 3, 1998, pp. 471-477.

Blanco, Richard. *The Prince of los Cocuyos: A Miami Childhood.* Ecco Press, Harper Collins, 2014.

Bost, Suzanne, and Frances R. Aparicio. "Introduction." *The Routledge Companion to Latino/a Literature*, edited by Suzanne Bost and Frances R. Aparicio, Routledge, 2013, pp. 1-10.

Cole, Pam B. *Young Adult Literature in the 21st Century.* McGraw-Hill Higher Education, 2009.

De León, Jason. *The Land of Open Graves: Living and Dying on the Migrant Trail.* U of California P, 2015.

Flores-González, Nilda. *Citizens but Not Americans: Race and Belonging among Latino Millennials.* New York UP, 2017.

García, Diana. "On Leaving." *Prairie Schooner*, vol. 88, no. 4, 2014, pp. 11-12.

_____. "On Staying Behind." *Prairie Schooner*, vol. 88, no. 4, 2014, pp. 12-13.

Gonzales, Roberto G. *Lives in Limbo: Undocumented and Coming of Age in America.* U of California P, 2016.

González, John Morán. "Introduction." *The Cambridge Companion to Latina/o American Literature*, edited by John Morán González, Cambridge UP, 2016, pp. xxiii-xxxv.

Luiselli, Valeria. *Tell Me How It Ends: An Essay in Forty Questions.* Translated by Lizzie Davis, Coffee House P, 2017.

Malvo-Juvera, Victor. "A Postcolonial Primer with Multicultural YA Literature." *English Journal*, vol. 107, no. 1, 2017, pp. 41-47.

Maslow, Abraham H. *A Theory of Motivation.* Martino Fine Books, 2013.

Mignolo, Walter. *Local Histories/Global Designs: Coloniality, Subaltern Knowledges, and Border Thinking.* Princeton UP, 2000.

Nazario, Sonia. *Enrique's Journey (The Young Adult Adaptation): The True Story of a Boy Determined to Reunite with His Mother.* Ember, 2014.

Patten, Eileen. *The Nation's Latino Population Is Defined by its Youth.* Pew Research Center, 2016.

Rodríguez, R. Joseph. *Enacting Adolescent Literacies across Communities: Latino/a Scribes and Their Rites.* Lexington Books, The Rowman & Littlefield Group, Inc, 2017.

_____. "Oh, America, Can You See Us?" Unpublished poem, 2018.

Sánchez, Erika L. *I Am Not Your Perfect Mexican Daughter.* Knopf Books for Young Readers, 2017.

US Census Bureau. "Facts for Features: Hispanic Heritage Month 2017." *Profile American Facts for Features*, 31 Aug. 2017, www.census.gov/newsroom/facts-for-features/2017/hispanic-heritage.html. Accessed 25 Oct. 2017.

Vargas, Jose Antonio. "Foreword." *Lives in Limbo: Undocumented and Coming of Age in America*, by Roberto G. Gonzales, U of California P, 2016, pp. xi-xiv.

Zinn, Howard, and Rebecca Stefoff. *A Young People's History of the United States: Columbus to the War on Terror.* Seven Stories P, 2009.

Aspiration and Disillusionment: Undocumented Experiences in Imbolo Mbue's *Behold the Dreamers*

Maryse Jayasuriya

Anna V. Ortiz Juarez-Paz has asserted that

> general discursive constructs of the immigrant continue to be negatively framed. Predominantly absent from the conversation is the humanity of undocumented immigrants. Their voice is rarely heard; most of the focus found in public discourse is on the number of undocumented immigrants living in the United States or on what anti-immigration policy has been proposed. Most notably, however, how are we going to take care of the problem, the border problem? (165-166).

At a time when the fear of deportation can make undocumented immigrants understandably hesitant to tell their stories, fiction can play a role in bringing attention to the experiences and the humanity of such immigrants. At the same time, the majority of narratives about undocumented immigrants tends to focus on specific demographics—primarily immigrants from Mexico or various countries in Central America. Undocumented immigrants who come to the United States from other regions are seldom depicted in fiction. One exception is Kiran Desai's Booker Prize-winning novel, *Inheritance of Loss*, which features Biju, a young man from a working-class family in India who arrives in New York City and works in a series of restaurants as part of a "shadow class" of undocumented immigrants who are desperate to remain in the country and therefore particularly vulnerable to exploitation. His story challenges the typical representation of South Asian immigrants to the United States as being part of a "model minority"—those who arrive in the United States pursuing or already armed with a tertiary education and who go on to make comfortable middle-class lives for themselves as professionals in the hostland.

Another exception to the dearth of fiction about undocumented immigrants from outside the Americas is Imbolo Mbue's recent and highly-acclaimed novel *Behold the Dreamers* (winner of the Pen/Faulkner Award for Fiction, a *New York Times Book Review* Notable Book of the Year, and named one of the best books of the year in numerous other venues, as the cover blurb proclaims). According to Mbue, herself an immigrant from Cameroon who lost her job in market research in New York during the financial crisis of the last decade, "I wanted to write about what it's like to be working class [. . . .] To be struggling with poverty, to be barely getting by in America. I wanted to write about what it's like to be an immigrant. I wanted to write about me" (Rocco 22). Her debut novel presents undocumented immigrants from Cameroon, who arrive not only after the events of 9/11 but around the time of the global financial crisis in 2007–2008. The novel explores what it means to be in pursuit of the much-vaunted American Dream without the aid of necessary documentation and at a particular moment in the recent history of the United States when people at all levels of American society were affected by the economic downturn.

Arjun Appadurai has asserted that imagination is no longer a mere fantasy, an escape from reality, or an act of contemplation; instead, it is "a form of work (both in the sense of labor and of culturally organized practice) and a form of negotiation between sites of agency ('individuals') and globally defined fields of possibility" (30). An instance of the kind of work that Appadurai refers to can be seen in the efforts made by the protagonists of Mbue's novel to bridge the gap between their place of origin and the locus of desire and, thereafter, the work they put in—the desperate measures they take—to stay in the desired location. My essay analyzes the way in which Mbue depicts how and why the hegemonic idea of the American Dream becomes ingrained in people outside the United States and what, if anything, can lead to its dissolution.

The novel begins with Jende Jonga, a young man from Cameroon, on the day he obtains employment as the chauffeur of Clark Edwards, a senior executive at Lehman Brothers, and it explores the developing relationship between employee and employer. While the focus is on Jende and his wife Neni's life in Harlem, there are flashbacks to their lives in their homeland in Central Africa and the series of events that led to their emigration. The novel also goes on to examine the subsequent interweaving of the lives of Jende, Neni, and their young son Liomi with those of Clark's wife Cindy and their sons Vince and Mighty as a result of Jende driving the Edwards family around and Neni doing temporary work for Cindy and getting to know the Edwards offspring. Similar to the upstairs/downstairs dynamic depicted in many Victorian novels and also in more recent novels, like *The Remains of the Day* and television productions such as *Downton Abbey*, Jende and Neni become privy to what goes on in the Edwards household— from Clark's marital infidelities and Cindy's seeking refuge in prescription pills and alcohol to Vince's growing disillusionment with the materialism and exploitation of the capitalist society in which he lives and Mighty's anxieties about his parents' crumbling marriage. While one family struggles to save money and get the much-desired "papiers" that will lead to permanent residency and citizenship, the other faces disintegration as a result of the stress caused by the imminent collapse of Lehman Brothers, which exacerbates the already dysfunctional relationships among the family members.

Mbue captures the precarity faced by undocumented immigrants in their daily lives. When Jende is being interviewed by Clark initially, he is petrified when the subject of documentation comes up, and he has to "keep his desperation from bursting through the thin layer of dignity it had been wrapped in throughout the interview" (Mbue 10). As undocumented immigrants, Jende and Neni have both been frequently cautioned against talking to anyone about their legal status even though this is what is uppermost in their minds: "You tell person say you no get paper, the lawyer had said, the day you get palaver with them, they go call Immigration, report you" (236). Consequently, they are hesitant to mention their anxieties to even their closest friends. They do not feel free to move around the country at will and returning to the homeland for visits is an option that is foreclosed to them. When Jende's father passes away suddenly, "his sorrow at not being able to bury his father was as heavy as his grief at the death" (303). Friends gather to console him, but none of them asks whether he will be going back home for the funeral because they do not want to broach the sensitive topic of immigration status: "They figured he would tell them if he was going, and if he wasn't going, well, no grown man should be made to tell anyone that he couldn't go home to bury his father" (301).

Undocumented immigrants like Jende and Neni are compelled to learn very quickly about the complexities of immigration policies in the United States as well as the implications of sudden changes to such policies. They read up about these policies online, discuss them with a trusted few friends and relations, and consult lawyers when possible. In the case of Jende, he has the help of his cousin Winston—who won a green card lottery and then joined the army, which allowed him to get an education and eventually become a successful lawyer working on Wall Street—and Bubakar, the Nigerian storefront immigration lawyer whose services they have procured. Jende had originally arrived on a three-month tourist visa, though his intention was always to stay on. As he ponders on the seeming naiveté of US immigration officials later,

> Who traveled to America only to return to a future of nothingness in Cameroon after a mere three months? Not young men like him, not people facing a future of poverty and despondence in their own country. No, people like him did not visit America. They got there and stayed there until they could return home as conquerors—as green card- or American passport-bearing conquerors with pockets full of dollars and photos of a happy life. (Mbue 19)

Once the tourist visa expired, he applied for asylum. As a result of a delay in an asylum hearing, his lawyer was able to get him his EAD (Employment Authorization Document), which in turn enabled Jende to save enough money to bring over his then-girlfriend and their son. His status as an asylum seeker with a work permit and a driver's license makes it possible for Neni to get a student visa and enroll in community college.

The information available or proffered to immigrants is not always reliable or sufficient, however. Instead of applying for political asylum, Jende offers as truthful a reason as he can come up with for his asylum application—the story that his wife's father will throw him in prison if he returns to Cameroon, even though he is not facing any such persecution in the homeland. He finds out too late that a more dire-sounding reason is required, even if that narrative has no connection to truth or reality. As Bubakar puts it, "How'd you think all these people who gain asylum do it? [. . .] You think they are all running away from something? Puh-leez. [. . .] I just won asylum last month for the daughter of a prime minister of some country in East Africa. [. . .] And here she is, saying she's afraid for her life back home" (Mbue 20). Jende and Neni also find out the many restrictions imposed on those who do not have US citizenship. Neni, for example, is selected for an honor society due to her excellent academic performance in community college but is not eligible for many of the scholarships that she so desperately needs to stay on in school.

In certain ways, Jende and Neni experience what all immigrants have to face as a result of their relocation. There is constant pressure from family and friends in the homeland for financial help, which strains the protagonists' meagre savings: "Someone back home would always need money from him; a month never went by without at least one phone call asking him for money. [. . .] relatives had no consideration for those who sent them money because they thought the streets of America were paved with dollar bills" (Mbue 86).

Immigrants have a type of "double consciousness" that enables them to observe and comment on the differences between their homeland and the hostland, as Homi K. Bhabha has observed in his famous apothegm that "the truest eye may now belong to the migrant's double vision" (Bhabha 8). This double consciousness is distinct from that which W. E. B. Du Bois defined in *The Souls of Black Folk* as "two souls, two thoughts, two unreconciled strivings; two warring ideals in one dark body" and identified as central to the African American experience in the United States (Du Bois 7). It does, however, offer certain analogies, as Jende and Neni view the United States through a Cameroonian lens, even as they are compelled to view themselves through an American lens. Jende, for example, is flummoxed by Cindy's job as a nutritionist: "People in this country, always worrying about how to eat, they pay someone good money to tell them: Eat this, don't eat that. If you don't know how to eat, what else can you know how to do in this world?" (Mbue 28). Neni freely attends African parties thrown by people whom she has never met before on the premise that: "most African people didn't care about fancy white-people ideas like attendance by invitation-only" (31). Through her protagonists' observations, Mbue is able to satirize certain American norms, values, and lifestyle choices.

Immigrants are also able to appreciate and be nostalgic for their country of origin despite the negative aspects of that country that have driven them to leave it. Like most first-generation immigrants, Jende and Neni have times when they are homesick and yearn for the familiarity of the lifestyle they enjoyed there. Jende refers to his hometown as a "town made of magic" and tells his employer that "in Limbe, we live simple lives, but we enjoy our lives well" (Mbue 38). He thinks longingly of the network of friends that he spent time with, while Neni savors the memory of market days and the pleasure of bargaining with vendors for the best deals.

At the same time, they both have specific reasons for leaving their homeland and their families and coming to the United States. For Jende, the reason relates to class—if he had stayed on in the country of his birth, he would never have been able to achieve his goals due to a lack of resources and connections, which preclude his obtaining a good education or a white-collar job and therefore any hope of upward mobility. As Jende tries to explain to Clark, "I stay in my country, I would have become nothing. I would have remained nothing. My son will grow up and be poor like me, just like I was poor like my father. But in America, sir? I can become something. I can become a respectable man. My son can become a respectable man" (Mbue 39). Jende goes on to say "Because . . . because in my country [. . .] for you to become somebody, you have to be somebody first. You do not come from a family with money, forget it. You do not come from a family with a name, forget it. That is just how it is, sir. Someone like me, what can I ever become in a country like Cameroon?" (40). Jende cites the case of Barack Obama, who at the time in which the novel is set was running for the presidency, as the perfect example of what a man who comes from nothing—someone without family wealth or influence like himself—can achieve in the United States. For Neni, on the other hand, gender is the reason for her desire to emigrate—the patriarchal society of Cameroon made life difficult and limited her choices as a high school dropout and single mother: "She'd been unable to get a job because there were too few jobs in Limbe, never mind one for a young woman who hadn't made it as far as high school. She had been bored and frustrated at home, unable to have any sort of independence because she was financially dependent on her parents, unable to marry Jende because her father would not let her marry a council laborer" (311-312). She feels that she is stagnating—in limbo in Limbe—and fantasizes about life in America as a panacea for her tribulations.

In a sense, like many who aspire to immigrate to the United States, Jende and Neni subscribe to the idea of the American Dream that has been promoted through the global dominance of American popular culture—the notion that the United States is a kind of utopia that guarantees success to all those who are willing to work hard. As Jende tells Clark, "Everyone wants to come to America, sir. Everyone. To be in this country, sir. To live in this country. Ah, it is the greatest thing in the world!" (Mbue 39). When Clark's elder son Vince, a law student, tries to list the devastation wrought by American policies and interventions in order to "unindoctrinate [Jende] on all the lies [he] has been fed about America," the latter assures Vince that he will never stop believing that "America is the greatest country in the world" (103). Due to the spread of American television programs and movies, the protagonists in Mbue's novel have internalized the idea that if you are determined and work hard, anything is possible in the United States.

It wasn't that [Neni] thought that life in America had no ills—she'd watched enough episodes of *Dallas* and *Dynasty* to know that the country had its share of vicious people—but, rather, because shows like *The Fresh Prince of Bel Air* and *The Cosby Show* had shown her that there was a place in the world where blacks had the same chance at prosperity as whites. [. . .] Even after she'd seen *Boyz n the Hood* and *Do the Right Thing*, she couldn't be swayed that the kind of black life depicted represented anything but a very small percentage of black life, just like Americans probably understood that the images they saw of war and starvation in Africa were a very small percentage of African life. (Mbue 312)

Another reason for the hold that the United States has on people's imagination is that everything shared by first-generation immigrants with friends and family members in the homeland is carefully curated. "Every picture [Neni had] seen of Cameroonians in America was a portrait of bliss: children laughing in snow; couples smiling at a mall; families posing in front of a nice house with a nice car nearby" (Mbue 312). Since only good fortune is publicized and other sorrows and misfortunes are kept hidden, it is not surprising that those who remain in the homeland assume that all immigrants inevitably succeed in the United States once they get there.

Initially, this assumption seems to hold true for Jende and Neni, as they inch toward their dreams. The former has been able to scrape enough money as a cab driver to get his now-wife (on a student visa) and his son (on a visitor's visa) to the United States. His job with Clark enables him to support his wife and son, send money home, and even save at a good rate for a "down payment for a two-bedroom in Mount Vernon or Yonkers," which is their ten-year goal (Mbue 30). Neni, meanwhile, revels in what she has been able to achieve within a year and a half of her arrival: "For the first time in her life, she had a job, as a home health aide through an agency that paid her in cash, since she had no working papers. She was a matriculated student for the first time in sixteen years. [. . .] And for the very first time in her life, she had a dream besides marriage and motherhood: to become a pharmacist" (13-14). She has to pinch herself to believe that she is really in New York City and often finds herself singing more than she ever has before as she goes about her work.

Mbue's story illuminates the ironies that haunt such initial optimistic impressions. The hegemonic belief in the accessibility of the American Dream is gradually eroded by the experiences that Jende and Neni undergo in the United States. The precarious nature of the life of an undocumented immigrant means that if just one aspect of this life goes awry, it can create a domino effect and lead to disaster. First, Jende's asylum application is denied, and he is informed that he will have to face an immigration judge, which leaves Jende and Neni tense, full of trepidation, and desperate to find enough money to appeal the decision. Neni cries for the first time since her arrival in the United States at the prospect of being deported, while Jende is haunted by the fear that he will have to return to Cameroon "empty-handed" and ashamed (Mbue 60). While they try to keep each other's spirits up, they are affected psychologically by this development, which hinders communication within their relationship.

> They encouraged each other to be hopeful, to believe that they would one day realize the dream of becoming Americans. But that night they each had nightmares that they told the other nothing of the next morning. Jende dreamed of knocks on the door and strange men in uniform taking him away from his fainting wife and crying children. Neni dreamed of returning to a largely deserted Limbe, a town devoid of the young and the ambitious. (Mbue 226-227)

Secondly, Jende is suddenly and unjustly dismissed from Clark's employment. His attempt to regain his previous job as a cab driver is unsuccessful due to the economic downturn, which means that there are too many people competing for work in such a capacity. Jende has to work two jobs as a restaurant dishwasher—working twice as hard to earn less than half the money he earned as Clark's chauffeur—and develops severe back problems due to stress. He starts to question whether his stress and suffering are worthwhile and begins to consider the possibility of returning to his homeland.

This series of events emphasizes how easily the arrangements that enable undocumented life can unravel.

Jende's plans to return to Cameroon get stiff resistance, however, from Neni, who cannot bear the idea of going back to the restrictions imposed on her as a woman by a highly patriarchal society. She sees in her husband an example of the gender norms in her homeland that she so resents—he has forced her to quit her job after she becomes pregnant with their second child and tells her to drop out of school for two semesters. "He had brought her to America. He paid her tuition. He was her protector and advocate. He made the decisions for their family. Sometimes he conferred with her about his decisions. Most times he did what he deemed best. Always she had no choice but to obey. That was what he expected of her" (Mbue 172). Neni understands she can expect more of these restrictions being imposed on her not only by her husband but also by society in general if she were to go back to Cameroon and therefore comes up with strategies to avoid going back.

She begs Cindy to get Jende his job with Clark back and, when that fails, blackmails her erstwhile employer with pictures of the latter in an inebriated state. She gathers information from a variety of sources—friends, newspapers, television programs, internet search engines, and social media. She starts frequenting a progressive church not just for spiritual comfort but also in hopes that she will get assistance from the pastor and congregation with regard to her immigration status: "I was watching on the news the other day about this family that was supposed to be deported and they ran to a church. The church people let them stay in the church—the government could not touch them there" (Mbue 229). Neni tells Natasha, the pastor of the church, about her deportation fears because "she believed there were Americans who wanted to keep good hardworking immigrants in America. She'd seen them on the news, compassionate Americans talking about how the United States should be more welcoming to people who came in peace. She believed these kindhearted people, like Natasha, would never betray them" (237). While her husband's pessimism about life in America grows, Neni steadfastly believes that the United States is better for herself and her children and that "doing nothing was not an option" (285). In her desperation, she even considers divorcing her husband to marry a friend's cousin who has citizenship for the sake of obtaining a green card. When she is compelled to reject this possibility as unfeasible and risky, she ponders leaving her eldest son in the United States to be adopted by her erstwhile professor and his husband. The contrasting responses of Jende and Neni to their predicament illustrates heterogeneity in the way that immigrants adhere to the pull of the American Dream based on factors such as gender.

The discord between husband and wife concerning whether to go back home or stay on in the United States strains Jende and Neni's relationship to near-breaking point and actually leads, for the first time in their relationship, to domestic violence. Both have changed: one feels emasculated by his helplessness to change his predicament in an unwelcoming hostland, while the other realizes her own strength and fortitude and the lengths to which she is willing to go— including breaking up her family relationships if it means that they do not have to give up the American Dream. While immigration allows for self-fashioning new identities, the pressures relating to their legal status make Jende and Neni at times unrecognizable to each other and even to themselves.

Ultimately, Jende's decision to leave the United States is based on what he is not willing to put up with—such as constant stress and uncertainty—or sacrifice—such as dignity—anymore, like Biju in Desai's novel or the first-person narrator in Mohsin Hamid's *The Reluctant Fundamentalist*. As Jende attempts to explain to his wife, "I don't like what my life has become in this country. I don't know how long I can continue living like this, Neni. The suffering in Limbe was bad, but this one here, right now. . . it's more than I can take" (Mbue 306). The man who once told Vince that he would never stop believing in America's greatness now sees that even if he had documentation, his lack of education, race, and immigrant status will not enable him to achieve stability in the United States, partly due to the complex system of racial oppression of which he has now become aware and especially as a result of the Great Recession. As he points out to Neni,

> "*Papier* is not everything. In America today, having documents is not enough. Look at how many people with papers are struggling. Look at how even some Americans are suffering. They were born in this country. They have American passports, and yet they are sleeping on the street, going to bed hungry, losing their jobs and houses every day in this . . . this economic crisis." (Mbue 307)

Jende's pessimism is partly informed by his experience of the economic crisis in Cameroon, which lasted from the mid-1980s to the late 1990s, and his fear that the economic crisis in the United States could also be a long-running one. Perhaps he has also considered the detrimental impact that Clark's focus on work and material success had on the Edwards family and re-evaluated what success and happiness might mean for himself. Despite his wife's resistance and his mother's astonishment that he would wish to return to Limbe when everyone else is trying to leave, Jende petitions for, and is granted, the option of voluntary departure by the immigration judge.

Though he is unable to obtain the holy grail of the green card, Jende does return to his hometown with "pockets full of dollars" (Mbue 19) at the end of the novel. With the money he and Neni have saved as well as what Neni extorted from Cindy and what was donated by Natasha and her congregation, the couple leave the United States knowing that—as a result of the highly favorable exchange rate—they will be able to build a house, buy a car, send their children to private schools and perhaps start a business. The American Dream, for Jende and Neni, is recalibrated and becomes a Cameroonian Dream. This circular trajectory—not just from a distant homeland to the United States, but back from the United States to the original homeland—captures patterns of migration that can easily be missed when readers assume that every ticket to the United States is a one-way ticket. The Cameroonian Dream with which Jende and Neni end their story suggests the diversity of immigrant experiences and the multiplicity of immigrant dreams.

Works Cited

Appadurai, Arjun. "Disjuncture and Difference in the Global Cultural Economy." *Theorizing Diaspora*, edited by Jana Evans Braziel and Anita Mannur, Blackwell, 2003, pp. 25-48.

Bhabha, Homi K. *The Location of Culture*. Routledge, 1994.

Desai, Kiran. *The Inheritance of Loss*. Grove Press, 2006.

Du Bois, W. E. B. *The Souls of Black Folk*. 1903. Edited by Henry Louis Gates Jr. and Terri Hulme Oliver, Norton Critical Edition, W.W. Norton, 1999.

Hamid, Mohsin. *The Reluctant Fundamentalist*. Mariner, 2007.

Ortiz Juarez-Paz, Anna V. "Undocumented Identity Storytelling: (Re) framing Public Relations." *International Journal of Media and Cultural Politics*, vol. 13, nos. 1 and 2, 2017, pp. 165-178.

Mbue, Imbolo. *Behold the Dreamers*. Random House, 2016.

Rocco, Fiammetta. "Things Come Together: A New Generation of African Novelists Take Flight." *1843*, February/March 2017, pp. 22-24.

Contemporary African Immigration and the Legacy of Slavery in Yaa Gyasi's *Homegoing*___

Brian Yothers

Some immigration stories hardly seem to be immigration stories at all. Such is the case with the Ghanaian American writer Yaa Gyasi's highly successful first novel *Homegoing*, which narrates the experiences of fourteen members of the same extended African family: seven of them on the side of the extended family that remained in Africa during the time of the slave trade and of European colonialism in Africa, and seven of them on the side of the same extended family that was abducted into slavery in the Americas. Only one of the fourteen characters who provide the shifting point of view for the novel is an immigrant at the time of her vignette: Marjorie, whose adolescence in Alabama as a Ghanaian American immigrant resembles the author's own life story. Marjorie's father is also an immigrant, but the portion of his life story that is narrated comes before Marjorie's birth and the family's subsequent departure for the United States.

Viewed from one angle, then, *Homegoing* is precisely 1/14 (or if her father is counted, 1/7) of an immigrant novel and thus an odd fit for a discussion of the immigrant experience. Viewed from another angle, however, Gyasi's novel is an extended accounting for what distinguishes African experiences of immigration to the United States from other varieties of immigrant experience, and this immigrant-authored novel is in a profound sense a novel of the immigrant experience from start to finish.

The central question that preoccupies Gyasi in the novel is one that she has raised in interviews about the book. Gyasi—who was born in 1989; immigrated to the United States as a child with her parents in 1991; and grew up in Huntsville, Alabama, from the time she was ten years old—has said that her goal in the novel was to work through the complexities of Black identity in the United States in all its diversity. In an interview with *The Guardian*, Gyasi foregrounded the influence of the immigrant experience on the dynamics of race in her novel:

> One thing I ran up against a lot as a child was that saying "black" or "Afro-American" implies a certain cultural identity that was different from mine as an immigrant. I found it difficult to feel I was being black in the right way. The older I got, the more I realised there's no right way, that everything I do and am is also allowed to be black. It took me a long time to realise that . . . the word "black" can seem to generalise everything. (Gyasi, "Slavery")

One striking aspect of the African immigrant experience in the United States that shapes Gyasi's novel is the complicated question of how to account for the relationship between African immigrant identities and African American identities. Marjorie, the character who comes closest to the role of authorial surrogate in the novel, reflects on this explicitly when her African American high school teacher asks her to write about her African American identity:

> She [Marjorie] wanted to tell Mrs. Pinkston that at home, they had a different word for African Americans. *Akata.* That *akata* people were different from Ghanaians, too long gone from the mother continent to continue calling it the mother continent. She wanted to tell Mrs. Pinkston that she could feel herself being pulled away too, almost *akata*, too long from Ghana to be Ghanaian. (Gyasi, *Homegoing* 273)

Marjorie's reflection on the complexities of her personal identity also points to the complexities of the literary identity of *Homegoing*: it is at once an African novel and an African American novel and, as such, is heir to two distinct literary traditions that often resemble each other but all too rarely intersect.

Six of the vignettes that make up *Homegoing* belong to the tradition of African literature set in Africa, and most specifically, they belong to a tradition that represents African village life in the colonial era. The most famous example of this sort of novel by far is Chinua Achebe's *Things Fall Apart.*

Part of what makes *Homegoing* an immigrant novel is precisely the way that it engages with African literature and history. Readers who are familiar with post-independence African literature from Ghana and its populous neighbor Nigeria will recognize *Homegoing*'s deep roots in a tradition that goes back to Achebe and the Ghanaian novelist Ayi Kwei Armah (author of *The Healers*, a novel dealing directly with the slave trade) of contending with the effects of colonization and seeking the roots of modern African life in precolonial village life and in acts of resistance to colonization and the slave trade. What such readers will not find in *Homegoing* is the sort of discussion of contemporary African political dilemmas that appears in Achebe's last novel, *The Anthills of the Savannah*, or of urban life in African cities that appears in Ama Ata Aidoo's *Changes: A Love Story*, or of postcolonial historical crises that appears in Chimamanda Ngozi Adichie's novel of the Biafran War, *Half of a Yellow Sun*. In some respects, this omission of certain aspects of contemporary West African literature may appear to be a flaw, but it is also a sign of how thoroughly enmeshed with questions of immigration this multi-generational family saga is.

An African Immigrant's Genealogy

The African side of the narrative begins with the story of Effia the Beauty, an African woman who is married off, as the result of her stepmother's machinations, to an English officer at the Cape Coast Castle, the point of departure for enslaved Africans being sent to the Western Hemisphere. The story of Effia builds toward the realization that Baaba, the woman whom she had always believed to be her mother and who had both nursed her and treated her with considerable cruelty as she was growing up, was not her biological mother at all. Effia is prevented from marrying the African man she intended to marry by the treachery of Baaba, and as a result, she is married off to James, the British officer who is complicit in the slave trade. At the moment when Effia leaves her father Cobbe and Baaba, Gyasi sketches the following very affecting scene:

Cobbe, big strong man that he was, began to weep openly, but Baaba stood tall. She walked over to Effia after Abeeku had left, and handed her a black stone pendant that shimmered as if it had been coated in gold dust.

She slipped it into Effia's hands and then leaned into her until her lips were touching Effia's ear. 'Take this with you when you go,' Baaba said. 'A piece of your mother.'

And when Baaba finally pulled away, Effia could see something like relief dancing behind her smile. (Gyasi, *Homegoing* 16)

The pendant that Effia is given will have an important role in Gyasi's project of bringing together the African and African American narratives that shape her novel. The mother to whom Baaba refers when she gives the stone to Effia is a girl who had been a captive of Cobbe's and whose connection to Cobbe was likely a matter of rape rather than a consensual relationship. This moment, then, is crucial to the unfolding of the various African and African American identities that appear throughout the novel, as Effia, the very first character we meet, has had her life shaped by the influence of the slave trade from the start of her life. In one sense, Effia is herself a migrant, as she moves from the village of her youth to the English society at Cape Coast Castle, with its alien constellation of customs and beliefs.

When the novel turns to the next generation on Effia's side of the family, Gyasi's emphasis is on the ways in which Africans could become complicit in the very trade that exploited them and enslaved their family members. This vignette is the story of Quey, the son of Effia and the English officer James. Quey develops a close friendship with a young African man named Cudjo, to whom he comes to realize he is physically attracted. He is sent away to England for his education, and when he returns, he initially imagines an idyllic life in Africa with Cudjo. Notably, the story of Quey is the novel's first story of African immigration and return: Quey has experienced life in London before he returns to the slave-trading Fante village led by Effia's younger brother, and he initially seems to want to disavow the European side of his identity by uniting with Cudjo. He is drawn into the slave trade by his uncle, however, and his absorption into the slave trade is confirmed when he marries an Asante princess, thus consolidating his own village's power. Gyasi uses free indirect discourse to summarize Quey's reasons for his morally questionable decision to forsake his attachment to Cudjo and to take up his family business in the slave trade and the loveless marriage that will enable his success in that trade: "This was how they lived there, in the bush: Eat or be eaten. Capture or be captured. Marry for protection. Quey would never go to Cudjo's village. He would not be weak. He was in the business of slavery, and sacrifices had to be made" (Gyasi, *Homegoing* 69). Quey denies his own sexuality, his affection for Cudjo, and his moral intuitions in order to carry on his father's family business: the slave trade.

Quey's choices are reversed almost completely by Effia's grandson, James, who is ironically named for his British slave-trading grandfather. If Quey has denied his own desires and conscience in the belief that it was his responsibility to do so, James renounces the idea that participating in the slave trade can ever be a morally acceptable choice, and he does so as a result of his love for an African woman. In a crucial moment, James declares, "I want to leave my family and move to Asanteland. I want to marry Akosua Mensah and work as a farmer or something small-small" (Gyasi, *Homegoing* 104). Akosua Mensah is a young woman in an Asante village who refuses to greet James because of his family's ties to the slave trade. Like Quey, James is married off in a politically useful but loveless match; unlike Quey, he renounces this match in order to follow his own moral intuitions and affective connections via his marriage to Akosua Mensah after a battle in which he feigns his own death. James's choice is the inverse of Quey's. Quey chooses a corrupted form of manhood when he rejects his erotic and affective connection to Cudjo in favor of what he believes to be his family responsibilities, but James chooses exile and penury rather than engage in further complicity in the slave trade.

There is an American dimension to the opposing choices made by Quey and James: both are responding to a trade that has its African end point in the Middle Passage of enslaved men and women to the Americas, and in this sense, their African identities have a dimension that interacts with the future African immigrant identity of their descendent Marjorie.

If James rejects the economically successful and morally bankrupt choices of his father, his daughter Abena struggles with resentment towards his own legacy of morally upright poverty. Abena never experiences wealth or power as she is growing up, unlike the first three generations, and even her romance with a childhood friend becomes strained by his inability to marry a woman who is impoverished. Ultimately, her lover is able to gain wealth and status by cultivating cocoa, but he is still unable or unwilling to marry her even as she is carrying his child. Like James, Quey, and Effia, she confronts the consequences of her ancestors' choices, and only when she is preparing to leave her village is she able to recognize her parents' moral courage, and when James passes the stone he inherited from Effia on to her, she finds that she feels a connection to her father that she had not previously recognized:

> Abena put on the necklace and hugged her father. Her mother was in the doorframe, watching them out in the dirt. Abena got up and hugged her mother too.
> The next morning, Abena set out for Kumasi, and when she arrived at the missionary church there, she touched the stone at her neck and said thank you to her ancestors. (Gyasi, *Homegoing* 153)

Abena's receipt of the stone continues the novel's theme of intergenerational continuity and struggle. Once again, as with each previous generation in the family, Abena shapes a new future through migration, this time to the missionary church as a result of her pregnancy, which makes her continued life in the village impossible.

The fifth generation of Effia's family marks the most significant intergenerational rupture. Akua is Abena's daughter, but she has vastly less connection to her mother than any member of her family before her has had and no connection at all to her father. Her rupture with the past is defined by her relationship to fire:

Akua couldn't remember the first time she'd seen fire, but she could remember the first time she'd dreamed of it. It was in 1895, sixteen years after her mother Abena had carried her Akua-swollen belly to the missionaries in Kumasi, fifteen years after Abena had died. Then the fire in Akua's dream had been nothing more than a quick flash of Ochre. Now the firewoman raged. (Gyasi, *Homegoing* 177)

Akua grows up as an orphan, cut off from her parents and raised by missionaries. She returns to the Asante heritage of part of her family through her marriage to an Asante man, and she has three children with him. Her dreams of the firewoman are reminiscent of the magical realist tradition in West African fiction, including Ben Okri's *The Famished Road*, and it helps to capture the persistence of the past in shaping Effia's descendants' lives. In a twist that helps to connect this narrative on the African side of the family with some of the most harrowing stories of slavery in the Americas (including those that inspired Toni Morrison's *Beloved*), Akua's confrontation with the past through her dreams results in her inadvertently killing two of her children and badly burning her one surviving child.

Akua's surviving son, Yaw, provides the connection between the past of the African village and the post-independence African city and, beyond that, the African immigrant experience. Like Akua, Yaw grows up disconnected from his ancestors, in this case because of the fact that Akua has killed his siblings and injured him severely in the fire that she sets. Yaw grows up to be an educator, and he marries only late in life. When he marries his much younger housemaid, his marriage provides an opportunity to reunite with his mother, and she provides one of the most eloquent moments of reflection in the novel: "'What I know now, my son [Yaw]: Evil begets evil. It grows, it transmutes, so that sometimes you cannot see that the evil in the world began as the evil in your own home. I'm sorry you have suffered" (Gyasi, *Homegoing* 242). Akua's remarks to Yaw point to a central theme in *Homegoing*: the moral weight of slavery and violence with which all of the characters in the novel must live. They suggest that Akua's dreams of the firewoman are not just a matter of mental illness, but rather an expression of the continuing historical legacy of her ancestors' decisions, perhaps even a manifestation of collective trauma.

Yaw is the father of Marjorie, the first character who appears to the reader as an African immigrant in the United States. Yaw and his wife have migrated to the United States in order for Yaw to take up an academic appointment in Alabama, and Marjorie grows up as an immigrant and the child of immigrants who seeks to come to terms with the meaning of her complex identity as a Black woman in the United States who is African but not African American in the usual sense. The story of the African American side of the family that starts with Effia's and Esi's mother provides a kind of extended answer to the questions that Marjorie has as an immigrant child who is and is not African, and American, and African American all at once.

The *Akata* Side of the Story

The way in which *Homegoing* engages with the African American literary tradition resembles its engagement with the Anglophone literary traditions of West Africa. The first story from the African American side of the family, that of Effia's half-sister, Esi, presents a story that runs parallel to Effia's. Esi grows up with a mother who loves her but who is haunted by sadness, and she comes to realize that her mother had herself been enslaved in another village, in part because of her powerful sense of sympathy with a young girl who has been enslaved in Esi's village. When it becomes clear that Esi and her fellow villagers will be enslaved, Esi's mother (who, we come to realize, is also Effia's) chooses death over enslavement, and she passes on a stone to Esi that is the counterpart of the stone that Baaba bestowed upon Effia. Esi is herself abducted and enslaved, and her narrative begins in Cape Coast Castle, where she and other women are raped and abused as they are being held before being transported to the Americas on the Middle Passage. What is most poignant in Esi's story is the way that both her hope for the future and her memories of the past are destroyed by the inescapable cruelty of slavery: "When she [Esi] wanted to forget the Castle, she thought of these things, but she did not expect joy. Hell was a place of remembering, each beautiful moment passed through the mind's eye until it fell to the ground like a rotten mango, perfectly useless, uselessly perfect" (Gyasi, *Homegoing* 28). Esi's situation in her chapter represents a profound moment of rupture: her past is irretrievably tainted by a present that has removed all hope of a better future, and the looming Middle Passage ensures that she will never be able to go back home again. This loss is expressed powerfully by the fact that, despite all her attempts to save it, including swallowing it at one point and digging it out of a pile of excrement, she is ultimately forced to leave the stone behind. This becomes a powerful comment on the difference between twentieth-century African immigration and the forcible enslavement and removal of eighteenth-century Africans: later in the novel, Marjorie has been able to carry the stone that she inherited from her distant ancestor Effia back and forth across the Atlantic, but Esi is unable to retain the only physical item that she was given by her mother.

The brutality of the rupture caused by the Middle Passage is thus at the center of the novel, and at the heart of the dialogue between African and African American identities that Gyasi stages. Gyasi does not attempt to represent the Middle Passage, but a portion of *The Interesting Narrative of the Life of Olaudah Equiano, or Gustavus Vassa, the African, Written by Himself* can provide a sense of what would follow for Esi:

> I was now persuaded that I was got into a world of bad spirits, and that they were going to kill me. Their complexions too differing so much from ours, their long hair, and the language they spoke, which was very different from any I had ever heard, united to confirm me in this belief. Indeed, such were the horrors of my views and fears at the moment, that, if ten thousand worlds had been my own, I would have freely parted with them all to have exchanged my condition with that of the meanest slave in my own country. When I looked round the ship too, and saw a large furnace of copper boiling, and a multitude of black people of every description chained together, every one of their countenances expressing dejection and sorrow, I no longer doubted of my fate, and, quite overpowered with horror and anguish, I fell motionless on the deck and fainted. When I recovered a little, I found

some black people about me, who I believed were some of those who brought me on board, and had been receiving their pay; they talked to me in order to cheer me, but all in vain. I asked them if we were not to be eaten by those white men with horrible looks, red faces, and long hair? They told me I was not; and one of the crew brought me a small portion of spirituous liquor in a wine glass; but, being afraid of him, I would not take it out of his hand. One of the blacks therefore took it from him and gave it to me, and I took a little down my palate, which, instead of reviving me, as they thought it would, threw me into the greatest consternation at the strange feeling it produced, having never tasted any such liquor before. Soon after this, the blacks who brought me on board went off, and left me abandoned to despair. (38-39)

Equiano here describes the sense of terror that the transatlantic voyage could involve for enslaved persons being transported to the Americas. In eloquent, moving terms, Equiano describes the sense of absolute loss and disconnection from his past life that his abduction from Africa has caused, and at many points in the narration of the Middle Passage in *The Interesting Narrative*, Equiano contemplates suicide. The fact that whether Equiano's discussion of the Middle Passage is actually autobiographical has been subject to debate even among his admirers, including his recent biographer Vincent Carretta, only reinforces the difficulty of narrating the stories of those who have been violently stripped of their stories.

Gyasi picks her narrative thread up again years after Esi's abduction and enslavement. With the appearance of Ness, Esi's daughter, slavery in the Americas enters the novel. If Esi lost all of her physical possessions and was subjected to horrific violence, including sexual violence, in her portion of the novel, Ness's dispossession is more extreme still. She has some connection to Africa through the oral stories that Esi has told her, and she reconstructs a connection to Africa through her meeting with Aku, a woman who has been brought from Africa and is able to teach Ness something of the Twi language of her Asante ancestors. One of the most heart-wrenching moments in the entire book comes when Ness realizes she will have to give up her son, Kojo, in order to save him. "In broken Twi, Ness called to Aku, who was further in the distance, holding baby Jo. 'Don't come down, whatever you do,' Ness said" (Gyasi, *Homegoing* 86). Here Gyasi draws on one of the most compelling aspects of nineteenth-century African American slave narratives and fictional works, from Harriet Beecher Stowe's *Uncle Tom's Cabin* to Toni Morrison's *Beloved*: the appalling choices that faced women attempting to save their children from enslavement. Ness returns to be tortured and to be forced to witness the murder of her children's father, and the narrative that Gyasi constructs for her revolves around her memories of these traumatic events and her struggles to give shape to her life even under slavery and even after she has experienced unimaginable horrors.

The third generation of Esi's family appears in the form of Ness's escaped son, Kojo, now known as Jo, who has grown up free in Baltimore, but who is still in a precarious position due to fugitive slave laws. He is married to a free black woman, Anna, whose papers stating her free status are valid, unlike his own, which are forged. In an especially bitter irony, it is Anna, pregnant with the couple's youngest child, not Jo, who is abducted into slavery from Baltimore. There is something particularly brutal about the moment when Jo realizes that he is unlikely ever to see Anna again. He has asked a white police officer if he has seen Anna, showing him her picture. "Then Jo heard the sound of paper tearing. He looked up to see Anna's nose, and ears, and strands of hair, the shredded bits of paper flying off in the wind" (Gyasi, *Homegoing* 128). In the economy of nineteenth-century American racism and slavery, Anna's status as a free woman only counts insofar as white authorities are prepared to let it count, which proves to be not at all. This moment is yet another instance of the ruptures caused by the slave trade, as Anna will not see her older children again, and Jo will never meet his youngest son.

The story of Jo and Anna's son, H, reveals the ways in which slavery persisted in new forms after the ostensible emancipation of the Civil War. H is the fourth generation of Esi's descendants, and he, like each of the generations before him, finds himself cut off from his ancestors. He knows only that his mother has died immediately after giving birth to him, and he has no way of accessing the stories of Esi,

Ness, or Jo. After Emancipation, moreover, H is almost immediately re-enslaved by the criminal justice system. After emerging from his time as prison labor, yet another rupture, H finds an opportunity for a new sort of identity in the labor movement, working alongside black and white laborers alike for justice. In a climactic moment, H demonstrates his moral development as a character, when he refuses violence in order to pursue justice through solidarity with the members of his union: "H wanted to throw the man down, down to meet the city underneath the earth, but he stopped himself. He was not the con they had told him he was" (Gyasi, *Homegoing* 174). This moment provides a powerful rebuttal to narratives of Black criminality that, as recent work such as the 2015 documentary *13* has argued, represented the continuation of slavery by other means.

H's daughter Willie experiences directly what W.E.B. DuBois identified as "the problem of the Twentieth Century": the "color-line" (5). Willie's story is also the story of one of the great demographic movements of the first half of the twentieth-century, the Great Migration of African Americans from the rural South to the urban North in the United States, a movement that has been powerfully described by Isabel Wilkerson in her study *The Warmth of Other Suns*. Willie's husband Robert is so light-skinned that he can pass as white, and ultimately he deserts her in order to pass as a white man with a white wife and family, while Willie and her son Carson remain on the opposite side of the color line from him. This is powerfully dramatized when Willie and Carson see Robert on the street in a white neighborhood:

> Robert smiled at her [Willie], but soon he turned to talk to the blond woman, and the three of them continued in a different direction.
> Carson followed Willie's gaze to where Robert had been. "Mama?" he said again.
> Willie shook her head. "No, Carson. We can't go any further. I think it's time we go back." (Gyasi, *Homegoing* 221)

Willie experiences a different sort of disconnection from that experienced by her ancestors: in this case, the color line has divided her from the husband of her youth, and Robert has made the reverse

---

decision from the embrace of solidarity between lighter-skinned and darker-skinned African Americans described and advocated by Charles W. Chesnutt in his short story "The Wife of His Youth." A noteworthy pattern that Gyasi established in her stories from both sides of the Atlantic is her engagement with major literary works in the African and African American literary traditions, and this chapter provides a particularly pronounced instance of that pattern.

When Sonny (the name that Carson prefers) grows up, his early engagement with DuBois has transformed into Black Nationalism. "What Sonny wanted was Africa. Marcus Garvey had been onto something" (Gyasi, *Homegoing* 244). As Esi's fifth-generation descendent, Sonny finds that he wishes to recover his connection to his family's distant past in Africa, even as his relationship to his mother is at times contentious. As with each of his ancestors since Esi, he experiences a profound rupture, as his relationship with the mother of his child is stretched to the breaking point by her heroin addiction. Notably, given his enthusiasm for Garvey, he names his son Marcus. As Isabel Wilkerson has commented in her generally glowing review of *Homegoing*, this chapter seems less substantial in its evocation of African American culture than many of the other chapters, and perhaps part of the reason for this is Gyasi's apparent commitment to building a rupture into the experiences of each generation. Nonetheless, this chapter continues a pattern of noting the ways in which the African and African American stories are entangled with each other.

If Sonny never makes it back to Africa, his son Marcus does, albeit by an unlikely route. Marcus, unlike his autodidact father, finds his way into Stanford, a central location for elite higher education in the United States. Like his father, he wrestles with the nature of his heritage and identity, and he finds answers when he comes into contact with a young woman studying at Stanford who turns out to be Marjorie. Marjorie accompanies Marcus on a trip to Ghana, and she takes him for a tour of the Cape Castle, the very site where Effia lived as the spouse of a British officer and Esi was held before being transported to the Americas in the Middle Passage. In a compelling moment at the close of the novel, Marjorie restores to Marcus the physical connection with his ancestors that Marcus's distant ancestor Esi lost. When Marcus and Marjorie wade in the sea after Marcus has had an historically portentous panic attack in the Cape Castle, they wade into the Atlantic, and Marjorie gives him the stone that is the counterpart of the stone that his distant ancestor Esi lost at Cape Castle: "'Here,' Marjorie said, 'Have it.' She lifted the stone from her neck and placed it around Marcus's. 'Welcome home'" (Gyasi, *Homegoing* 300). This moment brings the movement of the plot back to the beginning of the novel, when Esi's and Effia's mother escapes from Effia's father, and the contrasting narratives of the families begin.

To return to the initial question that framed this essay, what makes this book a novel of the African immigrant experience? The answer to this question consists in no small part in the rich investment in the connected histories of Africa and the Americas that shapes every aspect of Gyasi's narrative. On the African side of Effia's and Esi's shared family, continuous patterns of migration and displacement within Africa illustrate that Marjorie's childhood in the United States is in keeping with a broader story of mobility and exile associated with both the slave trade in Africa and British colonialism. Meanwhile, on the African American side of the family, both the experience of slavery, racism, and segregation and the family's often heroic response to it shape a lineage that is parallel to but distinct from that of their African cousins. The African immigrant experience in the United States, Gyasi implies, cannot and should not be separated from the wider history of colonialism and the slave trade, with profound implications for recent immigrants and historic African American communities in the Americas alike.

Works Cited

Achebe, Chinua. *Anthills of the Savannah.* Heinemann, 1987.

_____. *Things Fall Apart.* Heinemann, 1958.

Adichie, Chimamanda Ngozi. *Half of a Yellow Sun.* Knopf, 2006.

Aidoo, Ama Ata. *Changes: A Love Story.* Feminist Press, 1991.

Armah, Ayi Kwei. *The Healers.* East African Publishing House, 1978.

Carretta, Vincent. *Equiano, The African: A Biography of a Self-Made Man.* Penguin, 2007.

Chesnutt, Charles. "The Wife of His Youth." 1898. *The Portable Charles W. Chesnutt,* edited by William L. Andrews, Penguin, 2008, pp. 58-71.

DuBois, W. E. B. *The Souls of Black Folk.* 1900. Norton Critical Edition, edited by Henry Louis Gates Jr. and Terri Hume Oliver, W. W. Norton, 1999.

DuVernay, Ava, director. *13th.* Kandoo Films, 2016.

Equiano, Olaudah. *The Interesting Narrative of the Life of Olaudah Equiano, or Gustavus Vassa, the African, Written by Himself.* 1789. Norton Critical Edition, edited by Werner Sollors, W. W. Norton, 2001.

Gyasi, Yaa. *Homegoing.* Knopf, 2016.

_____. "Slavery is on people's minds. It affects us still." Interviewed by Kate Kellaway. *The Guardian,* 8 Jan. 2017. Accessed 12 December 2017.

Morrison, Toni. *Beloved.* Knopf, 1987.

Okri, Ben. *The Famished Road.* Jonathan Cape, 1991.

Wilkerson, Isabel. *The Warmth of Other Suns: The Epic Story of America's Great Migration.* Random House, 2010.

_____. "Isabel Wilkerson Reviews Yaa Gyasi's 'Homegoing.'" *New York Times,* 6 Jun. 2016. Accessed 12 December 2017.

RESOURCES

Works on the Immigrant Experience⸻⸻⸻⸻

Selected Primary Works

Africa

Adichie, Chimamanda Ngozi. *The Thing Around Your Neck*. Anchor, 2010.

Bulawayo, NoViolet. *We Need New Names*. Back Bay Books, 2014.

Gyasi, Yaa. *Homegoing*. Knopf, 2016.

Mbue, Imbolo. *Behold the Dreamers*. Random House, 2016.

Mengestu, Dinaw. *The Beautiful Things That Heaven Bears*. Riverhead, 2007.

Selasi, Taiye. *Ghana Must Go*. Penguin, 2014.

South Asia

Alexander, Meena. *Fault Lines*. 2nd edition. Feminist P, 2003.

⸻⸻⸻. *The Shock of Arrival: Reflections on Postcolonial Experience*. South End P, 1996.

Bhatt, Sheela, et al., editors. *Our Feet Walk the Sky: Women of the South Asian Diaspora*. Aunt Lute, 1993.

Bhattacharya, Piyali, editor. *Good Girls Marry Doctors: South Asian American Daughters on Obedience and Rebellion*. Aunt Lute P, 2016.

Desai, Kiran. *The Inheritance of Loss*. Grove Press, 2006.

Divakaruni, Chitra Banerjee. *Arranged Marriage*. Doubleday, 1995.

⸻⸻⸻. *The Mistress of Spices*. Random House, 1998.

⸻⸻⸻. *Queen of Dreams*. Anchor, 2004.

Ganeshananthan, V. V. *Love Marriage*. Random House, 2008.

Hamid, Mohsin. *Exit West*. Riverhead Books, 2017.

⸻⸻⸻. *The Reluctant Fundamentalist*. Mariner, 2007.

Lahiri, Jhumpa. *The Interpreter of Maladies*. Mariner Books, 1999.

⸻⸻⸻. *The Lowland*. Vintage, 2014.

⸻⸻⸻. *The Namesake*. Houghton Mifflin, 2003.

⸻⸻⸻. *Unaccustomed Earth*. Vintage, 2009.

Mehta, Rahul. *No Other World*. Harper Collins, 2017.

Mukherjee, Bharati. *Jasmine*. Grove P, 1989.

Naqvi, Tahera. *Dying in a Strange Country*. TSAR, 2001.

Reddi, Rishi. *Karma and Other Stories*. Harper Perennial, 2007.

Satyal, Rakesh. *No One Can Pronounce My Name*. Picador, 2017.

Sharma, Akhil. *Family Life*. W.W. Norton, 2014.

Sidhwa, Bapsi. *An American Brat*. Milkweed, 1993.

Sindu, S. J. *Marriage of a Thousand Lies*. Soho P, 2017.

East Asia

Bui, Thi. *The Best We Could Do: An Illustrated Memoir*. Abrams
     Comicarts, 2017.

Eaton, Edith Maude. *Becoming Sui Sin Far: Early Fiction, Journalism,
     and Travel Writing*. Edited by Mary Chapman, McGill-Queen's
     UP, 2016.

Jen, Gish. *Mona in the Promised Land*. Vintage, 1997.

_____. *Typical American*. Vintage, 2008.

_____. *Who's Irish?: Stories*. Vintage, 2000.

Jin, Ha. *A Free Life*. Pantheon, 2007.

_____. *The Writer as Migrant*. U of Chicago P, 2008.

Kingston, Maxine Hong. *The Woman Warrior: Memoirs of a Girlhood
     Among Ghosts*. Vintage, 1989.

Ko, Lisa. *The Leavers*. Algonquin, 2017.

Lee, Chang-Rae. *Native Speaker*. Riverhead, 1995.

Nguyen, Bich Minh. *Stealing Buddha's Dinner: A Memoir*. Penguin,
     2008.

Nguyen, Viet Thanh. *The Refugees*. Grove P, 2017.

_____. *The Sympathizer*. Grove P, 2016.

Okada, John. *No-No Boy*. U of Washington P, 1976.

Tan, Amy. *The Joy Luck Club*. Penguin, 1989.

Tran, GB. *Vietnamerica: A Family's Journey*. Villard, 2010.

The Caribbean

Alvarez, Julia. *How the Garcia Girls Lost Their Accents*. Algonquin Books, 2010.

_____. *In the Name of Salomé: A Novel*. Plume, 2000.

Danticat, Edwidge. *Breath, Eyes, Memory*. Vintage, 1994.

_____. *Brother, I'm Dying*. Knopf, 2007.

_____. *Create Dangerously: The Immigrant Artist at Work*. Vintage, 2010.

_____. *The Dew Breaker*. Knopf, 2004.

Díaz, Junot. *The Brief Wondrous Life of Oscar Wao*. Riverhead Books, 2007.

_____. *Drown*. Riverhead Books, 1996.

_____. *This Is How You Lose Her*. Riverhead Books, 2013.

Kincaid, Jamaica. *Lucy*. Farrar, Straus and Giroux, 2002.

Menendez, Ana. *In Cuba I Was a German Shepherd*. Grove Press, 2001.

Latin America

Cortez-Davis, Evelyn. *December Sky: Beyond My Undocumented Life*. In Xochitl In Cuicatl, 2003.

Grande, Reyna. *The Distance Between Us*. Washington Square P, 2012.

Henriquez, Cristina. *The Book of Unknown Americans*. Vintage, 2015.

Hernandez, Daisy. *A Cup of Water Under My Bed*. Beacon P, 2014.

Orduña, Jose. *The Weight of Shadows: A Memoir of Immigration and Displacement*. Beacon P, 2016.

Nazario, Sonia. *Enrique's Journey: The Story of a Boy's Dangerous Odyssey to Reunite with His Mother*. Random House, 2007.

Padilla Peralta, Dan-el. *Undocumented: A Dominican Boy's Odyssey from a Homeless Shelter to the Ivy League*. Penguin P, 2015.

Sánchez, Erika L. *I Am Not Your Perfect Mexican Daughter*. Knopf Books for Young Readers, 2017.

Tywoniak, Frances Esquibel, and Mario Garcia. *Migrant Daughter: Coming of Age as a Mexican American Woman*. U of California P, 2000.

Europe

Antin, Mary. *The Promised Land.* Houghton Mifflin Company, 1912.

Cahan, Abraham. *Yekl and the Imported Bridegroom.* Dover, 1970.

_____. *The Rise of David Levinsky.* Penguin Classics, 1993.

Cather, Willa. *My Ántonia.* Dover, 1994.

Chabon, Michael. *The Yiddish Policeman's Union.* Harper Perennial, 2007.

Halevi, Yehudah. *The Selected Poems of Yehuda Halevi.* Edited by Hillel Halkin. Nextbook, 2011.

Lazarus, Emma. *Emma Lazarus: Selected Poems.* Edited by John Hollander, Library of America, 2005.

Levine, Philip. *The Mercy: Poems.* Knopf Doubleday, 2011.

McCourt, Frank. *'Tis: A Memoir.* Simon and Schuster, 2000.

Riis, Jacob. *How the Other Half Lives.* Bedford, 1996.

Rosenfeld, Alvin H, editor. *The Writer Uprooted: Contemporary Jewish Exile Literature.* Indiana UP, 2008.

Roth, Henry. *Call it Sleep.* Farah, Straus and Giroux, 1994.

Shtenygart, Gary. *Absurdistan.* Random House, 2007.

_____. *Little Failure: A Memoir.* Random House, 2014.

Tóibín, Colm. *Brooklyn.* Scribner, 2015.

Yezierska, Anzia. *How I Found America: Collected Stories of Anzia Yezierska.* Persea Books, 1991.

Middle East

Abu-Jaber, Diana. *Crescent.* W.W. Norton, 2004.

_____. *The Language of Baklava.* Anchor, 2006.

Dumas, Firoozeh. *Funny in Farsi: A Memoir of Growing Up Iranian in America.* Random House, 2006.

Helal, Marwa. *I am Made to Leave I am Made to Return.* No Dear and Small Anchor Press, 2017.

Selected Secondary Works

Bald, Vivek. *Bengali Harlem and the Lost Histories of South Asian America.* Harvard UP, 2013.

_____. et al., editors. *The Sun Never Sets: South Asian Migrants in an Age of U.S. Power*. New York UP, 2013.

Behdad, Ali. *A Forgetful Nation: On Immigration and Cultural Identity in the United States*. Duke UP, 2005.

Bhabha, Homi K. *The Location of Culture*. Routledge, 1994.

Bhatt, Amy, and Nalini Iyer. *Roots and Reflections: South Asians in the Pacific Northwest*. U of Washington P, 2013.

Braziel, Jana Evans, and Anita Mannur, editors. *Theorizing Diaspora*. Blackwell, 2003.

Caminero-Santangelo. *Documenting the Undocumented: Latino/a Narrative and Social Justice in the Era of Operation Gatekeeper*. U of Florida P, 2016.

Cappell, Ezra. *American Talmud: The Cultural Work of Jewish American Fiction*. SUNY P, 2008.

Chow, Rey. *Writing Diaspora: Tactics of Intervention in Contemporary Cultural Studies*. Indiana UP, 1993.

Cowart, David. *Trailing Clouds: Immigrant Fiction in Contemporary America*. Cornell UP, 2006.

Daniels, Roger. *Coming to America: A History of Immigration and Ethnicity in American Life*. Harper Perennial, 2002.

_____. *Guarding the Golden Door: American Immigration Policy and Immigrants since 1982*. Hill and Wang, 2005.

Fadda, Carol. *Contemporary Arab American Literature: Transnational Reconfigurations of Citizenship and Belonging*. New York UP, 2014.

Flores-González, Nilda. *Citizens but Not Americans: Race and Belonging among Latino Millennials*. New York UP, 2017.

Gonzales, Roberto G. *Lives in Limbo: Undocumented and Coming of Age in America*. U of California P, 2015.

Hall, Stuart. "Cultural Identity and Diaspora." *Identity: Community, Culture, Difference*, edited by Jonathan Rutherford, Lawrence and Wishart, 1990, pp. 222-237.

Hassan, Wail. *Immigrant Narratives: Orientalism and Cultural Translation in Arab American and Arab British Literature*. Oxford UP, 2011.

Jain, Anupama. *How to be South Asian in America*. Temple UP, 2011.

Kraut, Alan M. *The Huddled Masses: The Immigrant in American Society, 1880–1921*. Wiley-Blackwell, 2001.

Leonard, Karen Isaksen. *Making Ethnic Choices: California's Punjabi Mexican Americans*. Temple UP, 1994.

Lowe, Lisa. *Immigrant Acts: On Asian American Cultural Politics*. Duke UP, 1996.

Miller, Kerby A. *Emigrants and Exiles: Ireland and the Irish Exodus to North America*. Oxford, 1988.

Muller, Gilbert G. *New Strangers in Paradise: The Immigrant Experience and Contemporary American Fiction*. UP of Kentucky, 2008.

Ratti, Rakesh, editor. *Lotus of Another Color: The Unfolding of South Asian Gay and Lesbian Experience*. Alyson Books, 1993.

Roediger, David R. *Working Toward Whiteness: How America's Immigrants Became White: The Strange Journey from Ellis Island to the Suburbs*. Basic Books, 2006.

Said, Edward. *Reflections on Exile and Other Essays*. Harvard UP, 2002.

Salaita, Steven. *Modern Arab American Fiction: A Reader's Guide*. Syracuse UP, 2011.

Socolovsky, Maya. *Troubling Nationhood in U. S. Latina Literature: Explorations of Place and Belonging*. Rutgers UP, 2013.

Bibliography

Aboulela, Leila. *Minaret*. Bloomsbury, 2005.

Achebe, Chinua. *Anthills of the Savannah*. Heinemann, 1987.

_____. *Things Fall Apart*. Heinemann, 1958.

Ada, Alma Flor, and F. Isabel Campoy. *Yes! We Are Latinos: Poems and Prose about the Latino Experience*. Charlesbridge, 2013.

Adichie, Chimamanda Ngozi. *Half of a Yellow Sun*. Knopf, 2006.

_____. *The Thing Around Your Neck*. Anchor, 2010.

Adorno, Theodor. *Minima Moralia: Reflections from Damaged Life*. Translated by E. F. N. Jephcott, Verso, 1978.

Ahmed, Sara. "'She'll Wake Up One of These Days and Find She's Turned into a Nigger': Passing through Hybridity." *Performativity and Belonging*, edited by Vicki Bell, Sage, 1999, pp. 87-106.

Aidoo, Ama Ata. *Changes: A Love Story*. Feminist P, 1991.

Akhtar, Ayad. *Disgraced*. New York: Little Brown, 2013.

Alexander, Meena. *Fault Lines: A Memoir*. Feminist P at CUNY, 2003.

_____. *The Shock of Arrival: Reflections on Postcolonial Experience*. South End P, 1996.

Ali, Mona. *Brick Lane*. Scribner, 2004.

Alvarez, Julia. *How the Garcia Girls Lost Their Accents*. Algonquin Books, 2010.

_____. *In the Name of Salomé: A Novel*. Plume, 2000.

Ammons, Elizabeth. "Audacious Words: Sui Sin Far's Mrs. Spring Fragrance." *Conflicting Stories: American Women Writers at the Turn into the Twentieth Century*. Oxford UP, 1991, pp. 105-120.

Anaya, Rudolfo A. "What Good Is Literature in Our Time?" *American Literary History*, vol. 100, no. 3, 1998, pp. 471-477.

André, Richard, Edwidge Danticat, and Junot Díaz. "The Dominican Republic and Haiti: A Shared View from the Diaspora." *The Americans Quarterly*, Summer 2014, americasquarterly.org/content/dominican-republic-and-haiti-shared-view-diaspora/. Accessed 19 Oct. 2017.

Antin, Mary. *The Promised Land*. Houghton Mifflin Company, 1912.

Appadurai, Arjun. "Disjuncture and Difference in the Global Cultural Economy." *Theorizing Diaspora*, edited by Jana Evans Braziel and Anita Mannur, Blackwell, 2003, pp. 25-48.

Arab American National Museum. "Arab American Immigration." *Reclaiming Identity: Dismantling Arab Stereotypes*, April 2011, www.arabamericanmuseum.org/Coming-to-America.id.18.htm/. Accessed 30 Nov. 2017.

Armah, Ayi Kwei. *The Healers*. East African Publishing House, 1978.

Badruddoja, Roksana. "The Fantasy of Normative Motherhood." *Good Girls Marry Doctors: South Asian American Daughters on Obedience and Rebellion*, edited by Piyali Bhattacharya, Aunt Lute P, 2016, pp. 19-26.

Bald, Vivek. *Bengali Harlem and the Lost Histories of South Asian America*. Harvard UP, 2013.

Bald, Vivek, et al., editors. *The Sun Never Sets: South Asian Migrants in an Age of U.S. Power*. New York UP, 2013.

Baldwin, James. *The Fire Next Time*. 1963. Vintage, 1992.

Bautista, Daniel. "Comic Book Realism: Form and Genre in Junot Díaz's *The Brief Wondrous Life of Oscar Wao*." *Journal of the Fantastic in the Arts*, vol. 21, no.1, 2010, pp. 41-53.

Beah, Ishmael. *Long Way Gone: Memoirs of a Boy Soldier*. Sarah Crichton Books, 2008.

Bechdel, Alison. *Fun Home: A Family Tragicomic*. Mariner, 2007.

Bennett, David Harry. *The Party of Fear: From Nativist Movements to the New Right in American History*. U of North Carolina P, 1988.

Berlant, Lauren. *Cruel Optimism*. Duke UP, 2011.

Bhabha, Homi K. *The Location of Culture*. Routledge, 1994.

Bhatt, Amy, and Nalini Iyer. *Roots and Reflections: South Asians in the Pacific Northwest*. U of Washington P, 2013.

Bhatt, Sheela, et al., editors. *Our Feet Walk the Sky: Women of the South Asian Diaspora.*Aunt Lute, 1993.

Bhattacharya, Piyali, editor. *Good Girls Marry Doctors: South Asian American Daughters on Obedience and Rebellion*. Aunt Lute P, 2016.

Bhattacharya, Piyali. "The Politics of Being Political." *Good Girls Marry Doctors: South Asian American Daughters on Obedience and*

Rebellion, edited by Piyali Bhattacharya, Aunt Lute P, 2016, pp. 33-40.

Blanco, Octavio. "Getting Deported Was the Best Thing that Ever Happened To Me." *CNN Money*, 24 Jun. 2017. money.cnn.com/2017/06/24/news/economy/deported-mexico-immigrant/index.html/. Accessed 15 Oct. 2017.

Blanco, Richard. *The Prince of los Cocuyos: A Miami Childhood.* Ecco Press, Harper Collins, 2014.

Blanco, Richard. "Translation for Mamá." *Directions to the Beach of the Dead.* U of Arizona P, 2005, pp. 24-26.

Bloch, Ernst. *The Principle of Hope.* Translated by Neville Plaice, Stephen Plaice, and Paul Knight, The MIT P, 1995.

Bost, Suzanne, and Frances R. Aparicio. "Introduction." *The Routledge Companion to Latino/a Literature*, edited by Suzanne Bost and Frances R. Aparicio, Routledge, 2013, pp. 1-10.

Bostrom, Annie. "*The Best We Could Do.*" *Booklist*, vol. 113, no. 14, 15 Mar. 2017, p. 33. *Academic Search Complete.* Accessed 3 Oct. 2017.

Braziel, Jana Evans, and Anita Mannur, editors. *Theorizing Diaspora.* Blackwell, 2003.

Bui, Thi. *The Best We Could Do: An Illustrated Memoir.* Abrams Comicarts, 2017.

Bulawayo, NoViolet. *We Need New Names.* Back Bay Books, 2014.

Cahan, Abraham. *Yekl and the Imported Bridegroom.* Dover, 1970.

Cainkar, Louse. "The Arab American Experience: From Invisibility to Heightened Visibility." *The Routledge Handbook of Asian American Studies*, edited by Cindy I-Fen Cheng, Taylor and Francis, 2016, pp. 1-19.

Calhoun, Charles. *Longfellow: A Rediscovered Life.* Beacon Press, 2006.

Caminero-Santangelo, Marta. *Documenting the Undocumented: Latino/a Narrative and Social Justice in the Era of Operation Gatekeeper.* U of Florida P, 2016.

_____. "DREAMers: Youth and Migration / American DREAMers and Mexico." *Modern Mexican Culture*, edited by Stuart A. Day, U of Arizona P, 2017.

Camus, Albert. "Create Dangerously." *Resistance, Rebellion and Death: Essays*. 1960. Translated by Justin O'Brian, Vintage, 1995, pp. 249-285.

Carretta, Vincent. *Equiano, The African: A Biography of a Self-Made Man*. Penguin, 2007.

Carter-Sanborn, Kristin. "'We Murder Who We Were': Jasmine and the Violence of Identity." *American Literature*, vol. 66, no. 3, 1994, pp. 573-593.

Cha, Theresa Hak Kyung. *Dictee*. California UP, 2001.

Chabon, Michael. *The Yiddish Policeman's Union*. Harper Perennial, 2007.

Chapman, Mary. "Finding Edith Eaton." *Legacy*, vol. 29, no. 2, 2012, pp. 263–269.

Chesnutt, Charles. "The Wife of His Youth." 1898. *The Portable Charles W. Chesnutt*, edited by William L. Andrews, Penguin, 2008, pp. 58-71.

Clifford, James. *Routes: Travel and Translation in the Late Twentieth Century*. Harvard UP, 1997.

Coates, Ta-Nehisi. *Between the World and Me*. Spiegel & Grau, 2015.

Cole, Pam B. *Young Adult Literature in the 21st Century*. McGraw-Hill Higher Education, 2009.

Danticat, Edwidge. *After the Dance: A Walk through Jacmel, Haiti*. Vintage, 2002.

_____. *The Art of Death: Writing the Final Story*. Graywood, 2017.

_____. *Breath, Eyes, Memory*. Vintage, 1994.

_____. *Brother, I'm Dying*. Knopf, 2007.

_____. *Claire of the Sea Light*. Knopf, 2013.

_____. *Create Dangerously: The Immigrant Artist at Work*. Vintage, 2010.

_____. *The Dew Breaker*. Knopf, 2004.

_____. *The Farming of Bones*. Vintage, 1999.

_____. *Krik? Krak!* Vintage, 1995.

DasGupta, Sayantani. "Good Girls Become Doctors." *Good Girls Marry Doctors: South Asian American Daughters on Obedience and Rebellion*, edited by Piyali Bhattacharya, Aunt Lute P, 2016, pp. 55-58.

Davis, Rocío G. "Layering History: Graphic Embodiment and Emotions in GB Tran's *Vietnamerica.*" *Rethinking History*, vol. 19, no. 2, 2015, pp. 252-67. *Academic Search Complete.* Accessed 3 Oct. 2017.

De León, Jason. *The Land of Open Graves: Living and Dying on the Migrant Trail.* U of California P, 2015.

De Robertis, Carolina. *Radical Hope: Letters of Love and Dissent in Dangerous Times.* Vintage, 2017.

Desai, Kiran. *The Inheritance of Loss.* Grove Press, 2006.

Dhillon, Kartar. *South Asian Digital Archives*, SAADA, 2017, www.saada. org/tides/author/kartar-dhillon/.

Díaz, Junot. *The Brief Wondrous Life of Oscar Wao.* Riverhead Books, 2007.

_____. "Radical Hope." *Radical Hope: Letters of Love and Dissent in Dangerous Times*, edited by Carolina De Robertis, Vintage, 2017. 11-14.

Divakaruni, Chitra Banerjee. *Arranged Marriage.* Doubleday, 1995.

_____. *The Mistress of Spices.* Random House, 1998.

_____. *Queen of Dreams.* Anchor, 2004.

Doreen, Massey, editor. *Space, Place, and Gender.* Polity P, 1994.

Du Bois, W. E. B. *The Souls of Black Folk.* 1903. Edited by Henry Louis Gates Jr. and Terri Hulme Oliver, A Norton Critical Edition, W.W. Norton, 1999.

Dumas, Firoozeh. *Funny in Farsi: A Memoir of Growing Up Iranian in America.* RandomHouse, 2006.

DuVernay, Ava, director. *13th.* Kandoo Films, 2016.

Eaton, Edith Maude. *Becoming Sui Sin Far: Early Fiction, Journalism, and Travel Writing.* Edited by Mary Chapman, McGill-Queen's UP, 2016.

Emecheta, Buchi. *Second Class Citizen.* George Braziller, 1974.

Engel, Patricia. *It's Not Love, It's Paris.* Grove Press, 2014.

Epes, Sargent. "A Life on the Ocean Wave." *American Melodies*, edited by George Pope Morris, Linen and Fennell, 1840, pp. 28-29.

Equiano, Olaudah. *The Interesting Narrative of the Life of Olaudah Equiano, or Gustavus Vassa, the African, Written by Himself.* 1789. Edited by Werner Sollors, A Norton Critical Edition, W. W. Norton, 2001.

Fadda, Carol. *Contemporary Arab American Literature: Transnational Reconfigurations of Citizenship and Belonging.* New York UP, 2014.

Fassler, Joe, and Edwidge Danticat. "All Immigrants Are Artists." *The Atlantic*, 27 Aug. 2013, www.theatlantic.com/entertainment/archive/2013/08/all-immigrants-are-artists/279087/. Accessed 30 Sept. 2017.

Faulkner, William. *Requiem for a Nun.* Vintage, 2012.

Flores-González, Nilda. *Citizens but Not Americans: Race and Belonging among Latino Millennials.* New York UP, 2017.

Gandhi, Triveni. "Good Girls Pray to Gods." *Good Girls Marry Doctors: South Asian American Daughters on Obedience and Rebellion*, edited by Piyali Bhattacharya, Aunt Lute P, 2016, pp. 65-72.

Ganeshananthan, V. V. *Love Marriage.* Random House, 2008.

García, Diana. "On Leaving." *Prairie Schooner*, vol. 88, no. 4, 2014, pp. 11-12.

_____. "On Staying Behind." *Prairie Schooner*, vol. 88, no. 4, 2014, pp. 12-13.

Ghert-Zand, Renee. "A Video Message to the Ultra-Orthodox: 'It Gets Besser.'" *The Forward*, 12 Jul. 2011, forward.com/schmooze/139753/a-video-message-to-the-ultra-orthodox-it-gets/. Accessed 21 Dec. 2017.

Gloria, Eugene. "Assimilation." *Returning a Borrowed Tongue: Poems by Filipino and Filipino American Writers*, edited by Nick Carbó, Coffee House P, 1995, pp. 102-3.

Golash-Boza, Tanya. "Racism, Citizenship, and Deportation in the United States." *Open Democracy*, 23 Jun. 2015, www.opendemocracy.net/beyondslavery/tanya-golashboza/racism-citizenship-and-deportation-in-united-states/. Accessed 26 Nov. 2017.

González, John Morán. "Introduction." *The Cambridge Companion to Latina/o American Literature*, edited by John Morán González, Cambridge UP, 2016, pp. xxiii-xxxv.

Gonzales, Roberto G. *Lives in Limbo: Undocumented and Coming of Age in America.* U of California P, 2015.

Goodwin, Mary. "Mapping Memory in Tran's *Vietnamerica*." *CLCWeb: Comparative Literature and Culture*, vol. 17, no. 3, Sept. 2015, n.p. *Literature Resource Center.* Accessed 3 Oct. 2017.

Gooneratne, Yasmine. *A Change of Skies*. Picador, 1991.

Grande, Reyna. *The Distance Between Us*. Washington Square P, 2012.

Gualtieri, Sarah. *Between Arab and White: Race and Ethnicity in the Early Syrian American Diaspora*. U of California P, 2009.

Gyasi, Yaa. *Homegoing*. Knopf, 2016.

_____. "Slavery is on people's minds. It affects us still." Interviewed by Kate Kellaway. *The Guardian*, 8 Jan. 2017, https://www.theguardian.com/books/2017/jan/08/yaa-gyasi-slavery-is-on-peoples-minds-it-affects-us-still-interview-homegoing-observer-new-review/. Accessed 12 Dec. 2017.

Halevi, Yehudah. *The Selected Poems of Yehuda Halevi*. Edited by Hillel Halkin, Nextbook, 2011.

Hall, Stuart. "Cultural Identity and Diaspora." *Theorizing Diaspora*, edited by Jana Evans Braziel and Anita Mannur, Blackwell, 2003, pp. 233-246.

Hamid, Mohsin. *The Reluctant Fundamentalist*. Mariner, 2007.

Hanna, Monica. "'Reassembling the Fragments': Battling Historiographies, Caribbean Discourse, and Nerd Genres in Junot Díaz's *The Brief Wondrous Life of Oscar Wao*." *Callaloo*, vol. 33, no. 2, 2010, pp. 498-520.

Harris, Wilson. *History, Fable and Myth in the Caribbean and Guianas*. Calaloux Publications, 1995.

Hartman, Michelle. "Grandmothers, Grape Leaves, and Khalil Gibran: Writing Race in Anthologies of Arab American Literature." *Race and Arab Americans Before and After 9/11: From Invisible Citizens to Visible Subjects*, edited by Amaney Jamal and Nadine Naber, Syracuse UP, 2008, pp. 170-203.

Harvey, Graham, and Charles D. Thompson Jr. "Introduction." *Indigenous Diasporas and Dislocations*, edited by Graham Harvey and Charles D. Thompson Jr., Ashgate, 2005.

Hassan, Wail. *Immigrant Narratives: Orientalism and Cultural Translation in Arab American and Arab British Literature*. Oxford UP, 2011.

Helal, Marwa. ")[[;".'.,:]](REMIXED." *I am Made to Leave I am Made to Return*. No Dear and Small Anchor Press, 2017.

_____. "generation of feeling." *I am Made to Leave I am Made to Return*. No Dear and Small Anchor Press, 2017.

_____. *I am Made to Leave I am Made to Return*. No Dear and Small Anchor Press, 2017.

_____. "if this was a different kind of story id tell you about the sea." *I am Made to Leave I am Made to Return*. No Dear and Small Anchor Press, 2017.

_____. "involuntary memory." *I am Made to Leave I am Made to Return*. No Dear and Small Anchor Press, 2017.

_____. "leaving note no. 3." *I am Made to Leave I am Made to Return*. No Dear and Small Anchor Press, 2017.

_____. "leaving note no. 6." *I am Made to Leave I am Made to Return*. No Dear and Small Anchor Press, 2017.

_____. "Made." *I am Made to Leave I am Made to Return*. No Dear and Small Anchor Press, 2017.

_____. "poem for palm pressed upon pane." *I am Made to Leave I am Made to Return*. No Dear and Small Anchor Press, 2017.

_____. "poem to be read from/ right/ to left." *I am Made to Leave I am Made to Return*. No Dear and Small Anchor Press, 2017.

_____. "poem to be read from right to left." *Winter Tangerine*, n.d., www.wintertangerine.com/helal-poem-to-be-read/. Accessed 30 Nov. 2017.

Hoffman, Eva. "Afterword." *The Writer Uprooted: Contemporary Jewish Exile Literature*, edited by Alvin H. Rosenfeld, Indiana UP, 2008, pp. 234-246.

Hollander, John. "Introduction." *Emma Lazarus: Selected Poems*, edited by John Hollander, Library of America, 2005, pp. xiii-xxiv.

Honig, Bonnie. *Democracy and the Foreigner*. Princeton UP, 2001.

Houston, Robert. "Expecting Angels." *New York Times Book Review*, 23 Apr. 1995.

Howe, Irving. *Jewish-American Stories*. Edited and introduction by Irving Howe, New American Library, 1977.

Iyer, Nalini. "Diasporic Subjectivity: Dhan Gopal Mukerji's *Caste and Outcast* and Sadhu Singh Dhami's *Maluka*" in *Crossing Borders: Essays on Literature, Culture, and Society in Honor of Amritjit Singh*, edited by Tapan Basu and Tasneem Shahnaz, Fairleigh Dickinson UP, 2016, pp. 109-118.

Jain, Anupama. *How to be South Asian in America*. Temple UP, 2011.

Jarmakani, Amira. "Arab American Feminisms: Mobilizing the Politics of Invisibility." *Arab and Arab American Feminisms: Gender, Violence, and Belonging*, edited by Rabab Abdulhadi, Evelyn Alsultany, and Nadine Naber, Syracuse UP, 2011, pp. 227-241.

Jen, Gish. *Who's Irish?: Stories.* Vintage, 2000.

Jin, Ha. *A Free Life.* Pantheon, 2007.

_____. "In Defense of Foreignness." *The Routledge Handbook of World Englishes*, edited by Andy Kirkpatrick, Routledge, 2010, pp. 461–70.

_____. *The Writer as Migrant.* U of Chicago P, 2008.

Kalma. "The Undocumented." *Papers: Stories by Undocumented Youth*, edited by José Manuel, et al. Graham Street Productions, 2012, p. 34.

Kaus, Alaina. "A View from the Vietnamese Diaspora: Memories of Warfare and Refuge in GB Tran's *Vietnamerica*." *Mosaic*, vol. 49, no. 4, Dec. 2016, p. 1. *Literature Resource Center.* Accessed 3 Oct. 2017.

Kawash, Samira. *Dislocating the Color Line: Identity, Hybridity, and Singularity in African-American Narrative.* Stanford UP, 1997.

Kincaid, Jamaica. *Lucy.* Farrar, Straus and Giroux, 2002.

Kingston, Maxine Hong. *The Woman Warrior: Memoirs of a Girlhood Among Ghosts.* Vintage, 1989.

Krogstad, Jens Manuel. "5 Facts about Latinos and Education." *Pew Research Center*, 28 Jul. 2016., www.pewresearch.org/fact-tank/2016/07/28/5-facts-about-latinos-and-education/. Accessed 26 Nov. 2017.

Kureishi, Hanif. *The Buddha of Suburbia.* Penguin, 1991.

Lahiri, Jhumpa. *The Namesake.* Mariner, 2003.

Lax, Leah. *Uncovered: How I left Hasidic Life and Finally Came Home.* She Writes Press, 2015.

Lazarus, Emma. *Emma Lazarus: Selected Poems.* Edited by John Hollander, Library of America, 2005.

_____. "1492." *Emma Lazarus: Selected Poems*, edited by John Hollander, Library of America, 2005, p. 87.

_____. "In Exile." *Emma Lazarus: Selected Poems*, edited by John Hollander, Library of America, 2005, pp. 77-78.

_____. "In the Jewish Synagogue at Newport." *Emma Lazarus: Selected Poems*, edited by John Hollander, Library of America, 2005, pp. 9-10.

_____. "The New Colossus." *Emma Lazarus: Selected Poems*, edited by John Hollander, Library of America, 2005, p. 58.

_____. "To R.W.E." *Emma Lazarus: Selected Poems*, edited by John Hollander, Library of America, 2005, p. 126.

Lear, Jonathan. *Radical Hope: Ethics in the Face of Cultural Devastation.* Harvard UP, 2006.

Lee, Chang-Rae. *Native Speaker*. Riverhead, 1995.

Lee, Yu-cheng. *Diaspora*. Asian Culture, 2013.

Leonard, Karen Isaksen. *Making Ethnic Choices: California's Punjabi Mexican Americans.* Temple UP, 1994.

Levi, Primo., S. J Woolf, and Philip Roth. *Survival in Auschwitz: The Nazi Assault On Humanity.* 1st Touchstone ed. New York: Simon & Schuster, 1996.

Levine, Philip. "The Mercy." *The Mercy: Poems*. Knopf Doubleday, 2011, p. 73.

Levy, Andrea. *Small Island*. Picador, 2010.

Ling, Amy. "Pioneers and Paradigms: The Eaton Sisters." *Between Worlds: Women Writers of Chinese Ancestry.* Pergamon, 1990, pp. 21-55.

Longfellow, Henry Wadsworth. "The Jewish Cemetery at Newport." *Longfellow: Selected Poems*, edited by J. D. McClatchy, Library of America, 2000, pp. 335-36.

Lopez-Calvo, Ignacio. "A Postmodern Platano's Trujillo: Junot Díaz's *The Brief Wondrous Life of Oscar Wao*, More Macondo than McOndo." *Antipodas: Journal of Hispanic and Galician Studies*, vol. 20, 2009, pp. 75-90.

Lorde, Audre. "The Uses of the Erotic: The Erotic as Power." *Sexualities and Communication in Everyday Life*, edited by Karen E. Lovaas and Mercilee Jenkins, Sage Publications, 2007, pp. 87-91.

Ludescher, Tanyss. "From Nostalgia to Critique: An Overview of Arab American Literature." *MELUS*, vol. 31, no. 4, Winter 2006, pp. 93-114.

Luiselli, Valeria. *Tell Me How It Ends: An Essay in Forty Questions.* Translated by Lizzie Davis, Coffee House P, 2017.

Machado Saez, Elena. "Dictating Desire, Dictating Diaspora: Junot Díaz's *The Brief Wondrous Life of Oscar Wao* as Foundational Romance." *Contemporary Literature*, vol. 52, no.3, Fall 2011, pp. 522-555.

Majaj, Lisa Suhair. "Arab-American Literature: Origins and Developments." *American Studies Journal*, vol. 52, no.2, 2008, pp.1-14.

_____. "Two Worlds Emerging: Arab-American Writing at the Crossroads." *Forkroads*, Spring 1996, pp. 64-80.

Malvo-Juvera, Victor. "A Postcolonial Primer with Multicultural YA Literature." *English Journal*, vol. 107, no. 1, 2017, pp. 41-47.

Maslow, Abraham H. *A Theory of Motivation.* Martino Fine Books, 2013.

Mbue, Imbolo. *Behold the Dreamers.* Random House, 2016.

McCourt, Frank. *'Tis: A Memoir.* Simon and Schuster, 2000.

Mehta, Rahul. *No Other World.* Harper Collins, 2017.

Mengestu, Dinaw. *The Beautiful Things That Heaven Bears.* Riverhead, 2007.

Mignolo, Walter. *Local Histories/Global Designs: Coloniality, Subaltern Knowledges, and Border Thinking.* Princeton UP, 2000.

Miller, T. S. "Preternatural Narration and the Lens of Genre Fiction in Junot Díaz's *The Brief Wondrous Life of Oscar Wao." Science Fiction Studies*, vol. 38, no.1, Mar. 2011, pp. 92-114.

Ming, Di. "An Interview with Ha Jin on Poetry Writing." *Time Missed: Selected Poems by Ha Jin.* Linking Books, 2011.

Morris, George Pope. "Woodman, Spare that Tree!" *American Melodies*, edited by George Pope Morris, Linen and Fennell, 1840, pp. 93-94.

Morrison, Toni. *Beloved.* Knopf, 1987.

Mukerji, Dhan Gopal. *Caste and Outcast.* 1923. Stanford UP, 2002.

_____. *Gay Neck: The Story of A Pigeon.* 1926. Dutton 1968.

Mukherjee, Bharati. *Jasmine.* Grove P, 1999.

_____. "An Interview with Bharati Mukherjee." With Alison Carb. *The Massachusetts Review*, vol. 29, 1998, pp. 645-54.

_____. "Beyond Multiculturalism: Surviving the Nineties." *Journal of Modern Literature*, vol. XX, no.1, 1996, pp. 29-34.

_____. *Jasmine.* Grove P, 1989.

"Myth." *Oxford English Dictionary*, 2015, en.oxforddictionaries.com/definition/myth/. Accessed 15 Apr. 2015.

Naber, Nadine. "Ambiguous Insiders: An Investigation of Arab American Invisibility." *Ethnic and Racial Studies*, vol. 23, no.1, 2000, pp. 37-61.

_____. "Introduction: Arab Americans and U.S. Racial Formations." *Race and Arab Americans Before and After 9/11: From Invisible Citizens to Visible Subjects*, edited by Amaney Jamal and Nadine Naber, Syracuse UP, 2008, pp. 1-45.

Naqvi, Tahera. *Dying in a Strange Country*. TSAR, 2001.

Nazario, Sonia. *Enrique's Journey (The Young Adult Adaptation): The True Story of a Boy Determined to Reunite with His Mother*. Ember, 2014.

Nielson, Him. "The Geek vs. the Goat: Popcultural Politics in Junot Díaz's *The Brief Wondrous Life of Oscar Wao*." *Contracorriente: A Journal of Social History and Literature in Latin America*, vol. 11, no. 2, 2014, pp. 256-277.

Noguchi, Irena. "A Vietnam Story Told through the Eyes of Refugee Parents." *KQED Arts*. KQED, 1 Sept. 2017, ww2.kqed.org/arts/217/09/01/a-vietnam-story-told-through-the-eyes-of-refugee-parents/. Accessed 4 Sept. 2017.

Nguyen, Bich Minh. *Stealing Buddha's Dinner: A Memoir*. Penguin, 2008.

Nguyen, Viet Thanh. *The Refugees*. Grove P, 2017.

Okada, John. *No-No Boy*. U of Washington P, 1976.

Okri, Ben. *The Famished Road*. Jonathan Cape, 1991.

Ondaatje, Michael. *Handwriting: Poems*. Vintage, 2000.

Ong, Aihwa. *Flexible Citizenship: The Cultural Logics of Transnationality*. Duke UP, 1999.

Orduña, Jose. *The Weight of Shadows: A Memoir of Immigration and Displacement*. Beacon P, 2016.

Ortiz Juarez-Paz, Anna V. "Undocumented Identity Storytelling: (Re)framing Public Relations." *International Journal of Media and Cultural Politics*, vol. 13, nos. 1 and 2, 2017, pp. 165-178.

Padilla Peralta, Dan-el. *Undocumented: A Dominican Boy's Odyssey from a Homeless Shelter to the Ivy League*. Penguin, 2015.

Patten, Eileen. *The Nation's Latino Population Is Defined by its Youth.* Pew Research Center, 2016.

Poe, Edgar Allan. "Marginalia [part XIII]." *Southern Literary Messenger*, vol. XV, no. 4, April 1849, pp. 217-222.

Quintana, Francisco. "Inter-American Court Condemns Unprecedented Situation of Statelessness in the Dominican Republic." *European Network on Statelenessness*, 27 Oct. 2014, www.statelessness.eu/blog/inter-american-court-condemns-unprecedented-situation-statelessness-dominican-republic. Accessed 18 Oct. 2017.

Rader, Pamela J. "'Trawling in Silences': Finding Humanity in the Paginas en Blanco of History in Junot Díaz's *The Brief Wondrous Life of Oscar Wao.*" *Label Me Latina/o*, vol. 2, Spring 2012, pp. 1-23.

Radhakrishnan, R. "Ethnicity in the Age of Diaspora." *Theorizing Diaspora*, edited by Jana Evans Braziel and Anita Mannur, Blackwell, 2003, pp. 119-31.

Ramirez, Dixa. "Great Men's magic: charting hyper-masculinity and supernatural discourses of power in Junot Díaz's *The Brief Wondrous Life of Oscar Wao.*" *Atlantic Studies*, vol. 10, no. 3, 2013, pp. 384-405.

Ramnath, Maia. *From Haj to Utopia: How the Ghadar Movement Charted Global Radicalism and Attempted to Overthrow the British Empire.* U of California P, 2011.

Rastogi, Pallavi. "Pedagogical Strategies in Discussing Chitra Banerjee Divakaruni's *Arranged Marriage.*" *Asian American Literature: Discourse & Pedagogies*, vol. 1, 2010, pp. 35-41.

Ratti, Rakesh, editor. *Lotus of Another Color: The Unfolding of South Asian Gay and Lesbian Experience.* Alyson Books, 1993.

Redden, Elizabeth. "International Enrollments: From Flat to Way Down." *Inside Higher Ed.*, 5 Sept. 2017, www.insidehighered.com/news/2017/09/05/some-universities-are-reporting-declines-international-enrollments-ranging-modest/. Accessed 30 Nov. 2017.

Riis, Jacob. *How the Other Half Lives.* Bedford, 1996.

Rocco, Fiammetta. "Things Come Together: A New Generation of African Novelists Take Flight." *1843*, February/March 2017, pp. 22-24.

Rodríguez, R. Joseph. *Enacting Adolescent Literacies across Communities: Latino/a Scribes and Their Rites.* Lexington Books, The Rowman & Littlefield Group, Inc, 2017.

_____. "Oh, America, Can You See Us?" Unpublished poem, 2018.

Roth, Henry. *Call it Sleep*. Farrar, Straus and Giroux, 1994.

Rushdie, Salman. "Imaginary Homelands." *Imaginary Homelands: Essays and Criticism 1981–1991*. Granta, 1991, pp. 9-21.

Said, Edward. *Reflections on Exile and Other Essays*. Harvard UP, 2002.

_____. "Introduction: Secular Criticism." *The World, the Text, and the Critic*. Harvard UP, 1983, pp. 1-30.

Salaita, Steven. *Modern Arab American Fiction: A Reader's Guide*. Syracuse UP, 2011.

Saldivar, José David. "Conjectures of 'Americanity' and Junot Díaz's 'Fuku Americanus'" *The Brief Wondrous Life of Oscar Wao*." *The Global South*, vol. 5, no.1, Spring 2011, pp. 120-136.

Saliba, Therese. "Resisting Invisibility: Arab Americans in Academia and Activism." *Arabs in America: Building a New Future*, edited by Michael Suleiman, Syracuse UP, 1999, pp. 304-319.

Sánchez, Erika L. *I Am Not Your Perfect Mexican Daughter*. Knopf Books for Young Readers, 2017.

Satrapi, Marjane. *The Complete Persepolis*. Pantheon, 2007.

_____. *Persepolis 2: The Story of a Return*. Pantheon, 2005.

Schor, Esther. *Emma Lazarus*. Schocken, 2006.

Scott, Derek B. *The Singing Bourgeois: Songs of the Victorian Drawing Room and Parlor*. Routledge, 2017.

Selasi, Taiye. *Ghana Must Go*. Penguin, 2014.

Selvon, Sam. *The Lonely Londoners*. Longman, 1989.

Shakir, Evelyn. "Coming of Age: Arab American Literature." *Ethnic Forum*, vol. 13-14, 1993-1994, pp. 63-80.

Shamsie, Kamila. *Home Fire*. Riverhead, 2017.

Shan, Te-hsing. "In the Ocean of Words: An Interview with Ha Jin." *Tamkang Review* vol. 38, no. 2, 2008, pp. 135–57.

Shomali, Mejdulene. "Scheherazade and the Limits of Inclusive Politics in Arab American Literature." *MELUS*, spring 2017. Forthcoming.

Shraya, Vivek. *The Boy and the Bindi*. Illustrated by Rajini Perera, Arsenal Pulp P, 2016.

Shteyngart, Gary. *Absurdistan*. Random House, 2007.

Sindu, S. J. *Marriage of a Thousand Lies*. Soho Press, 2017.

Smith, Zadie. *White Teeth*. Vintage, 2000.

Softky, Elizabeth. "Cross-cultural understanding spiced with the Indian diaspora." *Black Issues in Higher Education*, vol. 14, no.15, 18 Sept. 1997, p. 26. Academic Search Complete, EBSCOhost. Accessed 22 Oct. 2017.

Solberg, S. E. "Sui Sin Far/Edith Eaton: The First Chinese-American Fictionist." *MELUS*, vol. 8 no. 1, 1981, pp. 27–39.

Spiegelman, Art. *The Complete Maus*. Pantheon, 1997.

Suleiman, Michel. "Introduction: The Arab Immigrant Experience." *Arabs in America: Building a New Future*, edited by Michael Suleiman, Temple UP, 1999. pp. 1-21.

Tan, Amy. *The Joy Luck Club*. Penguin, 1989.

Tatum, Sophie. "Trump Administration to end Protective Status for Haiti." *CNN*, edition.cnn.com/2017/11/20/politics/dhs-temporary-protected-status-haiti/index.html/. Accessed 20 Dec. 2017.

Thangaraj, Stanley. "Playing through differences: black-white racial logic and interrogating South Asian American Identity." *Ethnic and Racial Studies*, vol.35, no.6, June 2012, pp. 988-1006.

Tölölyan, Khachig. "Rethinking *Diaspora*(s): Stateless Power in the Transnational Moment." *Diaspora*, vol. 5, no. 1, 1996, pp. 3-36.

Tran, GB. *Vietnamerica: A Family's Journey*. Villard, 2010.

"Undocumented and Unafraid." *YouTube*, Shatteredverve, 28 Feb. 2011, www.youtube.com/watch?v=xdOrxLLHo0U/. Accessed 11 June 2016.

"Undocumented and Unafraid 'In Loving Memory of Gaby'." *YouTube*, Guerra Production, 7 Dec. 2016, www.youtube.com/watch?v=VLnLC7Xv6S4/. Accessed 1 Nov. 2017.

US Census Bureau. "Facts for Features: Hispanic Heritage Month 2017." *Profile American Facts for Features*, 31 Aug. 2017, www.census.gov/newsroom/facts-for-features/2017/hispanic-heritage.html. Accessed 25 Oct. 2017.

Vargas, Jose Antonio. "Foreword." *Lives in Limbo: Undocumented and Coming of Age in America*, by Roberto G. Gonzales, U of California P, 2016, pp. xi-xiv.

Vassanji, M.G. *The In-Between World of Vikram Lall*. Vintage, 2005.

Vega-González, Susana. "Negotiating Boundaries in Divakaruni's *The Mistress of Spices* and Naylor's *Mama Day*." *Comparative Literature and Culture*, vol. 5, no.2, 2003. doi.org/10.7771/1481-4374.1186/. Accessed 13 Jan. 2018.

Volpp, Leti. "The Legal Mapping of U.S. Immigration, 1965–1996." *Crossing into America: The New Literature of Immigration*, edited by Louis Mendoza and S. Shankar, New Press, 2003, pp. 257-269.

Walker, Alice. *In Search of Our Mothers' Gardens*. Harcourt, 1983.

Wang, L. Ling-chi. "The Structure of Dual Domination: Toward a Paradigm for the Study of the Chinese Diaspora in the United States." *Amerasia Journal*, vol. 21, no. 1-2, 1995, pp. 149-69.

Washington, George. "To the Hebrew Congregation at Newport, Rhode Island." *Washington: Writings*, edited by John H. Rhodehamel, Library of America, 1997, pp. 766-67.

West, Kanye. "Runaway." *My Beautiful Dark Twisted Fantasy*. Roc-A-Fella Records, 2010.

White, J. Daniel. "Looking beyond the shallowness of imitation for a take on contemporary America." *Washington Independent Review of Books*. www.washingtonindependentreviewofbooks/. Accessed 13 Jan. 2018.

White-Parks, Annette. *Sui Sin Far/Edith Maude Eaton: A Literary Biography*. U of Illinois P, 1995.

Wickremesekera, Channa. *Distant Warriors*. Perera-Hussein, 2005.

Wilkerson, Isabel. *The Warmth of Other Suns: The Epic Story of America's Great Migration*. Random House, 2010.

_____. "Isabel Wilkerson Reviews Yaa Gyasi's 'Homegoing.'" *New York Times* 6 Jun. 2016. Accessed 12 Dec. 2017.

Wordsworth, William. "Preface to *Lyrical Ballads*." 1800. *Bartleby.com*, 2015, www.bartleby.com/39/36.html/. Accessed 3 Dec. 2017.

Yin, Xiao-huang. "The Voice of a Eurasian." *Chinese American Literature since the 1850s*. U of Illinois P, 2000, pp. 85-116.

Yezierska, Anzia. "America and I." *Children of Loneliness: Stories of Immigrant Life in America*. Funk & Wagalls, 1923.

_____. *How I Found America: Collected Stories of Anzia Yezierska*. Persea Books, 1991.

Young, Bette Roth. *Emma Lazarus in Her World: Life and Letters.* Jewish Publication Society, 1997.

Zinn, Howard, and Rebecca Stefoff. *A Young People's History of the United States: Columbus to the War on Terror.* Seven Stories P, 2009.

About the Editor

Maryse Jayasuriya is Associate Professor of English and Associate Dean in the College of Liberal Arts at the University of Texas at El Paso. She also teaches courses in Asian studies and women's and gender studies. She earned her MA and PhD from Purdue University and her BA from Mount Holyoke College. Her primary area of research is postcolonial literature and theory. Her research interests include South Asian, East and West African, Oceanian, Caribbean, and nineteenth and twentieth-century British literature. Her book, *Terror and Reconciliation: Sri Lankan Anglophone Literature, 1983–2009*, was published by Lexington Books (2012). She has published articles and reviews in *South Asian Review, Asiatic, Indialogs, Phoenix, Journal of Postcolonial Cultures and Societies, Journeys, Margins* and the edited collections *Postcolonial Urban Outcasts: City Margins in South Asian Literature* (2016), *Contemporary Immigrant Short Fiction: Critical Insights* (2015), and *South Asia and its Others: Reading the 'Exotic'* (2009). She has also guest-edited a special issue of *South Asian Review* (33.3) on Sri Lankan Anglophone Literature. She has served as the editor of the South Asian Literary Association (SALA) Newsletter and an executive board member of the South Asian Literary Association. She teaches classes in nineteenth and twentieth-century British literature, postcolonial studies, world literature, literature and film, and literary theory and criticism.

Contributors

Umme Al-wazedi is Associate Professor of Postcolonial Literature in the Department of English and Co-Program Director of Women's and Gender Studies at Augustana College, Rock Island, Illinois. Her research interest encompasses (Muslim) women writers of South Asia and South Asian Diaspora, Muslim feminism, and postcolonial disability studies. She has published in *South Asian Review, South Asian History and Culture*. She also coedited a special issue of *South Asian Review* titled Nation and Its Discontents with Madhurima Chakraborty, Columbia College Chicago, Chicago, Illinois. Her coedited book *Urban Outcasts in South Asian Literature* was published by Routledge in October 2016.

Marta Caminero-Santangelo is Director of the Center for Latin American and Caribbean Studies and a professor in the English Department at the University of Kansas. She teaches classes in US Latinx literatures and the literature of social justice. Her academic research in the field of twentieth and twenty-first-century US Latinx literary studies focuses on the conjunction between literature, group identity, and the ability to promote social change. She has published three books: *The Madwoman Can't Speak: Or Why Insanity Is Not Subversive* (Cornell UP, 1998); *On Latinidad: US Latino Literature and the Construction of Ethnicity* (UP Florida, 2007); and most recently, *Documenting the Undocumented: Latina/o Narrative and Social Justice in the Era of Operation Gatekeeper* (UP Florida, 2016). She earned a PhD in English from the University of California, Irvine.

Ezra Cappell is Associate Professor of English and Director of the Inter-American Jewish Studies Program at the University of Texas at El Paso. Cappell received his BA in English from Queens College, his MA in creative writing from The City College, and his MPhil and PhD in English and American literature from New York University. Cappell teaches and publishes in the fields of twentieth century and contemporary Jewish American literature, and he is a recipient of the University of Texas Regents' Outstanding Teaching Award. Cappell has published numerous articles on American and Jewish American writing, and he is the author of the book: *American Talmud: The Cultural Work of Jewish American Fiction* and co-editor of the forthcoming book: *Off the Derech: Post-Orthodox Jewish Writing*. Cappell is a frequent lecturer on Jewish American culture and Holocaust writing, and he serves as Editor of the SUNY Press book series Contemporary Jewish Literature and Culture.

Robert C. Evans is I. B. Young Professor of English at Auburn University at Montgomery (AUM). He earned his PhD from Princeton University in 1984. In 1982, he began teaching at AUM, where he has been named Distinguished Research Professor, Distinguished Teaching Professor, and University Alumni Professor. External awards include fellowships from the American Council of Learned Societies; the American Philosophical Society; the National Endowment for the Humanities; the UCLA Center for Medieval and Renaissance Studies; and the Folger, Huntington, and Newberry Libraries. He is the author or editor of roughly fifty books and of more than four hundred essays, including recent work on various American writers.

Nalini Iyer is Professor of English at Seattle University where she teaches postcolonial literatures. Her publications include: *Other Tongues: Rethinking the Language Debates in India* (coedited with Bonnie Zare); *Roots and Reflections: South Asians in the Pacific Northwest* (coauthored with Amy Bhatt); and *Revisiting India's Partition: New Essays in Memory, Culture, and Politics* (coedited with Amritjit Singh and Rahul K. Gairola). She is Vice President of South Asian Literature Association (SALA).

Asha Jeffers is Faculty Fellow at the University of King's College in Halifax, Nova Scotia. Her research focuses on literature about the children of immigrants, "the second generation," across national and ethnic lines, with a particular interest in how these texts represent coming of age, spirituality and myth, and intergenerational relationships. Her article "Means of Escape, Means of Invention: Hindu Figures and Black Pop Culture in Rakesh Satyal's *Blue Boy*" was published in *South Asian Review* 36.3, and her article "Unstable Indianness: Double Diaspora in Ramabai Espinet's *The Swinging Bridge* and M.G. Vassanji's *When She Was Queen*" appeared in *South Asian Review* 37.1. Her short story "The Scar" has been published in *The Puritan* magazine's issue 30.

Cynthia A. Leenerts is Associate Professor of English at East Stroudsburg University of Pennsylvania. She teaches British and postcolonial literatures, as well as courses on the graphic novel, literary criticism, and linguistics. In addition to other publications, she coedited (with Lopa Basu) *Passage to Manhattan: Critical Essays on Meena Alexander* (Cambridge Scholars Publishing, 2009) and (with George Bozzini) *Literature Without Borders: International Literature in English for Student Writers* (Prentice-Hall, 2001). An avid student of Chinese language, literature, and literary criticism, she is currently reinventing Literature Without Borders for students in China, as well as doing preliminary work (with Hema Chari) on Tagore's travel writings, and she serves on the editorial board of *South Asian Review*.

R. Joseph Rodríguez is the author of *Enacting Adolescent Literacies across Communities: Latino/a Scribes and Their Rites, Teaching Culturally Sustaining and Inclusive Young Adult Literature: Critical Perspectives and Conversations*, and several journal articles. He has taught English and Spanish language arts in public schools, community colleges, and universities. His areas of research include children's and young adult literatures, language acquisition, and socially responsible biliteracies. Joseph serves as coeditor of *English Journal*, a publication of the National Council of Teachers of English.

Marion Christina Rohrleitner is Associate Professor of English at The University of Texas at El Paso, where she researches and teaches contemporary American literature with a focus on Chicanx, Latinx, and Caribbean diasporic fiction and a special interest in historical fiction through the lenses of affect and queer theory. She is coeditor of *Dialogues Across Diasporas: Women Writers, Scholars, and Activists of Africana and Latina Descent in Conversation* (Lexington Books, 2013), and her scholarship has appeared in, for example, *American Quarterly, Callaloo, El Mundo Zurdo, Gender & Society, Latino Studies, Melus, Symbolism,* and *The European Journal of American Studies.* Her current book project, *Transnational Latinidades*, explores the production, translation, and marketing of Latinx fiction outside of the United States.

Te-hsing Shan is Distinguished Research Fellow of the Institute of European and American Studies, Academia Sinica, Taiwan. Besides journal articles and book chapters in Chinese and English, his publications include *Inscriptions and Representations: Chinese American Literary and Cultural Criticism, Transgressions and Innovations: Asian American Literary and Cultural Studies,* and *Edward W. Said in Taiwan.* To his credit are three collections of interviews, including *In the Company of the Wise: Conversations with Asian American Writers and Critics.* He has also translated nearly twenty books from English into Chinese, including *The Challenge of the American Dream, Representations of the Intellectual,* and *Power, Politics, and Culture: Interviews with Edward W. Said.* His research areas are comparative literature, Asian American literature, and cultural studies.

Mejdulene B. Shomali is a Palestinian American poet and Assistant Professor in Gender and Women's Studies at the University of Maryland, Baltimore County. Her work centers on queerness, femininity, Palestine, and transnational Arab culture. Her scholarship can be read or is forthcoming in *Multi-Ethnic Literature of the United States, Encyclopedia of Women and Islamic Cultures, Journal of Middle East Women's Studies, International Journal of Middle East Studies, Arab Studies Quarterly,* and *Social Justice.* Creative work can be read or is forthcoming in *McSweeney's Internet Tendency, Tinderbox, Diode, The Pinch Literary Journal, Mizna,* and *The Feminist Wire.*

Brian Yothers is the Frances Spatz Leighton Endowed Distinguished Professor of English at the University of Texas at El Paso. He is the author of *Reading Abolition: The Critical Reception of Harriet Beecher Stowe and Frederick Douglass* (2016), *Sacred Uncertainty: Religious Difference and the Shape of Melville's Career* (2015), *Melville's Mirrors: Literary Criticism and America's Most Elusive Author* (2011), and *The Romance of the Holy Land in American Travel Writing, 1790–1876* (2007). He is coeditor, with Jonathan A. Cook, of *Visionary of the Word: Melville and Religion* (2017); editor of *Critical Insights: Billy Budd, Sailor* (2017); and coeditor, with Harold K. Bush, of *Above the American Renaissance: David S. Reynolds and the Spiritual Imagination in Nineteenth-Century America* (2018). He is associate editor of *Leviathan: A Journal of Melville*

Studies; coeditor of the interdisciplinary journal *Journeys*; editor of the Camden House Press series Literary Criticism in Perspective; associate editor of *Melville's Marginalia Online*; and coeditor, with Wyn Kelley, of the *Moby-Dick*/Travel section of the *Melville Electronic Library*. He was a 2014 winner of the University of Texas Regents' Outstanding Teaching Award.

Watanna, Onoto 89
Watchmen 45
Weight of Shadows: A Memoir of Immigration and Displacement, The xiv, xix
We Need New Names xiv, xviii
Wessell, Henry 35
West, Kanye 127
whites 91, 94, 203
White Teeth xvii, xix
Who's Irish? xiii, xix
Wickremesekera, Channa xvii
Wilkerson, Isabel 220, 221, 223
Willie 220
Wing Sing viii, 89, 90, 91, 92, 93, 94, 95, 96, 97, 98, 99, 100, 101, 102, 103
Winston 199
Woman Warrior, The xiv, xix

Wong Chow 98
Wordsworth, William 59
World War II ix, xvi, 106, 122
Writer as Migrant, The 152
Wu, Nan 152

YA literature 184, 185, 186, 193
Yaw 215, 216
Yeats, William Butler 159
Yezierska, Anzia 5, 10, 19, 21, 135
Yiddish Policeman's Union, The 13, 20
Young Adult literature 184, 194
Young, Bette Roth 73
Yunior 34, 38, 40, 41, 42, 43, 44, 45, 46

Zafa 39, 46